The Weight of Whiteness

Philosophy of Race

Series Editor: George Yancy, Emory University

Editorial Board: Sybol Anderson, Barbara Applebaum, Alison Bailey, Chike Jeffers, Janine Jones, David Kim, Emily S. Lee, Zeus Leonardo, Falguni A. Sheth, Grant Silva

The Philosophy of Race book series publishes interdisciplinary projects that center upon the concept of race, a concept that continues to have very profound contemporary implications. Philosophers and other scholars, more generally, are strongly encouraged to submit book projects that seriously address race and the process of racialization as a deeply embodied, existential, political, social, and historical phenomenon. The series is open to examine monographs, edited collections, and revised dissertations that critically engage the concept of race from multiple perspectives: sociopolitical, feminist, existential, phenomenological, theological, and historical.

Recent Titles

The Weight of Whiteness: A Feminist Engagement with Privilege, Race, and Ignorance, by Alison Bailey

The Logic of Racial Practice: Explorations in the Habituation of Racism, edited by Brock Bahler

Hip Hop as Philosophical Text and Testimony: Can I Get a Witness?, by Lissa Skitolsky

The Blackness of Black: Key Concepts in Critical Discourse, by William David Hart

Self-Definition: A Philosophical Inquiry from the Global South and Global North, by Teodros Kiros

A Phenomenological Hermeneutic of Antiblack Racism in The Autobiography of Malcolm X, by David Polizzi

Buddhism and Whiteness, edited by George Yancy and Emily McRae

The Weight of Whiteness

A Feminist Engagement with Privilege, Race, and Ignorance

Alison Bailey

LEXINGTON BOOKS
Lanham • Boulder • New York • London

Published by Rowman & Littlefield
An imprint of The Rowman & Littlefield Publishing Group, Inc.
4501 Forbes Boulevard, Suite 200, Lanham, Maryland 20706
www.rowman.com

6 Tinworth Street, London SE11 5AL, United Kingdom

Copyright © 2021 by The Rowman & Littlefield Publishing Group, Inc.

All rights reserved. No part of this book may be reproduced in any form or by any electronic or mechanical means, including information storage and retrieval systems, without written permission from the publisher, except by a reviewer who may quote passages in a review.

British Library Cataloguing in Publication Information Available

Library of Congress Cataloging-in-Publication Data

Names: Bailey, Alison, 1961- author.
Title: The weight of whiteness : a feminist engagement with privilege, race, and ignorance / Alison Bailey.
Description: Lanham, Maryland : Rowman & Littlefield, [2021] | Series: Philosophy of race | Includes bibliographical references and index. | Summary: "The Weight of Whiteness invites white people to wade mindfully into the inherited epistemic and affective weight of whiteness. It examines the ways that white supremacy and privilege continue to anesthetize white people from the inherited damage that whiteness does to our collective humanity"—Provided by publisher.
Identifiers: LCCN 2020051679 (print) | LCCN 2020051680 (ebook) |
  ISBN 9781793604491 (cloth) | ISBN 9781793604507 (epub) |
  ISBN 9781793604514 (pbk)
Subjects: LCSH: Whites—Race identity. | Racism. | White nationalism. | Social justice.
Classification: LCC HT1575 .B35 2021 (print) | LCC HT1575 (ebook) |
  DDC 305.809—dc23
LC record available at https://lccn.loc.gov/2020051679
LC ebook record available at https://lccn.loc.gov/2020051680

For My Father,
with Abundant Gratitude

Contents

Acknowledgments ix

Introduction: Has the Weight of Whiteness Finally Come Up to Claim Us? xi

1 Understanding Privilege as Unearned Power Conferred Systemically 1

2 The Problem with White Talk: Ignorance and Epistemic Closure 33

3 Tracking Privilege-Preserving Epistemic Pushback in Feminist and Critical Race Philosophy Classes 59

4 The Weighty Conversation: How White Supremacy Damages White People 79

5 Inheriting the Weight of Whiteness 123

Bibliography 165

Index 175

About the Author 181

Acknowledgments

I sincerely believe that strong and loving relationships are what fuel our most stunning accomplishments. We never truly create anything alone. The thoughts we commit to paper are nurtured by countless conversations with friends, partners, family, colleagues, ancestors, scholars, neighbors, students, and yes, even the people who annoy us. They are our teachers, our critics, and our muses. The book you hold is also filled with decades of righteous anger, tears, anxiety, joy, frustration, depression, fear, and hope. I have been thinking about questions of race, ignorance, privilege, and whiteness for a very long time. I've witnessed my thoughts shift, crumble, grow, and reshape themselves in response to other scholars' observations and in my own encounters with the unforgiving racialized worlds we all inhabit.

Acknowledgement sections are fairly secure spaces, dedicated to the practice of gratitude for those who have helped us along the way. I hope that my appreciation for the communities that have brought me to this place is tangible throughout the book; nonetheless, acknowledgements are still in order. Especially heartfelt thanks go to Betye Saar (Roberts Projects) for permission to use the photograph of her mixed-media assemblage *The Weight of Whiteness* (2014). I'm honored to have such a powerful image grace the cover of this book. It could not be more perfect. Thanks also to Halie Hugenberg for her pen-and-ink illustration work. Some chapters are revised and updated versions of previously published material. I'm grateful for the permission to reprint them here. Many thanks to Nicholette Amstutz, Holly Buchanan, Jana Hodges-Kluck, Sydney Wedbush, and the staff at Lexington Press for all they did to expedite the publication of this book.

I'm indebted to the Monmouth County Historical Society, the Sayerville Historical Society, and local historians Verne James, Bernadette Rogoff, and Ed Campbell for their help with the Morgan family history. It's a great joy to have conversations with those who know parts of my family history so deeply. Special thanks to the Rev. Karen G. Johnston, Kristal C. Langford, and all the members of the Lost Souls Memorial Project of East New Brunswick, New Jersey, for their loving effort to the preserve and memorialize the names of the 137+ people who my New Jersey ancestors sold into permanent slavery in the south.

Thanks to my feminist posse, Melissa Johnson, Kass Fleisher, Cynthia Edmonds-Cady, and Kyle Ciani, for holding me when I fell apart, and for listening to me go on and on about my ancestry, whiteness, and the book project. Additional gratitude to Melissa for reading my early drafts and discussing my final chapters with me. I'm also indebted to Gaile Pohlhaus, Jr. and Allison B. Wolf for helping me to organize my ideas and for reading drafts at our feminist philosophy retreats and long-distance zoom discussions during the pandemic. And, in retrospect, gratitude to Sandra Kim for the lessons I took away from her Healing from Internalized Whiteness Workshop. It took me a full year to process the trauma her exercises triggered in me and to navigate and hold space with the lessons they contained.

I would be remiss not to thank the many scholars and colleagues who have influenced my thinking on these issues in recent years. You have been patient and encouraging with me and my thought process. I have had the great fortune of becoming a philosopher during a rich and exciting time in the history of our profession. Thanks to Barbara Appelbaum, Linda Martín Alcoff, Jackie Anderson, Nora Berenstain, Charlotte Brown, Lorraine Code, Chris Cuomo, Patricia Hill Collins, Kristie Dotson, Marilyn Frye, Laurie Fuller, Ann Gary, Sandra Harding, Sarah Hoagland, María Lugones, Charles Mills, Marianna Ortega, Erica Meiners, Ted Morris, Thomas P. Niebur, Maura Toro-Morn, Shireen Roshanravan, Nancy Tuana, George Yancy, and Kirsten Hotelling Zona. Thanks also to Xhercis Méndez, whom I met briefly, but whom gifted me with a direct and humbling question that stopped me in my tracks—Why do you do this work? In many ways the last two chapters of this book are my humble response to her direct query.

Thanks to the College of Arts and Sciences at Illinois State University for granting me a sabbatical leave for the academic year, and for the subventions funds required to secure permission to reproduce sections of this book and Betye Saar's image for the cover. I'm also grateful to Georgetown Law School for granting me visiting faculty status during my sabbatical.

I want to thank my father, Holmes Bailey, for instilling in me an insatiable interest in our family history, and for the enthusiasm and joy he brought to our summer genealogy road trips. And, especially for my beloved partner, Lawrence B. Solum: thank you for your patience, attentive feedback, and suggestions as I researched and wrote the book. I felt supported, encouraged, and loved through it all.

Introduction

Has the Weight of Whiteness Finally Come Up to Claim Us?

I write this introduction from a liminal space: an all too familiar place that I don't fully recognize. Like all liminal spaces this one is ripe with fear, hope, anxiety, and possibility. The nation been thrown into liminal spaces before; but, this one feels different. Americans are standing at the precipice of an era that will only be named once the chaos settles and the contours of a brave new geography become tangible. No one event has brought us to this place. The deadly combination of a growing global pandemic, malignant presidency, aggressive public misinformation campaigns, accelerated environmental destruction, economic recession, and growing social resistance to centuries of social injustice has finally caught up with us. We've snapped again. There are fissures of lucidity in this chaos. Three months of sheltering in place have pushed many of us to hold space with the world that surrounds us—to slow down, be still, and attend to one another with greater care. The busy public world, with its endless diversions and distractions, has evaporated. We have been left to feel our vulnerability. For the longest time I could not find a precise language to capture this mixture of horror and hope I feel. Pandemics have historically pushed us to break with old ways of organizing the world and to imagine new ways of being. As Arundhati Roy observes, "This one is no different. It is a portal, a gateway between one world and the next. We can choose to walk through it, dragging the carcasses of our prejudice and hatred, our avarice, our data banks and dead ideas, our dead rivers and smoky skies behind us. Or we can walk through lightly, with little luggage, ready to imagine another world. And be ready to fight for it."[1] I'm trying to walk forward lightly, attentively, and humbly because I do not want to lose touch with either the pain or the possibility the lies before us.

We have been entrusted with a chronic pain that has always surrounded us, and that we have been too numb to feel. It has forced us, once again, as a nation, to gaze deeply into James Baldwin's disagreeable mirror, and to attend to the violent colonial legacy we inherit. Are we finally becoming more sensitive to our own insensitivity? Are we finally feeling the weight of our history? Breonna Taylor is fatally shot in her own apartment by a three plainclothes Louisville Metro police officers executing a no knock warrant. George Floyd is murdered by a Minneapolis police officer in broad daylight before of crowd of bystanders. We've been here before, but this time feels different. White people (and the rest of the world) saw something that's been happening in America for centuries, and this time the weight has come up to claim more of us. This time it has broken open more of our hearts. Van Jones, believes that "a miracle has taken place. A continent of new common ground has emerged from beneath the waves. Where there are twenty, thirty, forty million white Americans saying—racism is real, more real than I thought. There is something wrong with our justice system, it's more broken than I knew. What can I do about it? As an African American man, it's a miracle... we're in the midst of some kind of an awakening. Somebody killed a Black man, and everybody cares."[2]

The sudden acceleration of these shifts offers unwelcome comfort. I've witnessed an entire parade of shifty moments over the past month. *Shift* . . . the confederate flag is banned at NASCAR races. Statues of confederate leaders and colonizers are being defaced, pulled down, or removed to storage. Businesses are flying Black Lives Matter flags. The city of Albuquerque removes the statute of conquistador Juan de Oñate, after an altercation between a local armed militia and protestors. One man was shot before the police arrived. *Shift* . . . Juneteenth magically appears on my Google calendar as U.S. public holiday. It wasn't there yesterday. Washington, D.C. Mayor Muriel E. Bowser renames a street in front of the White House "Black Lives Matter Plaza." She watches as local artists and city workers paint the slogan on the asphalt in massive letters with highly reflective yellow street paint. This inspires the New York City mayor to paint the slogan on the street in front of Trump Tower. *Shift* . . . concepts such as white fragility, white supremacy, systemic racism, intersectionality, and anti-black racism, which once circulated within the narrow confines of social justice movements, progressive social media sites, and academic conferences, now spring from the mouths of newscasters and late-night talk show hosts. *Super shift* . . . the Mississippi state legislature passes a bill to remove the confederate battle emblem from the state flag. Things have become heavier. Are we beginning to feel the weight? Has it come up to claim us? The future feels more hopeful. Senator Kamala Harris accepts the Democratic Party's nomination for vice president. Representative Alexandria Ocasio-Cortez evokes the sentiments expressed by black lesbian feminist Audre Lorde about the power of poetry and social change during her brief speech at the democratic convention. Is the weight lifting? Maybe not. The protests in Portland, Oregon become more violent. The police shootings continue: Jacob Blake is shot seven times in the back, in front of his three young sons, by a white police officer. The small city of Kenosha, Wisconsin is now on fire. And, it's not just police violence anymore, Americans continue to drag the carcasses of our prejudice and hatred through the streets. We are shooting one another. I feel my fear and anxiety return. I'm not sure what it will finally take for us to imagine another world, but I'm certain that attending to the historical weight of whiteness figures into this somewhere.

The Weight of Whiteness: A Feminist Engagement with Privilege, Race, and Ignorance is framed as a series of invitations to wade slowly and mindfully into the weight of whiteness, and to attend to the ways white supremacy has misshapen our nation, our communities, and our humanity. Black, Indigenous, and People of Color (BIPOC) feel the weight of whiteness every day. The systemic machinery of white privilege, however, is designed to anesthetize most white people to this unbearable weight. We can learn to feel our indifference, but the resistant habits of whiteness make this work difficult. Part of the problem is that white people, myself included, have spent too long trying to think our way out of our whiteness. When we rush from our hearts to our heads, however, we become insensitive and inattentive to the subtle ways that whiteness anesthetizes us to the damage it does to our collective humanity. White people are far more comfortable thinking about white supremacy in terms of what privilege does *for* us, than we are feeling what it does *to* us.

The invitations to the weighty conversation begin in the head and lumber slowly downward into the body toward the heart. People of color have repeatedly invited white people to attend to the weight, but most of us have failed to respond to their generous invitations. My first three chapters focus on the *overexposed side of white privilege*, the side that works to make the invisible and intangible structures of power more visible and tangible. The final two chapters invite white readers to explore the *underexposed side of white dominance*, the weightless side that is too painful for us to feel. Taken together these chapters are my deeply personal attempt to hold space with the weight of whiteness in my own being, and to consider the weight I've inherited from my settler colonial ancestors. The gravitational pull of white ignorance's comfort is stronger than the painful knowledge required for our collective liberation. It's easier to wrestle with white guilt and shame, than it is to confront the possibility that each of us carries the historical weight of whiteness in our bodies, and that we continue to blow the weight of our trauma through people of color's bodies and communities. I'm convinced that our collective survival on this planet depends on white people doing this work. And, I'm scared that the majority of white people will find this work far too painful to even begin and that most of us will choose anesthesia over knowledge.

The first chapter invites readers to "check their privilege." The invitation feels like a brisk and disorienting nudge. It's not a request for a one-time favor. It asks those of us with privilege to consider what we have been socialized to ignore. It's instructive to witness how white people habitually use silence and distraction to avoid the invitation. The nudge makes us defensive, anxious, and angry. Our defensiveness almost always relies on confused understandings of privilege. Stretchy definitions are a barrier to clarity. Answering this request then, presupposes a solid account of what privilege is and how it functions. We need to identify and define what we are invited to examine. But, here's the catch: Privilege is designed to be check proof. The obstacles to accepting the invitation are part and parcel of privilege itself. This is not accidental. Ignorance about white privilege and white supremacy help to sustain the painful injustices they repeatedly reproduce.

Resisting white supremacy demands a stable point from which to wade into the weight of whiteness. Chapter 1 offers readers a stretch-resistant account of privilege: one that expands upon, problematizes, and clarifies Peggy McIntosh's definition of privilege as an "unearned power conferred systemically."[3] I begin with a rough taxonomy of advantages. Privilege is a distinct species of systemically conferred advantages, which are distinct from perks, earned benefits, and legal rights. Privileges are marked by four interrelated features. First, privileges are capriciously granted to particular groups based solely on their membership in those particular groups. Next, privileges are experienced as invisible and weightless to those who have them. Privileges also function like 'wild cards' that confer dominant group benefits in a wide variety of circumstances. Finally, privileges have positive and negative dimensions. Even the most stretch-resistant definition of privilege will spark resistance. Many of the objections and counterexamples raised in response to my definition of privilege can be addressed by circling back to a basic taxonomy of advantages, and explaining how objectors habitually confuse systemically conferred privileges with nonsystemic advantages. However, this doesn't always work. Some objections always spring from within the parameters of the stretch-resistant definition. Answering them demands taking into account intersectional and historical understandings of the counterexamples that objectors put on the table. To illustrate this, I explore a few common 'members-of-oppressed-groups-have-privileges-too' objections, which objectors use to redirect our attention away from power. Remember, the invitation to check your privilege is disorienting. It evokes a discomfort strong enough to trigger a bottomless conversation.

The next two chapters highlight the relationships between privilege and willful ignorance. I invite white readers in particular, to hold space with two forms of resistance: *white talk* and *privilege-preserving epistemic pushback*. Like stretchy definitions of privilege, these tactics are used to derail conversations on race and to maintain white silence and comfort.

Chapter 2 explores the many ways that white talk functions as a barrier to understanding the problem of whiteness. You've heard white talk before, it sounds like this–*But I was in the streets protesting after police killed Breonna Taylor and George Floyd. My ancestors came here after the Civil War, so we are neither responsible for nor benefitted from the horrors of slavery and indigenous genocide.* The chapter explains why the question 'How does it feel to be a white problem?' cannot be answered in the fluttering grammar of white talk. The language of fluttering comes from W. E. B. DuBois's description of white people's discomfort during conversations about race. White talk is what white fragility sounds like. We flutter when we feel vulnerable. We flutter to avoid feeling the weight of our whiteness. Drawing on the stretch-resistant definition of privilege, I explore the advantages and disadvantages of using white talk as a route into understanding and feeling the problem of whiteness. My argument expands Alice MacIntyre's analysis of white talk to include the racialized bodily scripts, emotional content, and vocal tones that choreograph these utterances. White talk persists because it has an enduring moral, ontological, and epistemic pay off for white people. It bolsters our sense of well-being by pulling uncomfortable conversations toward evidence of our individual goodness and innocence. Ontologically, it re-inscribes historically fictitious accounts of whiteness as valuable, pure, and unproblematic. White talk is also used to defend our epistemic home terrain against information that upsets our worldview. These detours and distractions promote epistemic closure. I address each of these payoffs by highlighting the many ways white talk functions to maintain the illusion of white invulnerability. White talk, cannot be used to answer the question, how does it *feel* to be a white problem, because white talk functions to prevent white people from feeling the weight of whiteness in the first place. I suggest that white people might work to reduce our fluttering, by replacing white talk with a discourse of vulnerability, where vulnerability is defined not as weakness, but as a condition for potential and growth.

Chapter 3 combines my observations about white talk's epistemic payoff, with the realization that epistemic injustice scholarship offers educators a powerful resource for identifying white resistance to classroom discussions about gender and race. Classrooms are *unlevel knowing fields*, contested terrains where knowledge and ignorance circulate with equal vigor. Patterns of resistance are actively at play in these spaces. Awkward silences, closed body language, denial, angry responses, and verbal posturing are artifacts of white discomfort. The phenomenon I call privilege-preserving epistemic pushback is a species of willful ignorance that dominant groups deploy habitually during conversations that challenge their racialized worldviews. I want to work with, not against, this ground-holding reflex by offering a technique for tracking it productively. I focus on these ground-holding responses because they bear a strong resemblance to critical thinking practices.

Privilege-preserving epistemic pushback takes two forms. The first expression passes easily as critical thinking. The second expression is more sophisticated: it occurs when philosophical practices and critical concepts are enlisted in the service of strategic refusals to understand. I argue that this privilege-preserving form of ignorance counts neither as skepticism nor critical thinking. These performances of willful ignorance do a different kind of work. To make this tangible I treat these ground-holding gestures as '*shadow texts*;' that is, as the spoken copy that runs alongside the readings in ways that prevent epistemic friction. The word "shadow" brings to mind something walking closely alongside another thing without engaging it. Detectives shadow their suspects. Shadows are regions of visual opacity. Shadow texts then, point to these regions of epistemic opacity. They are artifacts of ignorance. I argue that shadow texts are a helpful way to track the production of ignorance and the harms of epistemic violence in classrooms. Learning to spot shadow texts, however, does offer discussants a common point of epistemic friction: It gets them to attend to what shadow texts *do*, rather than on the content what is being *said*. I offer a technique for tracking shadow texts in classroom settings. This is not just an intellectual exercise. Treating privilege-preserving epistemic pushback as a form of healthy skepticism or critical thinking creates a hostile learning environment. Permitting privilege-preserving epistemic pushback to circulate uncritically does psychological harm and epistemic damage.

Now let us shift from head to heart, remembering that white people are more comfortable discussing what white supremacy does *for* us, than we are feeling what it does *to* us. Peggy McIntosh has famously compared privilege to an invisible and weightless knapsack, but the majority of engagement with her famous article attends exclusively to the overexposed side of privilege; that is, to the task of making privilege's unearned advantages visible. Chapters 4 and 5 invite white readers to wade into the underexposed side of privilege, and to hold space with the weight of whiteness until we are able to feel the pain we'd rather not feel. Privilege feels weightless because it anesthetizes us not only to the daily violence against BIPOC bodies, but also to what white people have been forced to surrender in the name of belonging. There is an abrupt shift in the style and tone of these two chapters. Holding space with the weight of whiteness is not intellectual work. The act of holding space is a weight bearing gesture. It is healing work. I use weighty language and gravitational metaphors to call attention to how the anesthesia of privilege constructs white ways of being. I invite white readers in particular to hold space with white supremacy's gravitas long enough to feel how the weight of whiteness continues to misshape our humanity.

People of color have invited white folks to join the weighty conversation about what white supremacy does to our collective humanity for centuries. Chapter 4 invites you, dear reader, to begin opening those invitations. There is a deep wound in the white collective that people of color have witnessed for a very long time, but few white people have considered in a deep and sustained way. The weighty conversation is not about restoring white comfort. It's about touching and feeling the pain of the wound at the heart of whiteness long enough to move ourselves toward wholeness. I begin with a personal account of the racialized lessons my community instilled in me during the 1967 Newark Race Riots/Rebellion to illustrate how the layered messages about the value of whiteness took root in my young being. The daily gestures, unspoken scripts, and comments, which gradually introduced a fear of black and brown bodies into my being, were not installed painlessly. They damaged me, and to this day they remain in my flesh, my thoughts, and my nervous system. They have weight.

There are barriers to the weighty conversation. White ways of knowing contain a gravitas that shapes our conversations before they begin. Western epistemologies lean heavily on visual vocabularies to express what it means to know something. This makes it challenging to capture the untapped knowledge we touch when we mindfully attend to the weight of whiteness. The desire for perfection, comfort, mechanistic thinking, control, and other habits of whiteness also make responding to these invitations difficult. There is no painless way to open the weighty invitations, but open them we must. White supremacy relies on white people avoiding the weighty conversation. As long as we steer clear from the weight in own being the violence will continue. In the absence of a weighty epistemology, I offer a heavy vocabulary. Learning to feel the weight of whiteness begins by sensitizing ourselves to the ways its gravity pulls us away from the weighty conversation. I offer an extended account of this gravitas. We can't force ourselves to feel what we've been taught not to feel, but we can become extremely curious about why white people continue to say that they don't feel anything at all. Anesthesia is part of the master's tool kit. What if white people treated our inability to feel the weight of whiteness in our bodies as evidence that white supremacy functions like anesthesia? The call to wade into the weight, is a call to cultivate a sensitivity to our own insensitivity, by attending carefully to the moments we feel the anesthesia pulling us under. The weight will only make itself known when the anesthesia lifts. Recovering our humanity requires that we remain still long enough to feel the damage.

I begin with a few raw personal examples of how the weight of whiteness has come up to claim me. These include: the psychological costs of entitlement, fear, and hypervigilance; the social weight of strained friendships and alliances; the material weight of looting, hoarding, and the illusion of safety; historical and ancestral amnesia; and, the moral and epistemic costs of learning to see and judge the world wrongly. Naming the weight has allowed me to understand my brokenness; but, that brokenness still did not feel heavy to me. The habits I developed in response to the Newark lessons I learned as a child made the damage feel weightless. In looking back on these lessons I came to understand white identity as sedimented trauma numbed by white privilege. I'd long suspected that costs and losses of whiteness had a curious correspondence to the features of trauma response exposure. After all, trauma is about brokenness and we are wired to anesthetize ourselves to the pain of that brokenness. If the costs and losses of white supremacy share common features with trauma exposure, then the recent literature on trauma may offer a path toward healing. What if we treated the habits of white supremacy as the product of trauma exposure? My final section draws on the recent literature in polyvagal theory to explain why most white people choose to live our entire lives stuck in endless cycles of dirty pain and anesthesia. I rely on Resmaa Menakem's account of *white-body supremacy,* and the distinction between clean and dirty pain, to explain why white people continue to choose anesthesia over liberation. I sincerely believe that white people will never be able to feel the weight of whiteness until we make a conscious effort to metabolize the pain we inherit; only then can the healing begin. The weighty conversation can lead us down a path toward wholeness, connection, healing, reconciliation, and liberation, but only if have the courage to walk into the places and parts of ourselves that feel most heavy.

Chapter 5 extends the weighty invitation. It invites people with white ancestries—especially those of us with settler colonial pedigrees—to hold space with the discomfort, pain, and messiness of the weight we inherit from our ancestors. The forces that disfigure our humanity also distort our family histories. If there is trauma in our bodies, and trauma in our families, then there is most certainly trauma in our pedigrees. I begin with a brief history of genealogy as a social practice and suggest that the white genealogical practices commonly produce anesthetized pedigrees. In Chapter 4 I described the anesthetized body as an artificially settled body, a body that chooses addiction to repeated numbing over the clean pain of liberation. The same can be said about the *anesthetized pedigree.* Whiteness has a strong gravitational pull on the ways white people construct our family histories. There are parts of our family trees that most of us are unwilling to feel. Family genealogists choose the dirty pain of denial when we prune our family trees into pleasing topiaries designed to fit comfortably into colonial master narratives. When robbed of their historical context and complexity our ancestries become barriers to our collective healing. I use Henry Louis Gates's interview with

Ben Affleck as cautionary tale about the price of the anesthetized pedigree. Affleck's request to have all references to his slave-holding ancestors deleted from an episode of the popular PBS *Finding Your Roots* series, offers a powerful example of how we inherit the anesthetic habits of whiteness from those who came before us. The weighty conversation can lead us down the path toward healing, reconciliation, and collective liberation, but we have to find the courage to occupy the uncomfortably heavy limbs of our family trees without anesthetizing ourselves to what we'd rather not find. We must summon the courage to do genealogy without anesthesia.

Medicinal genealogies offer an antidote to the anesthetized pedigree. Genealogy does more than excavate lost ancestors and place them into neatly organized pedigree charts. Genealogy can be used medicinally, in ways that recognize how our ancestral past may provide us with the stories we need to make ourselves whole. Aurora Levins Morales offers an inspiring account of history's healing power, which is easily extended to cover family histories. The medicinal value of genealogy lies in the courage hold the family weight that reaches up to claim you. Practicing ancestry without anesthesia is an act of historical and psychological recovery. Genealogy has the power to make the historical personal. Joy DeGruy's scholarship is not specifically about genealogy, but it carefully attends to the importance of naming and feeling the pain black people inherit from the traumas of slavery and colonization. Genealogists of color are well aware of the weighty imprint of colonization on their family trees. Their narratives are ripe with the language of remembrance and healing. A handful of white genealogists have held space with the inconvenient truths in their ancestral trees long enough for the anesthesia to lift. I use the family histories written by Warren Read, Serene Jones, Edward Ball, Katrina Browne and the DeWolf family to illustrate some of the ways white people have chosen to hold space with their ancestors and to use that pain and knowledge in the service of collective healing. I've come to think of these offerings as *medicinal white genealogies*. These narratives have inspired me to hold space with my own ancestors long enough to affectively engage what my family has long forgotten. Researching my family history made the violence of colonization tangible to me in deeply personal ways. The success of colonial projects in general depended on colonizers learning to anesthetize themselves to the horrors of colonization. My family lines run through some of the more perceptible atrocities of North American colonization: I was astounded by how many stories had been lost, erased, forgotten, or buried. My eighth great-grandmother, Mary Barnes (1626–1663) was the last person in Connecticut to be publicly hung during the Wethersfield Witch Panic of 1662. Dozens of my ancestors participated in genocidal campaigns against indigenous peoples during the Pequot War, King Philip's War, and the Black Hawk War. My Dutch, Welsh, and English ancestors played a central role in the colonization of New Jersey and lower Manhattan. But, for the purposes of this chapter, I've chosen to hold space with my Morgan and Van Wickle ancestors, who engineered a plan to sell over 137+ free, bonded, and enslaved people of African descent into permanent slavery in the south. My desire to hold space with them is rooted in a feeling I cannot seem to shake. The wound at the heart of whiteness is generations deep. It predates my childhood Newark lessons. And so, I feel called upon to hold space with the historical circumstances that gave rise to their deeds and to make the pain I feel sacred, so that we can mourn and heal together. Holding space is a collective endeavor. And, I was extremely fortunate to find a community that had already begun this healing work.

NOTES

1. "The Pandemic Is a Portal," *Yes! Magazine*, April 17, 2020, https://www.yesmagazine.org/video/coronavirus-pandemic-arundhati-roy/

2. Tara Brach, "Van Jones on Racial Justice," *YouTube video*, 5:09, June 18, 2020. https://www.youtube.com/watch?v=-oHHRv—8fc&feature=youtu.be&mc_cid=c1ba4f14c6&mc_eid=60a0cce755

3. Peggy McIntosh, "White Privilege and Male Privilege: A Personal Account of Coming to See Correspondences through Work in Women's Studies," in *The Feminist Philosophy Reader*, eds. Alison Bailey and Chris J. Cuomo (New York: McGraw Hill, 2008), 61–69.

Chapter 1

Understanding Privilege as Unearned Power Conferred Systemically

The invitation to "check your privilege" is a disorienting demand.[1] It asks those of us with white, male, nondisabled, cisgender, age, or class privileges to examine what we have been socialized not to perceive. This is not a request for a simple favor. It's an invitation to join a bottomless conversation that asks us to consider carefully how systems of power create advantages for some groups at the expense of others. How do dominant-group privileges fasten themselves to our being? How do we unknowingly animate the unearned entitlements that shape our decisions and actions? How are the habits of privilege inherited? How do they shape our interactions and structure how we move through that world? In what contexts do these privileges have currency? Whose flesh nourishes them?

These questions make most readers defensive, anxious, and angry. "Privilege," as Peggy McIntosh remarks, is "an elusive and fugitive subject. The pressure to avoid it is great, for in facing it [we] must give up the myth of meritocracy."[2] Most of us want to believe that the world is fair and that we are good-hearted people, innocent of any wrongdoing. It's instructive to attend to the ways that we push back against the request to check our privilege. Our defensive responses usually rely on confused and underdeveloped accounts of what privilege means and these are barriers to clarity. Taking up the request to check our privilege presupposes a working understanding of what it means to have privilege. It requires that we name these privileges and explain how they function. After all, we can't check what we can't perceive, and I don't think this invisibility is accidental. "We have built into all of us," as Audre Lorde tells us, "old blueprints of expectation and response, old structures of oppression" [and privilege], but "they are difficult to access."[3] Privilege is designed to be check proof. Its structures are lodged deeply within us. Our ignorance about how privilege functions is a large part of what sustains the injustices that hold privilege in place. The request to check your privilege, then, is a request to draw privilege out into the open, to name it, to observe it, feel its weight, and track its movements.[4]

I want to explain, in the clearest terms possible, what it means to understand privilege as a complex system of domination rather than as a mere advantage or perk. My goal is to leave readers with a stretch-resistant account of privilege: one that expands upon, problematizes, and clarifies McIntosh's definition of privilege as "unearned power conferred systemically," without stretching it to the point of meaninglessness.[5] I start with Marilyn Frye's account of oppression because it lays the clearest foundation for understanding the ways that systemic barriers generate privileges. Next, I make a distinction between privilege and advantage that parallels Frye's distinction between oppression and harm. I also recognize the conceptual limits of her birdcage metaphor. Frye's single-system focus, however, obscures how interlocking systems of oppression (e.g., white supremacy, heteropatriarchy, colonialism, ableism, or antisemitism) work in concert to discipline and confine some groups. Her metaphor does not lend itself easily to an intersectional reading of how oppression and privilege work together seamlessly in particular contexts. My thick account of privilege is intersectional; it explains how privilege and oppression rely on one another for their meaning. My distinction between unearned privileges and earned advantages begins with a rough taxonomy of advantages. I argue that privileges are a special class of advantage marked by four interrelated features. The benefits granted by privilege are unearned and conferred systemically to members of dominant groups; capriciously and unjustifiably granted to those groups by virtue of their membership; and are invisible to those who have them. Privileges also have an unconditional "wild card" quality that extends benefits to cover a broad range of conditions. I conclude by using this thick account of privilege to respond to common objections triggered by the "check your privilege" request. My final discussion highlights the usefulness of the thick definition to illustrate how a complete privilege check requires intersectional thinking and additional research.

UNDERSTANDING OPPRESSION SYSTEMICALLY

Marilyn Frye's "Oppression" remains required reading in university courses with feminist content. Its greatest merit lies in illustrating how traditional social practices (e.g., men opening doors for women), metaphors equating oppression with double binds, and descriptions of how birdcage-like power structures reveal the architecture of oppression. Anyone who teaches Frye's essay knows how challenging it is to get students to appreciate how Frye uses "oppression" to distinguish systems of domination from individual prejudices and random harms. When I teach this article, I try to move the discussion one step further, prompting students to connect oppressive barriers with the privileges they generate. Echoing Frye's concerns, I caution students not to use privilege in ways that "stretch the term to meaninglessness."[6] Yet when I offer instances of how racial oppression maintains white supremacy and white privilege, or how male privilege relies on the devaluation of feminized bodies, or how homophobia and transphobia hold heterosexual and cisgender privilege in place, students who are otherwise on board with Frye's account of oppression as a birdcage-like macroscopic structure, resist extending her metaphor to privilege. They are reluctant to consider the view from outside of the birdcage, so to speak.

Unsurprisingly, invitations to check your privilege mirror the resistance Frye describes at the beginning of her essay. Requests that ask men to check their male privilege are met with a range of responses. "Women are privileged too, they are not expected to pay for dinner and drinks on dates. Women don't have to register for the selective service. Women are more likely to get child custody after a divorce. And, there are no domestic violence shelters for men."[7] Claims about white privilege are met with similar resistance. "But, people of color get affirmative action benefits. black students get more scholarships and white students can't apply for tuition assistance marked for students of color." Before same-sex marriage became legal in the United States, I used to hear students remark that gay, lesbian, bisexual, transgender, or queer couples had privileges too because local domestic partnership ordinances gave them "special rights." If students really understand oppression as the product of *systemically* related barriers and forces not of one's own making, then why does the request to check your privilege collapse so quickly into claims about privilege not being real because everyone has some kind of advantage?

Systemically Produced Barriers and Double Binds

The main reason most of us find it difficult to understand oppression systemically is that we are in the habit of focusing on isolated events, bad people, cruel intentions, and harmful actions, without placing them into their historical, social, or political systemic contexts. According to Frye, to "be oppressed is to have an absence of choices. Oppressed persons are constantly confronted with double binds, or situations in which options are reduced to a very few and all of them expose one to penalty, censure, or deprivation."[8] To illustrate the bind, Frye describes how women are boxed in by a sexual double standard that disciplines both their sexual choices and other people's judgments about those choices.[9] This is not an isolated example. Members of oppressed groups are quick to recall what it takes to navigate the structural double binds they encounter on a daily basis. These obstacles are not just pesky additional stressors and annoyances. They are patterned experiences. They happen over and over again and their repetition has a cumulative impact on a person's long-term health and well-being.[10] So, it's important to consider their lived implications. Sara Ahmed's account of violence against women and girls makes this real: "The personal is structural. His violence is justified as natural and inevitable: that is structure. A girl is made responsible for his violence: that is structure. The policeman who turns away because it is domestic violence: that is structure. A judge who talks about what she is wearing: that is structure."[11]

Double binds narrow our choices. They confine our movements on a daily basis.[12] Members of oppressed groups find themselves oriented to the world in a way that puts particular responses, opportunities, and aspirations out of reach, and that's structural.[13] In "Facing Down the Spooks," Angela Mae Kupenda describes the challenges she faced as a young black law professor. During an annual evaluation, her supervisor reminded her that he likes black people, has black friends, and that he has funded her to go to a "Black conference" to support her scholarship. In the same breath, he tells her that she "is spending too much time with people of color" and recommends that she "shun black folks and focus on white folks to help her image and that of the school."[14] How should she respond? If she takes his advice and spends more time with white folks, then she risks losing the support of her friends and colleagues of color. If she ignores his advice, then she risks losing departmental support. What should she do? In "The Ethics of Living Jim Crow," Richard Wright describes the bind he was forced to navigate after he took a job at an optical company. Morrie, a white co-worker, falsely claimed that Wright referred to their boss Mr. Pease as "Pease." This was a direct violation of Jim Crow etiquette, which required people of color to address all white people (including children) by their title and last name. Mr. Pease calls Wright to his office and says, "Richard, Mr. Morrie here tells me you called me Pease."[15] How should he respond? If he apologizes, then he admits that he treated a white man disrespectfully. If he denies it, then he is calling a white man a liar. Either response puts him in harm's way. These binds are not relics of the past. Eighty years later, Ta-Nehisi Coates vividly recalls the mental energy it took him to navigate the streets as a young black man. He describes an "array of lethal puzzles and strange perils that seem to rise up from the asphalt itself. The streets transform every ordinary day into a series of trick questions, and every incorrect answer risks a beating down, a shooting, or a pregnancy. No one survives unscathed."[16] How is it possible to negotiate his way through those streets safely?

Finally, it's worth mentioning the high stakes dilemmas Hillary Clinton repeatedly faced during her 2016 presidential campaign. The privileges of her class, whiteness, marital status (along with her experience as the First Lady), and her role as both a U.S. Senator, and Secretary of State were not enough to eclipse the ageist sexism directed at her by her opponent and the press. A headline in *Psychology Today* described her as "pathologically ambitious," Britt Hume complained about her "sharp lecturing tone," remarking that it was "not attractive." As Sady Doyle observed, "she can't be sad or angry, but she *also* can't be happy or amused, and she also can't refrain from expressing any of these emotions. There is literally no way out of this one. Anything she does is wrong."[17] The classic double bind, however, is not reducible to a simple catch-22 situation. As Deborah Tannen explains:

> A double bind is far worse than a straightforward damned-if-you-do, damned-if-you-don't dilemma. It requires you to obey two mutually exclusive commands: Anything you do to fulfill one violates the other. Women running for office, as with all women in authority, are subject to these two demands: Be a good leader! Be a good woman! While the qualities expected of a good leader (be forceful, confident and, at times, angry) are similar to those we expect of a good man, they are the opposite of what we expect of a good woman (be gentle, self-deprecating and emotional, but not angry). Hence the double bind: If a candidate—or manager—talks or acts in ways expected of women, she risks being seen as under confident or even incompetent. But if she talks or acts in ways expected of leaders, she is likely to be seen as too aggressive and will be subject to innumerable other negative judgments—and epithets—that apply only to women.[18]

Double binds indicate the presence of structural barriers that are not of the individual's own making. These barriers are created and shaped by forces which are neither accidental nor avoidable. This is structure. They are related to one another in ways that narrowly confine individual choices to the extent that movement in any direction is penalized. Frye's birdcage metaphor offers an image of the systemic barriers that produce these binds.

> [Oppression is] the experience of being caged in. . . . Consider a birdcage. If you look very closely at just one wire, you cannot see the other wires. If your conception of what is before you is determined by this myopic focus, you could look at that one wire, up and down the length of it, and be unable to see why a bird would not just fly around the wire . . . it is only when you step back, stop looking at the wires one by one, microscopically, and take a macroscopic view of the whole cage, that you can see why the bird does not go anywhere; and then you will see it in a moment.[19]

Failure to understand oppression macroscopically, as harms produced by systemically related forces and barriers not of ones own making, blurs the rough distinction between oppressive and non-oppressive harm.

All Oppression is Harm, but Not All Harm is Oppression

For oppression to be a useful concept, the distinction between oppressive and non-oppressive harms needs sharpening. All oppression is harmful, but not all harm is oppression. All persons who are oppressed are harmed, but not all persons who are harmed are oppressed. Social expectations that prevent men and boys from crying in public, or that prevent white students from applying for NAACP scholarships, are in some sense harmful in the sense that some emotional responses and opportunities are closed off to you; but, this is not oppression. There are no double binds or mutually exclusive demands here. The standards of heteronormative masculinity that pressure men and boys to choke back their tears are psychologically harmful, but there is no double bind here. There is a way out—not crying in front of other men makes you manly. You appear strong, courageous, and steady and these characteristics have cultural capital. They mark your status as a leader, protector, or provider. As harmful as it may be, stuffing your tears is a way to earn respect. White students ineligible for NAACP scholarships may feel like they are being treated unfairly, because *one* scholarship opportunity among many is closed to them, but this is not oppression. When you are used to having every option open to you, then having one closed to you feels unfair, but it's not. These scholarships are not for white people. The choice is not between the NAACP scholarship and no scholarship. White students may be oppressed because they grew up in impoverished neighborhoods with substandard schools and, as a result, received a poor education that put many scholarships out of reach. Or, their family income may have put a college education out of their reach altogether. But, there are no *racial* barriers in these cases that leave scholarship-seeking white students with severely limited options.

Intersectionality and The Limits of Frye's Birdcage Metaphor

While double binds may be a central feature of oppression for Frye, we should not take this to mean that they neutralize oppressed people's agency, rendering them completely helpless. Oppressed subjects are also resisting subjects.[20] Members of oppressed groups regularly use strategies and tactics to navigate double binds in ways that minimize risk and damage. They also seek out resistant communities and spaces where their identities are less likely to box them in. Frye's birdcage metaphor helps us to understand systemic oppression, but, like all metaphors, it has limited explanatory power.

It confines us to imagining only one siloed system of domination at a time. There is the heteropatriarchy birdcage, the white supremacy birdcage, the antisemitism birdcage, and so on. As a result, we may lose touch with how complex systems of domination rely on one another for their meaning and power. Learning to re-conceptualize oppression as a series of interconnected systems requires our effort and attention. For the sake of clarity, it makes sense to focus on one system so that you come to understand how barriers connect. A more accurate understanding, however, has to recognize that double binds have intersectional dimensions. They are best understood as constellations of interlocking systems.[21] So, it is more accurate to re-imagine Frye's birdcage as one of those chain-linked cyclone fences with zig-zagging wires that form interlocking diamond patterns.

The barriers Kupenda, Wright, Coates, and Clinton faced were never the exclusive product of one system. The blended effects of sexism and racism played out differently for Kupenda than for her non-black colleagues. The administrator's words kept her "from being able to experience academia in [the] same way a white male with similar credentials can."[22] The intersectional effects of sexism and ageism played out differently for Clinton than for her Republican opponent. Ageism is racialized and gendered: Despite the overwhelming evidence of his cruelty, corruption, predatory sexual behaviors, repeated business failures, arrogance, dishonesty, ignorance, narcissism, and incompetence many voters saw in Mr. Trump a successful businessman and qualified leader. Senator Clinton's extensive experience in the U.S. government was eclipsed by the perception that she was dishonest, shrewish, and just plain unlikeable.

ALL PRIVILEGES ARE ADVANTAGES, BUT NOT ALL ADVANTAGES ARE PRIVILEGES

Systems of oppression generate systems of privilege. Unearned disadvantages create unearned advantages.[23] As Beth Berila notes: "Systems of oppression use privilege as one way to keep themselves working smoothly. When they work properly, the people who receive privilege remain oblivious to the benefits they receive and to the fact that marginalized groups do not receive them."[24] If we are going to check our privilege, then we need to work with an understanding of privilege that mirrors an understanding of systemic oppression. For the purpose of clarity, I'll be focusing primarily on white privilege, but I'll bring in intersectional considerations along the way.

Peggy McIntosh defines privilege as "unearned power conferred systemically."[25] Her account, along with her well-known list of forty-six white privileges, should be treated as a contemporary version of W. E. B. DuBois's original insights on the value of whiteness. Careful readers will notice the strong parallels between DuBois and McIntosh's lists of privileges. DuBois was one of the first scholars to address the privileges attached to whiteness directly.[26] In *Black Reconstruction in America* (1935), he describes the public and psychological "wages of whiteness," and summarizes the many ways the social value of whiteness is marked. White people, he says, are granted "public deference and titles of courtesy," and access to "public functions, public parks and the best schools ... the police were drawn from their ranks, and the court, dependent upon their votes, treated them with such leniency as to encourage lawlessness." It was "their votes that selected public officials," "their race is represented in newspapers in ways that are flattering," and "they have the freedom to behave violently against others with little or no accountability."[27]

Today the social currency of whiteness is expressed in the language of privilege, but the definition remains elusive. So, it's best to start with what I *don't* mean by privilege. When members of dominant groups are asked to check their privilege, the word "privilege," is not being used in Joel Feinberg's broad juridical sense as something synonymous with mere liberties or the absence of duty.[28] To say that individuals or groups have privilege in this sense means they are at liberty to take a particular action; that is, they have no duties or obligations that prevent them from acting. For instance, when I say that Maureen is free to accept the head surgeon position at the Barnes Jewish Hospital I mean that she has no existing and binding obligations (i.e., an existing job contract, a noncompetition agreement, or a promise to live near her elderly parents) that prevent her from accepting the job offer. Although privilege, in the sense that I use it, does imply greater freedom of movement and choice, there is nothing about Maureen's social identity which implies that she has a duty to decline or accept the position.

Next, I'm not using privilege to mean a legal entitlement that is not a right. Privileges in this sense are valuable benefits that institutions (e.g., the State of Illinois, the U.S. Government, or the Catholic Church) grant to persons or organizations at their discretion. Having an Illinois driver's license, voting entitlements, or permission to officiate Holy Communion are privileges in this sense. Because my driving or voting privileges may be revoked at any time, say, for reckless driving or treason, these privileges count as legal entitlements. The state does not have a duty to grant me these benefits. Living in Illinois neither entitles me to a driver's license nor grants me the right to keep it once I pass the examination. While judicial institutions and legal practices have historically played, and continue to play a central role in holding heterosexual privilege, male privilege, white privilege, and class privilege in place, my account of privilege is not captured by the language of legal entitlement.[29] Still, this can be confusing. While it's true that privileges are not rights, it is also true that the absence of privilege sometimes translates into an absence of rights. As Terrance MacMullan observes "whiteness became valuable in the late seventeenth century not because of new benefits enjoyed by European Virginians, but because African Virginians and Native peoples living with the colonies *lost* important rights (the right to vote, to walk freely on the roads, to choose to marry or not, etc.)."[30] Naomi Zack also discusses the relationship between privileges and rights. She describes privilege as a "special treatment that goes beyond a right. It's not so much that being white confers privilege, but that not being white means being without rights in many cases. Not fearing that the police will kill your child for no reason isn't a privilege. It's a right. But, I think this is what white privilege is meant to convey, that whites don't have many of the worries nonwhites, especially blacks, do."[31] So, the request to check your privilege, is a request to examine how unearned *power* conferred *systemically* nourishes and sustains the privileges (or in some cases rights) that move some groups forward at the expense of other groups. Think of power this way: Privilege draws its power from systems of domination in much the same way that hurricanes draw their energy from heated water. Water vapor fuels hurricanes. Patriarchy fuels male privilege. White supremacy fuels white privilege.[32]

The distinction I want to make between (unearned) privilege and (earned) advantage parallels Frye's distinction between oppression and (non-systemic) harm. All oppression counts as harm, but not all harm counts as oppression. All privilege counts as advantageous, but not all advantages count as privileges. Like the difference between (non-systemic) harm and oppression, the difference between (earned) advantages and (unearned) privilege rests on the systemically conferred nature of these unearned powers. To determine whether a particular harm qualifies as oppression, Frye asks us to examine the bigger (macroscopic or systemic) picture of how some groups are placed repeatedly in harm's way. She encourages us to ask ourselves what role, if any, these placements play in maintaining racism, heterosexism, antisemitism, etc. Likewise, if we want to determine whether a particular advantage qualifies as a privilege, then we have to examine that particular advantage macroscopically to determine whether, like hurricanes, it is fueled by larger systems. This requires clarifying and expanding McIntosh's distinction between "earned strength" and "unearned power conferred systemically." She explains:

> Power from unearned privilege can look like strength when it is in fact, permission to escape or to dominate. But not all privileges . . . are inevitably damaging. Some, like the expectation that neighbors will be decent to you, or that your race will not count against you in court, should be the norm in a just society and should be considered as the entitlement of everyone. Others, like the privilege

not to listen to less powerful people, distorts the humanity of the holders as well as ignored groups. Still others, like finding one's staple foods everywhere may be a function of a numerical majority. Others have to do with not having to labor under pervasive negative stereotyping and mythology.[33]

McIntosh distinguishes between strengths that are earned and powers that are unearned. She cautions readers that the power of unearned privilege can sometimes appear as strength, when in reality it is just permission to dominate or discriminate against others. I understand her point, but I believe this distinction can be made more clearly if we start by acknowledging two kinds of assets: (unearned, systemically conferred) privilege, and other (earned) advantages, and then discuss how the assets associated with privilege cut two ways. After all, some privileges, like the expectation that store clerks, neighbors, and medical doctors will treat you respectfully, are just basic human decency (and should not be called privileges), and others are rooted deeply in social practices of domination.[34]

The distinction I want to make between unearned privileges and earned advantages begins with a rough taxonomy of privilege as a special class of advantages. The privileges DuBois and McIntosh list are a special class of advantages and are marked by four interrelated features: (1) privileges are granted capriciously and rarely justifiable; (2) privileges are invisible and not recognized as privileges by those that have them; (3) privileges have an unconditional "wild card" quality that extends the benefits to cover a broad range of conditions; and (4) privileges have positive and negative dimensions.

EXPOSING PRIVILEGE AS A SPECIAL CLASS OF ADVANTAGE: A ROUGH TAXONOMY

Let's begin with a rough taxonomy of advantages. The words "advantage" and "advance" share a common late Latin root–*abante* meaning "in front of" or "before." To have an advantage is to possess a skill, talent, asset, or condition favorable to success that is acquired—either by birth or by intentional cultivation—that helps you to rise to a higher rank, move yourself forward, lift yourself up, or to otherwise progress. Privileges are, by definition, advantageous, but not all advantages are privileges. Recognizing this requires attending carefully to the distinct character of this ill-gotten species of advantage. Advantages that are not privileges I'll call *earned* advantages; that is, benefits and strengths attached to any earned condition, skill, asset, or talent that helps a person to move forward. Earned advantages run the gamut from mere perks to significant benefits. Perks are earned in the weakest sense of being earned. They include fast food "buy one get one" promotional offers, frequent flyer award programs, and getting free drinks on ladies' night at the local bar. I'm not too concerned with perks. They don't do much conceptual work, so I use the term "earned advantages" to refer only to advantages that are earned in the *strong* sense. These include working to put yourself through college so you can have a fulfilling career, studying to become fluent in a second language, practicing your cello so that you can audition for the city orchestra, or working overtime so you can afford an apartment in a well-funded school district.

The distinction between privileges as unearned powers conferred systemically and earned advantages is not hard and fast; but, I want to hold onto it loosely because the two rarely operate independently from one another. Privilege places some people in a position where more advantages will fall within their reach. For instance, the ability to earn frequent flyer miles presupposes that you have enough money to actually buy airline tickets in the first place. Here class privilege opens up more advantages. The ability to work extra hours, so you can afford to live in a safer neighborhood assumes you are able-bodied, have transportation, and that landowners will rent to you. Regardless of gender or class privilege, real estate redlining practices continue to prevent families of color from moving into so-called "good neighborhoods."

This distinction between unearned privilege and earned advantage must also avoid a popular misconception about the intersections between privileges and oppressions. A common defensive response to the "check your [white] privilege" request usually comes from poor white people who insist that poverty (class oppression) is not only detachable from white privilege but also completely consumes and nullifies their race privilege. Poor and working-class white people are eager to point out that white privilege did not put more advantages within their reach. They had to work really hard for what they have. But, this is an inaccurate reading of what happens when class oppression intersects with race and gender privilege. *Class oppression complicates white privilege it does not erase it.* In some contexts, class oppression may devalue the currency of white privilege, but it never neutralizes it. Gina Crosely-Corcoran's initial remark that her "white skin didn't do shit to prevent [her] from experiencing poverty . . . the kind of poverty that people don't want to believe exists in this country," suggests that class oppression eclipses white privilege to the point where white privilege is drained completely of its power. She later realizes that her white, English-speaking, U.S. citizen, cisgender, able-bodied privileges, along with her ambitious nature, have value independently of her impoverished childhood. This constellation of privileges, she admits, is what enabled her to marry up, by partnering with a white middle-class man who fully expected her to earn a college degree.[35] As Sara Ahmed puts it, "bodies 'move up' when their whiteness is not in dispute."[36] The impact of oppression may soften when a marginalized person becomes a well-respected member of the larger community. Consider the lesbian community leader or the working-class philanthropist who, by virtue of their outstanding community service, is granted the status and authority commonly associated with heterosexual or class privilege. Members of dominant groups frequently make exceptions for individuals with good civic reputations. "She's not like most Mexican immigrants. She's not the stereotype." Or, "He's not your typical gay man." Closeted gay men or light-skinned Latinas can also be extended privileges episodically when they are straight-passing or are white-passing, a subject I'll return to later.

My point, then, is not that earned advantages and privileges are necessarily distinct, or that oppression completely drains the value from privilege. I'm arguing that advantages are earned more easily when they are accompanied by gender, heterosexual, cisgender, able-bodied, or white privilege. Privileges and earned advantages overlap when privilege places a person in a better position to earn *more* advantages—to move forward *more* quickly. The connection between earned advantages and privileges means that people with white or male privilege are in a position to earn additional assets (e.g., control over community resources, access to quality education, titles of respect, the attention of government officials, prestigious and well-paying jobs, or safe places to live) with greater ease and frequency than those without them. Failure to recognize the difference between earned and unearned assets prompts those with privilege to put unearned power conferred systemically on equal footing with earned advantages. Former Texas governor Ann Richards's, humorous remark that George H. W. Bush "was born on third base, and to this day believes he hit a triple," illustrates how easily people with privilege blur this distinction.[37] To give a more recent example, Brent Kavanaugh really believes that he got into Yale Law School and then onto the Supreme Court based *exclusively* on his own merits. When Christine Blasey Ford testified that he sexually assaulted her at a high school party, Kavanaugh angrily pulled out his academic pedigree like a get-out-of-jail free card—"I went to Yale! I went to Yale!" He seemed to sincerely believe that his academic pedigree entitled him to move smoothly, without obstruction, from his judicial seat onto the Supreme Court.

The most direct route to privilege, then, is to be born into it. In its classic sense, "privilege is meant to pick out precisely the benefits and advantages that accrue to individuals solely by virtue of their membership by birth into an elite caste," more contemporary notions of privilege recognize that "such unearned advantages are illegitimate."[38] Consider how, in the United States, legal entitlements like voting privileges were granted automatically to free adult white property-owning tax-paying males. Suffrage was later *extended* to white women in 1920, to indigenous peoples in 1924, and to African

Americans in 1965. Or, consider how state-sanctioned marriages were automatically available to heterosexual couples. It wasn't until 2015 that marriage privileges (civil rights) were *extended* to same-sex couples in all fifty states, but this only happened because activists fought for this privilege in the same way that Mildred Jeter Loving and her husband Richard fought to have their interracial marriage recognized by the Commonwealth of Virginia in 1967. Being granted the privilege to marry because you are heterosexual, or the privilege to vote because you are an adult white property-owning male, is unearned. These advantages are tied to fortunate accidents of birth. The less fortunate always have had to organize and fight to attain the rights and privileges that were granted automatically to dominant groups.

Privileges Are Capriciously Granted and Rarely Justifiable

This brings us to the first feature of privilege. The etymological roots of privilege point to its capricious nature. The word privilege comes from the Latin *privilegium*, meaning a law applying to one person, a bill of law in favor of or against an individual. It comes from *privus*, meaning private, individual, or particular, and from *lex*, or law.[39] So, privilege literally means private or individual law. One legal definition holds that "[p]rivileges are special rights belonging to the individual or class and not to the mass."[40] Historically, privilege refers to having a right or immunity, granting a particular benefit, advantage, or favor, such as those attached to holding a particular office or position. For instance, the "privilege from arrest" clause in the U.S. Constitution exempts members of Congress from civil arrest while going to, returning from, or attending legislative sessions. Ambulance drivers and police officers are legally exempt from the burdens and liabilities of public traffic laws (e.g., speed limits or traffic signals) while on duty. Since emergency care demands getting to the hospital quickly, it is reasonable to grant ambulance drivers immunity from speeding laws. Paramedics have "special rights" in this sense, but speeding privileges are justifiable in these cases. So, private laws are acceptable when they are attached to job duties, but not when they are attached to a particular perceived social identity.

In her essay "White Debt," Eula Biss recounts how the private laws of whiteness attached to her identity after she was arrested for wheat-pasting "Bomb the Suburbs" event posters all over Amherst. She explains:

> The first question the Amherst Police asked was whether I was aware that graffiti and "tagging," a category that included posters, was punishable as a felony. I was not aware. Near the end of the interrogation, my campus officer stepped in and suggested that we would clean up the posters. I was not charged with a felony, and I spent the day working side by side with my officer, using a wire

brush to scrub all the bombs off Amherst. Even as the police spread photos of my handiwork in front of me, I could tell by the way they pronounced "tagging" that it wasn't a crime invented for me. I was subject less to the law as it was written, than I was to the private laws of whiteness."[41]

Biss compares the version of justice in her police encounter with the violence Sandra Bland, a young black woman, experienced when she was pulled over by a white Texas trooper for her failure to signal a lane change. Biss's encounter began with a call into the Amherst police station. It ended with a request to scrub off the posters. Bland's encounter began with police lights in her rearview mirror. She was pulled over, thrown face down on the road, and arrested. It ended with her death in a jail cell. Private law means being given the benefit of the doubt because you are presumed innocent and nonthreatening. Privilege, then, is a particular class of unearned benefits and immunities enjoyed by people who, by moral luck or accident of birth, are perceived as belonging to a group that is understood to be innocent until proven guilty. These privileges are granted capriciously. They are held in place not only through legislation and public policy but also through social interactions and representations (i.e., informal and subtle expressions of speech, bodily reactions, gestures, malicious stereotypes, aesthetic judgments, and media images). In this way the capricious nature of privilege is systemically granted and culturally nourished. The understanding of privilege as "special right" or "private law" demonstrated in Eula Biss's story about the Amherst police should now be clear.

Privileges Are Invisible to Those Who Have Them

The request to check your privilege contains a grave irony. Privileges are designed to be check proof; so, we need to make them visible before we can take an inventory. Analogies and metaphors are the standard route into the irony. What Frye's birdcage metaphor does for oppression, Peggy McIntosh's invisible weightless knapsack analogy and Jona Olsson's word-processing software metaphor do for privilege.[42] McIntosh foregrounds privilege's epistemic dimensions when she describes privilege as an "invisible package of unearned assets that I can count on cashing in each day, but about which I was meant to remain oblivious. White privilege is like an invisible weightless knapsack of special provisions, assurances, tools, maps, guides, code books, passports, visas, clothes, compass, emergency gear, and blank checks."[43] Olsson compares white privilege to a user-friendly word-processing program. Her metaphor draws attention to the ways privileged knowers are oblivious to how privilege operates in the background when we perform many of our daily tasks. When you use word-processing software to create a document, the font, margins, line spacing, type size, and footnotes appear in a pre-set standard format. The software checks and corrects your spelling and grammar in ways that are structurally concealed from you. It automatically produces a document in an acceptable style, font, and layout. You come to expect and eventually take the professional appearance of your written work for granted. You eventually forget about what is happening in the background and begin to attribute your perfectly polished documents to your skills as a writer. Privilege, like software and virus scan programs, works silently and invisibly in the background of all we do.

Olsson's account reminds us not to read those grocery-list style inventories of privileges too narrowly. These lists tell us what privileges are, but they do not tell us how they function, and this is something we can't overlook. Annotating McIntosh's list clarifies what white privilege *does*: It confers value, visibility, privacy, security, respectability, and the public trust.

- I can, if I wish, arrange to be in the company of people of my race most of the time. *This is about the value of belonging, comfort, and safety. If you are fluent with the social norms of a community, then you don't have to be hyper-aware of what you say, how your body moves, or how you behave. Being around people who look and act like you is less stressful than being surrounded by people who don't share your social norms and may misread them.*
- I can be certain that my children will be given curricular materials that testify to the existence and accomplishments of their race. *This is about the value of visibility and the worth that comes from having your existence and experiences acknowledged, affirmed, and engaged. When you see your people represented positively in literature, on the news, or in history books, it sends the message that their accomplishments are valuable and important.*
- I am never asked to speak for the people in my racial group. *This is about the value of privacy and security. It means that you will not be singled out to educate people (who may be hostile to what you have to say) about issues of race. When you are not put on the spot, your privacy and integrity are respected.*
- I can swear or have bad manners without having my behavior attributed to my race. *This is about respectability. We might lose respect for white people who swear, dress poorly, and eat like pigs, but "whiteness" is never given as the reason for their bad manners or behavior.*
- Whether I use checks, credit cards, or cash I can be fairly sure that my skin color will not count against the appearance of my financial reliability. *This is about the value of public trust. Most white people are assumed to be trustworthy, financially solvent, honest, and reliable until proven otherwise.*

The starting assumption for white people is that we wouldn't write a bad check.

Our annotated list reveals a double ignorance. In addition to being unaware of white privilege itself, most white people are unaware of the damaging effects that exercising these privileges have on people of color. The value of whiteness is predicated upon the devaluation of bodies of color. The fact that whiteness is invisible to white people (especially well-meaning ones) is what makes it particularly dangerous. As bell hooks remarks, when "liberal whites fail to understand how they can and/or do embody white supremacist values and beliefs even though they may not embrace racism as prejudice or domination (especially domination that involves coercive control), they cannot recognize the ways their actions support and affirm the very structure of racist domination and oppressions that they profess to wish to see eradicated."[44]

McIntosh's list of white privileges is written from the center, from the perspective of a white woman; but, it's valuable to consider how these lists would sound if we centered people of color's voices. What if they were read from the grounds upon which people of color stand?[45] Unpacking the knapsack from the margins forces to the surface how white privilege fails to extend basic humanity to all people of color. It also makes visible the habits of vigilance people of color require to survive under white supremacy, and the costs and losses associated with having to navigate the world with such vigilance. Such a list might read:

- I must always be concerned about whether my appearance or presence will make white people fearful or uncomfortable.
- When I'm in white spaces with my Spanish-speaking family members, I must always be on high alert in case some white person decides to harass them for not speaking English.
- When I go shopping, I always assume that I'm being watched and that I might be confronted or harassed by the management.
- I have to constantly convince white people that my accomplishments and achievements are due to my talents and hard work and not to an affirmative action policy.
- I never assume that my rights will be respected or that I will be treated fairly under the law.
- My children will rarely be given curricular materials that testify to their existence or to our people's histories. I've come to expect this erasure and know I will have to supplement their education with family stories, genealogies, and the histories of our people.
- When I move, I never assume that people will rent to me or that realtors will show me houses in the neighborhoods where I want to live.

- I realize there will be times when I will be unable to protect my children from someone who might not like them because of how they look, act, or speak.
- I can never be certain that if I need medical or legal help, or if I'm applying for positions, that my race or appearance will not be working against me.

The background machinery of privilege has always been visible to marginalized groups whose survival depends on knowing how to navigate these barriers as safely as possible. Privilege means getting to do with impunity what others have to think about doing twice over.[46] People of color have a practical wisdom about the best ways to navigate whiteness. Consider how Cherríe Moraga uncomfortably acknowledges how her *güera* (light-skinned) appearance is something she can use to her advantage in a wide variety of difficult circumstances.

> Then [my friend] Tavo say to me, "you see at any time [you] decide to use your light skinned privilege [you] can. I say, "Uh huh. Uh huh." He says, "You can decide that you are suddenly no Chicana."
> That I can't say, but once my light-skin and good English saved my lover from arrest. And, I'd use it again. I'd use it to the hilt over and over to save our skins.
> "You get to choose." Now I want to shove those words right back into his face. You call this a choice! To constantly push against the wall of resistance from your own people or to fall nameless into the mainstream of this country, running with our common blood?"[47]

Moraga's words illustrate the lived experience that is implicit, but not tangible, in McIntosh's list. The double invisibility of this default position means that white people are rarely aware of how many times our light skin, white mannerisms, or clear English rescue us. Moraga's observations reinforce Eula Biss's story about how her whiteness saved her from formal arrest for wheat-pasting posters. Claudia Rankine's description of her conversation with a friend, who recently become the mother of a black son, offers a heart-wrenching account of the costs at which the value of white privilege is purchased.

> I asked another friend what it's like being the mother of a black son. "The condition of black life is one of mourning," she said bluntly. For her, mourning lived in real time inside her and her son's reality: At any moment she might lose her reason for living. Though the white liberal imagination likes to temporarily feel bad about black suffering, there really is no mode of empathy that can replicate the daily strain of knowing that as a black person you can be killed

for simply being black: no hands in your pockets, no playing music, no sudden movements, no driving your car, no walking at night, no walking in the day, no turning onto this street, no entering this building, no standing your ground, no standing here, no standing there, no talking back, no playing with toy guns, no living while black.[48]

Rankine's narrative points to the presence of white privilege in the most ordinary human activities. Who gets to put their hands in their pockets? Who gets to talk back? Who gets to run in public? Can you run in an airport if you are wearing a hijab or a dastaar? Can you run to catch the bus if you are undocumented? What happens when black and brown people run after their children in Walmart? Whose running inspires fear in white folks? Whose running signals the need for help? Whose running calls for bystanders to step up and help?[49]

Sara Ahmed addresses the flip side of my question: who gets stopped and how does it feel to be stopped? As she puts it: "Being stopped is not just stressful: it makes the 'body' itself the 'site' of social stress," and it depletes you. Privilege, she observes, "is an energy-saving device. Less effort is required to be or to do."[50] Interlocking systems of oppression distribute power unevenly and this has an unequal impact on our bodies. Ahmed continues, "some bodies become depleted because of what is required to go somewhere, to be somewhere, and to stay somewhere. . . . You often become even more conscious of a feeling when it dissipates. When we leave the spaces of whiteness, which is where I have lived and worked and accounts for most of the space I have been in, we become even more aware of how wearing whiteness is."[51] Who gets to have enough energy to make it through the day and to spend quality time with their family?

The energy-saving feature of privilege is invisible to white people. We are ignorant of the emotional, mental, psychological, and physical energy it takes for people of color to constantly navigate spaces where they feel unwelcome. Moraga, Rankine, and Ahmed's words offer a clear answer to my opening question about whose flesh nourishes the privilege that remains invisible to most white people. When these scholars say that white privilege is invisible to white people they mean that white people are not aware of the extent to which our whitely habits are artifacts of inherited histories of conquest, colonization, and segregation. This is an ignorance born of our failure to perceive the distance between the conscious good intentions of the majority of white people, and the unconscious historical scripts that remain active in our bones. White behaviors and judgments (e.g., who is regarded with suspicion, who is trustworthy, or whose art and history is important) are artifacts from earlier era, but they remain with us. This is our colonial inheritance.

Privileges Have a "Wild Card" Value

Understanding how privilege functions makes its value visible. The difference between the value of earned advantages and the value of unearned privileges is analogous to the difference between high-value cards and wild cards in some card games. All playing cards are "cards," so to speak; but, the rules of most card games assign more value to wild cards than to face cards, and more value to face cards than numerical cards. Wild cards can be played as if they were any card in the deck. Wild cards work to the player's advantage in ways that high-value cards do not. High-value cards, like aces and face cards, can strengthen a *particular* hand, but only when they fit with the other cards in that hand. Unlike wildcards, they cannot be used to stand in for the particular card a player needs to strengthen the hand she was dealt. Earned advantages function like high-value cards. They advance a person in limited contexts. They move a person forward only under narrow circumstances. For example, earned advantages like frequent flyer miles are only advantageous if I need to travel by air. Living in a neighborhood with a good school district is only beneficial if I have young children. Being bilingual is only an asset if I live or spend time in communities where I need to speak more than one language.

When McIntosh compares privileges to passports, blank checks, and code books, she is referencing the wild card value of privilege as something works to a person's advantage across a broad variety of situations. Consider the extraordinary value of whiteness. Whiteness gets people's attention. It calms police officers, enhances credibility in courtroom testimonies, and it makes employers think you are a "good fit" for the position. It signals honesty, virtue, reliability, leadership, and trustworthiness. White privilege works to white people's advantage in every single hand we are dealt. Privilege means that the immunities and benefits attached to your social identity extend beyond the boundaries of your comfort zones, neighborhood, circles of friends, or what María Lugones refers to as the familiar "worlds" in which you are at ease.[52] Although people with dominant-group privileges can and do feel ill at ease outside of the comfort of their own "worlds," this lack of ease does not signal a loss of privilege. It only signals a temporary loss of comfort.

The immunity granting wild cards have pecuniary value. In *Two Nations*, Andrew Hacker describes a thought experiment he use to conduct with his white students as a way of prompting them to assign a monetary value to white privilege. He asks them to imagine that they will be visited by an official they have never met, who informs them that according to his organization's records they were to have been born black. Since the error must be rectified immediately, at midnight they will become black and expect to live out the rest of their lives as a black person in America. Since this is the agency's error, they are entitled to compensation. Hacker then asks the white students how much money they would request in compensation. Years ago, when I tried to replicate Hacker's exercise, I discovered a predictable pattern in white student's responses. Those who asked for compensation requested amounts between $250,000 and $250 million dollars, but a significant number of white students vehemently refused any compensation. When I asked why they failed to write down an amount, they argued that asking for *any* money was racist. It implied that whiteness was more valuable and they insisted that everyone was equally valuable. In short, they flat out refused to even consider that whiteness had any wild-card value at all. I understand why Hacker conducted this exercise, but I have mixed feelings about how it works in cross-racial classrooms. White students' answers were frightfully depressing to witness. Those who accepted compensation admitted freely that whiteness had value. Students who refused compensation conflated the request with a guilty admission of racism, so they retreated to color-blind explanations (i.e., "all lives are valuable" or "the price we choose should be the same for everyone"). They refused to play. Better to opt out of the experiment entirely than to enter into a conversation that makes white value visible and raises awkward questions about white goodness, innocence and our complicity in racism. Hacker's exercise was eye-opening for most white students, but it triggered anger and pain for students of color, who had to witness white students' strategic refusals to consider what whiteness gave them. The assignment highlights the tight connections between white student's comfort and students of color's suffering. The emotional dynamics prompted by this realization were tangibly felt in our classroom. And in the end, white student's education came at the expense of a painful classroom experience for students of color. When I realized this, I stopped using the exercise.

Privileges Have Positive and Negative Dimensions

Now that the four interrelated features of privilege are in place, I want to return to my earlier point about privilege cutting two ways, because it illustrates two sources of value. Privileges are *negative* when their wild card value offers immunity from systemic barriers, but they are *positive* when they put people in positions to receive additional advantages. The negative dimensions of privilege (freedom from barriers) allow some groups to escape the double binds, harms, and that energy-draining effects interlocking systems of oppression have on our lives. Straight-passing men have "freedom from" most forms of sexually based street harassment. But this does not exempt some from being harassed for other reasons, such as body size or ability. The positive side of privilege points to additional perks that are not captured by immunity to structural barriers. Positive privileges are those wild cards that offer individuals the freedom to do something. Heterosexual couples, for example, are free to engage in public displays of affection without stopping to consider whether or not it is safe to do so.

The distinction between positive and negative privilege is not simply two ways of expressing the same phenomenon. I first realized this during a conversation I had with Bryan, a young white man in my Gender, Sex, and Power class. Once he understood the value of his white cisgender straight male privilege, he was eager to use it in politically supportive ways. Our community holds an annual Take Back the Night March, which at the time, was restricted to women and girls. Bryan reasoned that since most men can go out at night with very little risk of sexual assault, that he might use his straight, cisgender, white male privilege to protect the marchers from street harassment during the event. So, what's problematic about using privilege to protect women and girls while they marched for the basic human right to feel safe at night? Isn't using privilege to protect march participants being a good ally or active bystander? And, how does this illustrate my point about positive and negative privilege not being two sides of the same coin?

Certainly, there are occasions when it makes perfect sense for allies to use privilege supportively, but this is not one of them. The original purpose of the Take Back the Night movement was to create space for women and girls to reclaim the night *for themselves*. Symbolically, when we take back the night, we are taking it back from those who made it unsafe for us in the first place. Women and girls must do this for ourselves, so we can cultivate both an embodied understanding of what it feels like to be safe at night, and to rely on other women for protection and support. When male protectors step in, regardless of their heartfelt good intentions, the symbolism of the march is undermined; when men march protectively along the route, they deny us the experience of feeling safe independently of male protection. Historically, offers of protection have not always been offers of solidarity, so negotiating these offers is a tricky business. As Charlotte Perkins Gilman boldly recalls:

> A stalwart man once sharply contested my claim to this freedom to go along. "Any true man," he said with fervor, "is always ready to go with a woman at night. He is her natural protector." "Against what?" I inquired. "As a matter of fact, the thing a woman is most afraid to meet on a dark street is her natural protector."[53]

Now, I'm not suggesting that Bryan was secretly a predator or that his offer was insincere. My point is structural: the protector/protected dichotomy is integral to heteropatriarchal systems that organize sex and gender into strict binary categories. I'm not sure how the dynamics of protection work in queer communities, but historically protector/protected roles have fallen neatly in line with heteronormative understandings of sex and gender. The male-as-protector role can only exist if there is a population that is in constant jeopardy. Sarah Hoagland describes this as a protection racket, "there can be no protectors unless there is a danger. A man cannot identify himself in the role of protector unless there is something which needs protection."[54] Bryan doesn't notice how offers of protection fall neatly into the logic of domination. "The Master's Tools," as Lorde famously put it, "cannot dismantle the Master's House."[55] Offers of protection are part of the master's tool kit. In this context using these tools does not dismantle the master's house—it sharpens his tools.

Here's how this works in the context of white supremacy. One positive dimension of white privilege captures what has been called a reputational interest in being perceived as white. Whiteness—the lived and embodied expression of white privilege—means more than just being granted immunity from demeaning stereotypes and the removal of barriers to good housing, medical care, or education. Returning to Crosley-Corcoran's earlier point, being white (or white-passing) does not automatically free you from misfortune: even for impoverished whites, whiteness has value. If whiteness is associated with reliability, citizenship, trustworthiness, industriousness, then being white in America is a culturally valued identity. Recall that the "reputational interest in being regarded as white" was used as grounds for Homer Plessy's case in *Plessy vs. Ferguson* (1896). When Plessy, a white-passing man of mixed European and African descent, boarded a railway car reserved for whites, he was arrested for violating a Louisiana Jim Crow statute mandating separate cars for white and so-called "colored" passengers. Plessy's grievance was not that his race placed an additional barrier in his journey by denying him access to the best seats on the train. As a white-passing man he may have become accustomed to having Jim Crow barriers lifted for him (a negative privilege). His objection, however, was not that the railroad placed an additional barrier in his path. The company's refusal to seat him in the white passenger car deprived him of a positive privilege—the reputation of being white, which prompted others to treat him with respect, dignity, attention, and kindness. Being treated as white has actual pecuniary value.[56] His humanity was fully honored when people thought he was white.

COMPLICATING PRIVILEGE: COUNTEREXAMPLES AND CONSIDERATIONS

Hopefully, the invitation to check your privilege now feels a little less disorienting. Learning to perceive privilege systemically takes time, patience, and practice. Remember, privilege is designed to be check proof, and many of you reading this chapter may still feel the urge to push back against the invitation itself. The invitation to check your privilege is not a one-and-done task like checking to see if your seatbelt is fastened. It's a request to stop, investigate, and hold space with what you find. This takes considerable time and practice. Even those of us who think we understand privilege find ourselves suddenly disoriented by its shape-shifting tenacious nature. A meticulous privilege check requires more than a working taxonomy. It requires additional histories, facts, and figures, all of which need to be checked through an intersectional lens. To illustrate this, I want to revisit a few common responses to the invitation to check your privilege.

Let's start with some easy cases, the ones that can be settled quickly by appealing to my thick definition of privilege. When heterosexual men object that women have privileges too because men customarily pay for dinners out, or that women drink for free on ladies' night at the local bar, they confuse privileges with perks. Free drinks and invited dinners are not wild cards: They do not move you forward across a variety of circumstances. These are invitations and promotions that are confined to specific locations. In fact, when we examine the social practice of men paying for things systemically, we realize how these practices buttress heterosexism and patriarchy. Ladies' night is a marketing strategy that uses women as bait to lure straight men into bars where they can pick up women without having to pay for their drinks. The social etiquette that prompts men to pay for a night out is rooted in traditional [white] masculine breadwinner, provider and protector roles. So, this is not an example of women's privilege; it is an artifact of gendered pay inequity under patriarchy, which understands women's work as less valuable. Historically men have paid for entertainment because few women could afford to.

The scholarship and affirmative action objections are more complicated. White people who object that people of color get identity-based scholarships or affirmative action benefits confuse white privilege with earned advantages. Scholarships are, by definition, *earned* advantages. Scholarship applications require candidates to offer evidence of their eligibility and excellence. Some private scholarships, like the League of United Latin American Citizens (LULAC) or the American Association of University Women (AAUW) have ethnicity and identity as part of their eligibility criteria. These scholarships are neither lotteries nor insider deals. They are merit-based competitions. The fact that white people habitually raise raced-based scholarships as an example of how people of color have privileges too speaks to their sense of entitlement. All possible educational resources should be open to them, or it's not fair. Dominant-group privilege skews privileged peoples' perception of equality. If the machinery of privilege has been operating in the background for most of your life, then systemic advantages feel earned, and they experience genuine equality as loss.

Some invitations to check our privilege require more than an appeal to the taxonomies and interlocking features that I've outlined above. Objections that appeal to affirmative action, access to domestic violence shelters, child custody, and mandated military service as evidence of what might be called reverse privilege demand a working historical and intersectional knowledge of how these institutions came into being in the first place. So, in closing, I want to briefly explore why these go-to objections do not count as privileges in the sense that I'm using the term.

The perceived injustices of affirmative action are habitually raised in response to questions of privilege. To understand why affirmative action is not privilege, we need to stop to consider what affirmative action actually does. When you have privilege, policies aimed at leveling the playing field feel like requests to forfeit earned advantages. In spirit, affirmative action is a legal instrument designed to give qualified members of historically disenfranchised groups the same access to opportunities that members of privileged groups simply take for granted. This does not mean that universities are required to admit or that corporations are required to hire unqualified applicants in order to level the playing field. Affirmative action policies are not designed to throw the order of power into reverse. Affirmative action is the policymaker's response to *opportunity hoarding*, which happens when privileged groups restrict access to valuable and scarce resources to members of their own groups through legal, economic, cultural, and social processes of exclusions and other monopolies.[57] Consider how legacy admissions, social connections, tuition costs, low standardized test scores, or lack of access to high school advanced placement classes restrict people of color's access to higher education. There is evidence that race-neutral or merit-based admissions practices disproportionately favor white and Asian students.[58] So, race- and gender-conscious admissions plans, scholarships, and job applicant pools don't count as privileges. Returning to our definition, these advantages are not granted capriciously. They are not wild cards. They don't waive basic job and scholarship requirements in favor of a candidate's race or gender. They are policy-based antidotes to educational and employment opportunity hoarding, so they count as *historically earned* compensation for past injustices.

Let's check the "women have privileges too" objection to the check-your-privilege invitation. I often hear people say, "there are domestic violence shelters for women but not men, women are more likely to get child custody after a divorce, and women don't have to register for the selective service." These responses are intended to pick out unique instances where gender harms men and benefits women. At first glance, these claims fit neatly into my thick definition of privilege. The harms and benefits *are* produced systemically by heteropatriarchal structures. They are tied to traditional [white and middle-class] gender roles that portray men as protectors and women as caregivers. If masculinity is tied to protection, then the state will draft men in times of war. If femininity is tied to nurturing and caring, then courts will reward child custody to mothers more than fathers. So, one might argue that these instances are in line with the original definition of privileges as unearned advantages conferred systemically. Legal exemptions from military duty, being awarded child custody, or having access to social services during times of crisis are clearly advantageous. Military service puts one in harm's way, losing custody of one's children is heartbreaking, and not having a safe place to live in times of crisis is traumatizing.

Yet, I'm reluctant to characterize these counterexamples as privileges based solely on my thick definition. Such cases demand a much deeper understanding of what it means for something to be conferred systemically. The cases I've mentioned require additional information in order for the macroscopic view to come into sharper focus. These so-called "privileges," like access to shelters, child custody, and military service, might be more accurately characterized *earned advantages born of political struggle*. Unlike everyday earned advantages, which require individual effort and merit over one's lifetime, earned advantages born of struggle demand organized community efforts across generations. Second-wave feminists, civil rights activists, and their allies fought to create, staff, and fund shelters and resources for sexual assault survivors. These shelters and counseling programs are the fruits of decades of resistance to interlocking systems of oppression, not the fruits of the dominant systems themselves. Racialized patriarchy did not create shelters and support systems, resistance to racialized patriarchy did. These services were brought into existence by sustained grassroots movements responding to systemic indifference to violence against women and girls. They persist because violence against women and girls has been, and continues to be, a historical constant.

Yet this account is too simple. History all too frequently collapses into whiteness, so the invitation to check our privilege needs an additional level of vigilance. Intersectional considerations complicate the shelter example because race, immigration status, gender identity, and family history create additional obstacles for some survivors. Most shelters won't take women if they have older male children with them. Transwomen are routinely denied access to shelter services even though they are statistically more vulnerable to violence. Few shelters are able to accommodate immigrant women who speak languages other than English and Spanish. The taxonomy of privilege and advantage cannot capture these cases accurately. So, responding to they-have-privilege-too objections requires a deeper check. Being cisgender or English-speaking is definitely an advantage when it comes to accessing these services. I'm not claiming that transmen, men, and boys should not have access to crisis services. Recent statistics demonstrate that men suffer from intimate partner violence more than previously acknowledged, and the instances of intimate partner violence in transgender communities are demonstrably higher than they are for cisgender men and women.[59] What I am claiming is that domestic violence shelters are a response to patriarchal patterns of violence against women and girls, not a privilege granted by interlocking systems of oppression.

Next, the claim that mothers are privileged because they are overwhelmingly awarded child custody after a divorce or separation is another predictable objection to my definition of privilege. At first glance, one could argue that custody benefits count as unearned advantages produced by heteropatriarchal systemic structures, which understand mothers as better caregivers; and, that this fact works to women's advantage in most custody cases. Like the other examples in this section, this case must be supplemented with an intersectional understanding of how custody is awarded. It's true that women are awarded custody of their children in an overwhelming majority of divorce and separation cases, but it is not for the reasons most of us think. As it turns out, ninety-one percent of the custody cases are decided independently of the family court system. In heterosexual relationships mothers gain custody not because the courts favor women as caregivers; it's because the fathers chose to give custody to the mother.[60] So, the language of systemically conferred advantages doesn't fit here. It's inaccurate to describe an agreement made between two parties as a maternal privilege. Yet, if objectors insist that the statistics speak for themselves, I would reply that under heteropatriarchy, childcare is one of the very few contexts in which women's choices and desires are heard. Gender works in their favor when it comes to doing unpaid caregiver work. Hooray! Women are socially rewarded for mothering and domestic work. I'd also encourage objectors to think intersectionally about which women are culturally understood to be "good mothers," and which women have had their children taken from them because they are perceived to be bad mothers, or mother's trying to immigrate so they can give birth to so-called "anchor babies."

The claim that women are privileged because they are not required by law to register for the Selective Service fairs no better. Again, we need to move beyond the taxonomy and features of privilege. We need additional information, histories, and statistics to determine whether this advantage is truly conferred systemically. All American citizens and resident aliens between the ages of eighteen and twenty-five who were assigned the male sex at birth, are required to register for the selective service. But, enrollment only truly puts you in harm's way if there is an actual military draft, or if the country is at war.[61] The objection is not as strong as it appears. The claim would be stronger if the military were exclusively male, and if females were never permitted to serve, but this is not the case. At present military ranks are populated by "a poverty draft"; drawn disproportionately from communities of color and poor white communities. Women from these communities usually enlist for economic reasons. For many, it's the only way to access an education or career skills. Currently, women comprise nearly one in five active duty personnel in the Air Force (19%), make up eighteen percent of the Navy, fourteen percent of the Army, and eight percent of the Marines.[62] While military service comes with grave risks (including risk of sexual harassment and sexual violence), it also comes with veteran's health benefits, career training, and a pension. So, this instance is not a strong example of "women get privileges too." There is no sense in which exemptions to selective service registration can be described as unearned advantages conferred systemically. There are not really any wild cards associated with exemptions from military service, and these privileges are not given capriciously.[63] Women don't need to register, but we can enlist. And, this was an earned advantage born of political struggle.

My goal in this chapter has been to offer readers a starting point for checking our privileges, one that simultaneously acknowledges the dangers of stretching privilege to meaninglessness and the fact that simple definitions have a limited ability to complete the task fully. Stretch-resistant definitions of privilege reduce some confusion between privileges and other kinds of advantages. Difficult cases, however, require sustained attention to how complex systems of domination have functioned historically and intersectionally. I stress the importance of thinking clearly about privilege, because I believe that the general confusion about what privilege is, and how it works, is a function of the check-proof nature of privilege itself. The strategic refusal to understand how privilege functions can be more damaging than silence. Remember, the invitation to check your privilege is a disorienting request. It evokes discomfort and fear and generates a bottomless set of questions. When taken up with courage and humility, however, it becomes possible for us to perceive the world with greater clarity and complexity.

NOTES

1. This chapter contains previously published material reprinted from Alison Bailey, "Privilege: Expanding on Marilyn Frye's 'Oppression,'" *Journal of Social Philosophy* 29, no. 3, published by John Wiley & Sons in 1998. Copyright © 1998 *Journal of Social Philosophy*.

2. Peggy McIntosh, "White Privilege and Male Privilege: A Personal Account of Coming to See Correspondences through Work in Women's Studies," in *The Feminist Philosophy Reader*, eds. Alison Bailey and Chris J. Cuomo (New York: McGraw Hill, 2008), 66.

3. Audre Lorde, "Age, Race, Class and Sex," in *Sister Outsider: Essays and Speeches* (Freedom, CA: The Crossing Press), 123.

4. This chapter addresses privilege's *overexposed* side; that is, those approaches to the topic that focus on making the unacknowledged structural advantages of privilege tangible. Privilege also has an *underexposed* side that focuses on costs and losses. I'll address the underexposed side in my fourth chapter and fifth chapters.

5. McIntosh, "White Privilege and Male Privilege," 66.

6. Marilyn Frye, "Oppression," in *The Politics of Reality: Essays in Feminist Theory* (Freedom, CA: The Crossing Press, 1983), 1.

7. See, "Does Female Privilege Exist?," *Everyday Feminism Magazine*, May 29, 2016, accessed February 2, 2020, https://everydayfeminism.com/2016/05/does-female-privilege-exist/

8. Frye, "Oppression," 2.

9. If she enjoys sex too much, then she is a slut. If she chooses her partners carefully or remains celibate, then she is a tease or a virgin. The double standard is heteronormative. Being called lesbian or queer is way of disciplining straight women who are not overtly sexually active. How is it possible to navigate the options offered by theses binds without penalty?

10. See, Anderson J. Franklin, Nancy Boyd-Franklin and Sholanda Kelly, "Racism and Invisibility: Race-Related Stress, Emotional Abuse and Psychological Trauma for People of Color," *Journal of Emotional Abuse* 6, no. 2–3 (2006), 9–30.

11. Sara Ahmed, *Living a Feminist Life* (Durham, NC: Duke University Press, 2017), 30.

12. David Owen argues that "a consequence of racial oppression is that white people also face double binds," but the contradiction not a logical contradiction. It is inherent in social systems characterized by oppression. White people are constrained by white supremacy, but the binds we face are nowhere nearly as harmful. See, "Cornered by Whiteness: On Being a White Problem," in *White Self-Criticality beyond Anti-Racism: How Does it Feel to Be a White Problem?*, ed. George Yancy (Lanham, MD: Lexington Books, 2015), 151. I use to call this the dilemma of white privilege awareness. See, Alison Bailey, "Despising an Identity They Taught Me to Claim: Exploring a Dilemma of White Privilege Awareness," in *Whiteness: Feminist Philosophical Narratives*, eds. Chris J. Cuomo and Kim Q. Hall (Totowa, NJ: Rowman and Littlefield, 1999), 85–107.

13. I'm drawing on Sara Ahmed's observation that "whiteness is an orientation that puts certain things within reach." It follows that orientations also put certain things out of reach for others. See, "The Phenomenology of Whiteness," *Feminist Theory* 8, no. 2 (2007), 158.

14. Angela Mae Kupenda, "Facing Down Spooks," in *Presumed Incompetent: Intersections of Race and Class for Women in Academia*, eds. Yolanda Flores, Gabriella Gutiérrez y Muhs, Carmen G. González Neimann, and Angela P. Harris (Boulder: University of Colorado Press, 2012), 26.

15. Richard Wright, "The Ethics of Jim Crow," in *Uncle Tom's Children* (New York: Harper Perrenial, 2008), 6.

16. Ta-Nehisi Coates, *Between the World and Me* (New York: Spiegel and Grau, 2015), 22–23.

17. These examples are from Rebecca Solnit, "Milestones in Misogyny," in *Call Them by Their True Names* (Chicago: Haymarket Books, 2018), 24–25.

18. Deborah Tannen, "Our Impossible Expectations of Hillary Clinton and All Women in Authority," *The Washington Post*, February 20, 2016, https://www.washingtonpost.com/opinions/our-impossible-expectations-of-hillary-clinton-and-all-women-in-authority/2016/02/19/35e416d0-d5ba-11e5-be55-2cc3c1e4b76b_story.html?noredirect=on&utm_term=.645dfb9546f2

19. Frye, "Oppression," 5–6.

20. Double binds are the product of an imagined unified self. María Lugones argues that these binds don't erase an oppressed subject's agency completely, although they can neutralize it on some terrains. Oppressed groups are at once oppressed and resisting. So, the structures they must navigate are not closed completely. They have fissures. See, "Structure/Anti-Structure and Agency under Oppression," in *Pilgrimages/Pereginajes: Theorizing Coalition against Multiple Oppressions* (Lanham, MD: Rowman and Littlefield, 2003), 53–65.

21. Kimberlé Crenshaw coined the term "intersectionality" to name approaches to discrimination that treated oppressions as multiplicative (i.e., white-supremacist-capitalist-patriarchy) rather than additive (i.e., white supremacist+capitalist+patriarchy). Intersectional thinking renders homogenously siloed categories politically suspect by situating individuals within networks of relations. See, "Mapping the Margins: Intersectionality, Identity Politics and Violence against Women of Color," *Stanford Law Review* 43, no. 6 (July 1991), 1241–99.

22. Kupenda, "Facing Down Spooks," 21.

23. See, George Lipsitz, *The Possessive Investment in Whiteness: How White People Profit from Identity Politics* (Philadelphia: Temple University Press, 2006), 105–17.

24. Beth Berila, *Integrating Mindfulness into Anti-Oppression Pedagogy: Social Justice Pedagogy in Higher Education* (New York: Routledge, 2016), 91.

25. McIntosh, "White Privilege," 66.

26. The focus on lists of privileges and "unpacking knapsacks" has met with criticism. There are worries about re-centering whiteness, focusing too much on privilege and not enough on white supremacy, and substituting rituals of confession and forgiveness for collective action. See Andrea Smith, "Unsettling the Privilege of Self-Reflexivity," in *Geographies of Privilege*, eds. France Winddance Twine and Bradly Gardener (New York: Routledge, 2013), 264–79.

27. W.E.B. DuBois, *Black Reconstruction in America: Toward a History of the Part Which Black Folk Play in the Attempt to Reconstruct Democracy in American, 1860–1880* (New York: Routledge, 2017), 700–02. Albert Memmi lists the privileges of colonizers: "should he ask for or have need of anything, he need only show his face to be prejudged favorably by those in the colony who count. . . . He enjoys the respect of the colonized themselves, who grant him more than those who are the best of their own people, who for example, have more faith in his word than in that of their own population . . . The colony follows the cadence of his traditional holidays. . . . The weekly day of rest is that of his native country; it is his nation's flag which flies over the monuments, and his mother tongue which permits social communication.

Even his dress, his accent and his manners are eventually imitated by the colonized. The colonizer partakes of an elevated world from which he automatically reaps the privileges." See, *The Colonizer and the Colonized* (Boston: Beacon Press, 1991), 56–58.

28. Joel Feinberg, *Social Philosophy* (Englewood Cliffs, NJ: Prentice Hall, 1963), 58–59. My comments follow his examples. See also, "Privilege," in *Black's Law Dictionary*, 6th edition (St. Paul, MN: West Publishing, 1990), 500.

29. Cheryl Harris makes a convincing case for whiteness as property. It is fundamentally, a legal concept that white people constructed to grant themselves protections under the law that they denied to people of color. Whiteness is something that white people own, in effect, and as long as they own it, it protects them. See, "Whiteness as Property," *Harvard Law Review* 106, no. 8 (June 1993), 1710–91.

30. Terrance MacMullan, *The Habits of Whiteness: A Pragmatist Reconstruction* (Bloomington: Indiana University Press, 2009), 137.

31. Georgy Yancy and Naomi Zack, "What White Privilege Really Means," *New York Times*, November 25, 2014, https://opinionator.blogs.nytimes.com/2014/11/05/what-white-privilege-really-means/

32. Robin DiAngelo clarifies the relationship between white supremacy and white privilege, when she says: "White supremacy does not refer to individual white people *per se* and their individual intentions, but to a political-economic social system of domination. This system is based on the historical and current accumulation of structural power that privileges, centralizes, and elevates white people as a group . . . I do not use the term to refer to hate groups. I use the term to capture the pervasiveness, magnitude and normalcy of white dominance and assumed superiority." See, *What Does It Mean to Be White?: Developing White Racial Literacy* (New York: Peter Lang, 2012), 126.

33. McIntosh, "White Privilege," 66.

34. Lewis Gordon argues for abandoning white privilege as a trope because these are not privileges, they are basic rights that should be common to all human beings. See, "Critical Reflections on Three Popular Tropes in The Study of Whiteness," in *What White Looks Like: African American Philosophers on the Whiteness Question*, ed. George Yancy (New York: Routledge, 2004), 173–94. Others favor reframing privilege as loss. See, Gayatri Chakravorty Spivak and Sarah Harasym, *the Post-Colonial Critic: Interviews, Strategies, and Dialogues* (New York: Routledge, 1990).

35. Gina Corcoran-Crosley, "Explaining White Privilege to a Broke White Person," *Huffington Post*, May 8, 2014, https://www.huffingtonpost.com/gina-crosleycorcoran/explaining-white-privilege-to-a-broke-white-person_b_5269255.html

36. Ahmed, "The Phenomenology of Whiteness," 160.

37. Thanks to Jona Olsson for demonstrating the appropriateness of Ann Richards's remark in this context.

38. Michael Monihan, "The Concept of Privilege: A Critical Appraisal," *The Journal South African Journal of Philosophy* 33, no. 1 (2014), 74.

39. My definition follows the *Oxford English Dictionary*. Privilege [from old French and middle English] *privilegium* a bill in favor of or against an individual; fr. L. *priv-us*, private, peculiar+*lex, legem* law.

40. Given the etymology of privilege, it's ironic that policies designed to protect particular ethnic, religious, or sexual minorities are re-framed as "special rights," by those who oppose these protections. Equal rights are not special rights. Disenfranchised groups require additional protections because the policies on the books fail to protect members of these groups in the first place.

41. Eula Biss, "White Debt: Reckoning with What Is Owned—and What Can Never Be Repaid—for White Privilege," *New York Times*, December 2, 2015, https://www.nytimes.com/2015/12/06/magazine/white-debt.html

42. This metaphor comes from Jona Olsson's unpublished antiracism work. White Privilege Workshop, 19th Annual Womyn's Music Festival, Hart, Michigan, August 10, 1994.

43. McIntosh, "White Privilege," 62.

44. bell hooks, *Killing Rage: Ending Racism* (New York: Henry Holt, 1995), 185.

45. For example, Lori Lakin Hutcherson, "What I Told My White Friend When He Asked for My Black Opinion on White Privilege," *Everyday Feminism*, August 25, 2016, accessed May 12, 2020, https://everydayfeminism.com/2016/08/told-white-friend-black-opinion/

46. See, Bonnie Mann, "Trump's New Taunt, Kavanaugh's Defense and Misogyny Rules," *New York Times*, October 3, 2018, https://www.nytimes.com/2018/10/03/opinion/kavanaugh-misogyny-epistemic-worlds.html

47. Cherríe Moraga, *Loving in the War Years: Lo Que Nunca Paso por Sus Labios* (Boston: South End Press, 1983), 97.

48. Claudia Rankine, "The Condition of Black Life is One of Mourning," *New York Times*, June 22, 2015, https://www.nytimes.com/2015/06/22/magazine/the-condition-of-black-life-is-one-of-mourning.html

49. Ahmed, *Living a Feminist Life*, 161.

50. Ahmed, 125.

51. Ahmed, 164.

52. María Lugones, "Playfulness, World Traveling and Loving Perceptions," in *Pilgrimages/Pereginajes: Theorizing Coalition against Multiple Oppressions* (Lanham, MD: Rowman and Littlefield, 2003), 77–103.

53. Charlotte Perkins Gilman, *The Living of Charlotte Perkins Gilman: An Autobiography* (New York: Appleton-Century Company, 1935), 72.

54. Sarah L. Hoagland, *Lesbian Ethics: Toward New Value* (Palo Alto, CA: Institute of Lesbian Studies, 1988), 30.

55. Audre Lorde, "The Master's Tools Will Never Dismantle the Master's House," in *Sister Outsider: Essays and Speeches* (Berkeley, CA: The Crossing Press, 1984), 112.

56. See, Derek Bell, "Property Rights in Whiteness—Their Legal Legacy, Their Economic Costs," in *Critical Race Theory: The Cutting Edge*, ed. Richard Delgado (Philadelphia, PA: Temple University Press, 1995), 75–83. And, Cheryl Harris, "Whiteness as Property," 1746.

57. The phrase "opportunity hoarding" comes from Charles Tilly's *Durable Inequality* (Oakland, CA: University of California Press, 1999). For an extended discussion in the context of educational opportunities, see Stacy Hawkins. "Race-Conscious

Admissions Plans: An Antidote to Educational Opportunity Hoarding," *Journal of College and University Law* 43, no. 2 (2017), 151–66.

58. Hawkins, "Race-Conscious Admissions Plans," 159–62.

59. In the United States, 1 in 7 women and 1 in 4 men have been injured by an intimate partner, and 1 in 10 women have been raped by an intimate partner. Data is unavailable for male victims. 1 in 7 women and 1 in 18 men have been stalked by an intimate partner. Intimate partner violence in trans communities is significantly higher: between thirty-five and fifty percent of transgender people experience intimate partner violence at some point in their life. See, *No More*, "Domestic Violence in the Transgender Community," and, NCADV, "Domestic Violence Fact Sheets," https://www.speakcdn.com/assets/2497/domestic_violence2.pdf

60. See, Cathy Meyer, "Dispelling the Myth of Gender Bias in the Family Court System," *Huffington Post*, August 10, 2012, https://www.huffpost.com/entry/dispelling-the-myth-of-ge_b_1617115

61. At present, people assigned "male" at birth are required to register. This includes people who have transitioned or are in the process of transitioning. At the time of this writing transwomen could file a claim for exemption if they receive an order to report for examination or induction. Transmen are not required to register.

62. Kim Parker, Anthony Cilluffo, and Renee Stepler, "Six Facts about the U.S. Military and Its Changing Demographics," Pew Research Center, April 13, 2017, accessed February 10, 2018, http://www.pewresearch.org/fact-tank/2017/04/13/6-facts-about-the-u-s-military-and-its-changing-demographics/

63. This is not to say that veterans get no affirmative action benefits (e.g., extra consideration for government positions), or that active duty personnel don't receive perks like service discounts.

Chapter 2

The Problem with White Talk
Ignorance and Epistemic Closure

Quick. How does it feel to be a white problem?[1] I want to hear what it's like for you. How do you think being white is a problem? Tell me in your own words. Tell me how you exist in your whiteness. How does whiteness feel? Tell me about the ease with which you move through the world. Tell me about the tension and the numbness. What's so special about living in a white body? What's valuable about being white? Tell me, how does it feel to be a white problem?

What do you mean by a white problem? You see, this is really NOT my problem. I'm a good person. I'm not prejudiced. My ancestors never owned slaves. My family immigrated after the Civil War. Anyway, even if some of them were slave owners, that was a long time ago. I'm not responsible for the Indian Removal Act, Japanese internment or the Black Codes. I wasn't even born yet. Yes, I know that racism and genocide drove American colonization, but our nation has come a long way. And, you can't dwell on the tragedies of U.S. history—that was in the past. We can't teach our children about the horrors of our colonial past if we want them to be proud of this country. Things are much better now. And, anyway, I'm not the problem—it's only racists that are the problem, like those white supremacists who marched in Charlottesville, Virginia. I'm not like my bigoted uncle. I don't care if you're black, red, or yellow with polka dots; everyone should be treated equally. The problem is that there are really bad white people who don't treat others equally. It's really not a white problem; I didn't choose to be born white. Anyway, I have black friends. I regularly send money to the Dolores Huerta Foundation. My church does charity work in the Chicago barrios. I'm from a poor white family. We suffered too and you don't hear us complaining. The problem is that people of color make everything about race. I don't think of you as black. Right, I understand the problem; I've read James Baldwin and bell hooks. I'm a lesbian, so I know what it feels like to be oppressed. I feel so awful about my whiteness. I don't think of myself as white—I'm really Irish, Dutch, and German. I've always felt as if I were an Indian in another life. It's not like I'm a member of the Aryan Nation or some Arizona militia group or something. . . . You can trust me! I'm on your side! I'm open-minded, fair, supportive, and empathetic. My heart is in the right place. I mean well. I'm innocent. I'm good! I'm a good white person! It's all good! There is no problem here.

It's no accident that these responses are often the first words out of white people's mouths when we talk about race, white privilege, and racism. They are not a random constellation of utterances. What Alice McIntyre calls "white talk" is a predictable set of discursive patterns that white folks habitually deploy when we are asked directly about the connections between white privilege and institutional racism.[2] I used to believe that white talk was a welcomed response to the request that I examine my whiteness. I routinely (and very sincerely) made many of the above declarations. Sometimes, in moments of defensiveness, I still do. I used to imagine that my remarks would be interpreted as expressions of solidarity, compassion, friendliness, and support. I thought that by pointing to my own perceived goodness that people of color would feel safe around me, and see me as a trustworthy ally, one of the good ones, an exception.[3] I was wrong. It's so much more complicated.

FLUTTERING AROUND THE WHITE PROBLEM

White talk has a long and annoying history. W. E. B. DuBois alludes to it in the opening lines of *The Souls of Black Folk* (1903) where he reflects on his many conversations with white people about what at the time was called "the Negro problem." He begins:

> Between me and the other world there is an ever-unasked question: unasked by some through feelings of delicacy; by others through the difficulty of rightly framing it. All, nevertheless flutter round it. They approach me in a half-hesitant sort of way, eye me curiously or compassionately, and then, instead of saying directly, How does it feel to be a problem? They say, I know an excellent colored man in my town; or, I fought at Mechanicsville; or, Do not these Southern outrages make your blood boil. At these I smile, or am interested, or reduce the boiling to a simmer, as the occasion may require. To the real question, how does it feel to be a problem? I answer seldom a word.[4]

DuBois's exchange not only marks the burdens of blackness but also points to white peoples' discomfort with the possibility that the so-called Negro problem's origins are closer to home. It lies not in the character of some "problem people," but in white peoples' general fears and anxieties. Lerone Bennett, Jr. later observed how deviously cleaver it was for white Americans to give black Americans the name of their problem so that attention to the problem would be permanently focused on the symptoms of the problem rather than on its causes. His essay, "The White Problem in America," makes this abundantly clear.

> When we say that the causes of the race problem are rooted in the white American and white community, we mean that the power is in white Americans and so is the responsibility. We mean that the white American created and invented the race problem and that his fears and frailties are responsible for the urgency of the problem.
> When we say that the fears of white Americans are at the root of the problem, we mean that the white American is a problem to himself, and that because he is a problem to himself he has made others problems to themselves.
> When we say that the white American is a problem to himself, we mean that racism reflects personal and collective anxieties lodged deep in the hearts and minds of white Americans.
> By all this we must understand that Harlem is a white-made thing and that in order to understand Harlem we must go not to Harlem but to the conscience of white Americans and we must ask not what is Harlem, but why have you made Harlem? Why did you create it? And why do you need it?[5]

DuBois's interlocutors' implicit queries can be traced back to white fears and anxieties. They flutter not only around the race problem but also around their whiteness. James Baldwin traced these fluttering responses to white folks' "personal incoherence," and observed they were "heard nowhere more plainly than in those stammering, terrified dialogues" which white Americans have with black men.[6] He continues, "the nature of this stammering can be reduced to a plea: Don't blame *me*. I was not there. I did not do it. My history has nothing to do with Europe and the slave trade. Anyway, it was *your* chiefs who sold *you* to *me*. I was not present on the middle passage. I'm not responsible for the textile mills of Manchester, or the cotton fields of Mississippi. Besides, consider how the English, too, suffered in those mills and in those awful cities!"[7] A century later, white people continue to rehearse this familiar chorus: "my best friend is black"; or, "I marched with women of color at the Women's March in Washington"; or "doesn't the murder of George Floyd, by Minneapolis police, in broad daylight, in front of witnesses, make your blood boil?" We flutter.

My project in this chapter is to explain why the question, "How does it feel to be a white problem?" cannot be answered in the fluttering grammar of white talk. The whiteness of white talk lies not only in its having emerged from white mouths but also in its evasiveness—in its attempt to suppress fear and anxiety, and its consequential (if unintended) inscription and legitimation of racist oppression. For this reason, it is ontologically impossible for white talk to answer the question, "How does it feel to be a white problem?"[8] White talk is designed, indeed scripted, for the purposes of evading, rejecting, and remaining ignorant about the injustices that flow from whiteness and its attendant privileges. White talk, by definition, is a tactic for avoiding the question! So, I want to suggest a new point of entry—a way to flip the script, so to speak.

I begin with some basic observations about the advantages and disadvantages of using white talk as a route into the white problem. My account develops an expanded version of Alice MacIntyre's definition of white talk that is attentive to the racialized bodily scripts and vocal tones that accompany white talk. I argue that white talk endures because it has a persistent and powerful moral, ontological, and epistemic pay off for white people. I explore each pay off with attention to clarifying how white talk functions to maintain the illusion that we are invulnerable human beings. Next, I pause to reply to the popular objection that my critique of white talk silences white people in conversations on race. If we cannot address the question "how does it feel to be a white problem" in the fluttering grammar of white talk, then how shall we begin? In closing, I suggest that we might reduce our fluttering by replacing white talk with a discourse of vulnerability, where vulnerability is defined not as weakness but as a condition for potential. I offer some general guidelines for how to begin this conversation.

WHY START WITH WHITE TALK?

I regularly use white talk as an entry point into classroom discussions on race. There are good reasons for this. First, white talk is a manageable artifact of the white problem.[9] It offers an accessible and tangible illustration of white people's resistance to understanding our complicity in maintaining racial inequalities. Understanding this requires that we focus not on what white talk says but on what it does. White talk is also a convenient point of agreement: it undeniably exists. It's evidence of white discomfort and fragility. Well-meaning white people can't explain away white talk with the same finesse as we explain away white privilege. No one says, "You're making this up. Maybe white people used to talk this way, but things have changed. White people don't say these things anymore!" Instead, we blush. *Yes! I've said many of these things. I hear myself in these utterances.*

There are also very good reasons for not using white talk as an entry point into the conversation. With rare exceptions, the burden of patiently listening, educating, correcting, and explaining racism regularly falls on people of color. As a friend of mine once said to me after a three-day antiracism workshop: *No offense, but I'm so tired of having the race conversation with white people. It's frustrating and it always leaves me feeling tired, depressed, and vulnerable. I don't think white folks know how much courage it took for me to tell y'all what it's like to go through the day in a black woman's body. It's hard to trust white folks to begin with, but sometimes, in settings like this, I just take a chance. I share my stories in hopes that someone will believe me when I tell them that racism is still very real for us. I always hope that a few white folks will be empathetic, and some are, but most of them don't listen. I know that when I'm talking, that you are up in your head all that time trying to explain my words away. Then, you find some reason to tell me that it's all in my head. You say I'm just seeing things, that I'm too sensitive, or too angry, or that I'm not trying hard enough. White people always politely say to me, maybe it's this, or maybe it's that. But, they rarely say: Thanks for having the courage to share this with us. Are you okay? Does this frequently happen to you? Do you think you were given the run around because you are black and the white guy at the bank teller's window assumed that you were scamming him? I'm tired of white folks insisting that I must be mistaken about my own experience. I'm tired of them assuming that I'm the problem. You deal with them. I don't have the energy. Maybe they will get it if they hear it from a white person. You talk with them.*[10]

I've heard people of color say these things over and over again. At some point in my journey I learned to hear what was being said. I stopped trying to explain away the harms by attributing them to individual character flaws. I started looking for patterns. I became curious and started asking questions. I walked toward my fear instead of away from it. So, I ask that white readers hold these voices in our heads and hearts.[11] I ask that we attend to these generous voices with the same love and care that we listen to the voice of a good friend or close family member. I ask that we center these voices, engage them, and feel their weight during our conversations.

WHAT IS WHITE TALK?

White talk is the *lingua franca* of race talk for white people. White talk is what white fragility sounds like. It is a privilege-preserving discourse that springs from our lips without notice. Robin DiAngelo coined the term "white fragility" to capture white people's intolerance for even the smallest amount of racial stress. Even the very suggestion that whiteness has meaning or that whiteness is a problem triggers a chorus of defensive responses. These include emotions such as anger, fear, and guilt and behaviors such as argumentation, silence, and withdrawal from the stress-inducing situation. These responses work to reinstate white equilibrium as they repel the challenge, return our racial comfort, and maintain our dominance within the racial hierarchy. I conceptualize this process as *white fragility*. Though white fragility is triggered by discomfort and anxiety, it is born of superiority and entitlement. White fragility is not weakness *per se*. In fact, it is a powerful means of white racial control and the protection of white advantage.[12]

White fragility is an expression of white fear and that fear makes us dangerous to people of color. Bell hooks describes how black folks live constantly with the possibility that they will be terrorized by whiteness.[13] Fear triggers a number of reactions, including running away, freezing/shutting down, fawning, and fighting. This is physiologically true of all human beings. Under white supremacy, however, people of color have to be particularly mindful of white fragility and fear because they never know which response will be triggered, and given the history of white violence directed at communities of color, it makes sense to be prepared for an aggressive response.

White people's words are almost always ahead of our thoughts on matters of race. I'm continually surprised at the ease with which I slide into white talk when I feel fearful and defensive. White people habitually fall back on white talk as a way to avoid considering the possibility that many of our actions, utterances, and thoughts contribute to the perpetuation of racial injustices and that we bear some responsibility for these harms. White talk anesthetizes us: we don't want to feel like we are the problem. It's an audible artifact of how much we fear thinking about the damage white supremacy does to our collective humanity. As Alice McIntyre argues, white talk "serves to insulate white people from examining our individual and collective role(s) in the perpetuation of racism. It is the result of whites talking uncritically with/to other whites, all the while resisting critique and massaging each other's racist attitudes, beliefs and actions."[14] White talk is a family of verbal strategies that whites regularly deploy to excuse us "from the difficult and almost paralyzing task of engaging [our] own whiteness."[15] We resist attending to how the unearned benefits of white privilege continue to move us forward. We refuse to feel what the weight of whiteness costs us. We use white talk to derail conversations on race, to dismiss counterarguments, to retreat into silence, to interrupt speakers and topics, and to collude with other whites in creating a "culture of niceness" that makes it difficult to critique the white world.[16]

White talk restores white comfort. It mirrors Elizabeth Spelman's remarks on boomerang perception—"I look at you, and come right back to myself."[17] White talk is a "boomerang discourse": I talk to you but come right back to myself. James Baldwin's account of white people's "stammering, and terrified dialogues" illustrates the swiftness with which our words boomerang back to us as pleas to hear *our* suffering and to see *our* goodness. "Don't blame *me*. I was not there. I did not do it."[18] This boomerang process points to another important aspect of white talk. In addition to its responsibility-dodging function, white talk also works to construct the speaker as an imagined non-racist self. That is, it creates a discursive space for well-meaning white folks to boomerang back to when we feel that the sense we have of ourselves as good is being challenged. When we perform white talk publicly, especially in people of color's company, our utterances act as a ritual of moral purification. We virtue signal, hoping that people of color will affirm our goodness. Since white people are adept at seeing only the self we want to see, we are habitually pulled to interpret people of color's patience and kindness as affirmations of our innocence. *LaKeesha didn't get mad at what I said; she knows I'm a good person.* It's also common for white folks to imagine that people of color have mistakenly overlooked our goodness. *Diego is so trapped by his own oppression and victimhood that he can't seem to understand that I'm his ally.* Boomeranging back to goodness and innocence allows white people to avoid, rather than own up to, the white problem. As Barbara Applebaum famously remarks, "Being a good white is part of the problem, rather than the solution to systematic racism."[19]

McIntyre's account is clearly intended to nudge white people into thinking about the ways white talk is used to maintain white domination. Her focus on the content of these utterances, however, overlooks the additional information that vocal tone and bodily comportment contribute to white talk. I think it's a huge mistake to confine our understanding of white talk exclusively to the content of its utterances. There is information in the timber, texture, tone, and rhythms of white talk as it is spoken. When white talk is put into writing, as it was in the introduction to this chapter, its emotional content is flattened.[20] White talk is a performative. Attending carefully to what is being said is equally as important as attending to the way it is said—to how our bodies move, react, and perform what is spoken. Attending to how white bodies perform white talk is essential to understanding what these utterances do, if only for the reason that what our words communicate and what our bodies communicate are not always in concert. Over the years, I've cultivated the habit of watching people's bodies during conversations on race. I regularly hear white people offer examples of why they haven't a racist bone in their bodies. Yet as they speak, I watch their bodies tighten, squirm, and withdraw, and their eyes dart about the room looking for a comfortable place to rest their gaze. Here is what I've learned. Most white speakers attribute our goodness to the content of our utterances, even when our words spring from white bodies that are unsettled, restless, fearful, and anxious. White fragility reveals itself in stunning ways when we attend to the tension between our bodies and our words. The stress between the two offers an honest glimpse into the hearts and souls of white folks. Body language is a form of nonverbal communication: our posture, facial expressions, the rhythms of our breath, and our subtle gestures offer additional information about white talk's emotional content.[21]

White talk—its utterances, tones, and accompanying gestures—marks our fluttering. The verb "to flutter" is etymologically linked to "float," which connotes a feeling of remaining on the surface of things, failing to go deep. White talk, then, is a way of communicating that confines our racial attention to the thinnest surfaces of power. We flutter when we resist lighting upon or dwelling in spaces where we feel uncomfortable, anxious, and vulnerable. We flutter when we search for detours and distractions. We flutter when we shut down, numb our feelings, and become unreachably silent. We flutter when we blame others, react defensively, and treat people of color as our confessors. We flutter when we tune out people of color's testimonies. Cherríe Moraga's description of white women's fluttering illustrates the embodied, affective, and relational nature of white talk that I have in mind.

> I watch white women shirk before my eyes, losing their fluidity of argument, of confidence, pause awkwardly at the word, "race," the word, "color." The pauses keeping the voices breathless, the bodies taut, erect—unable to breathe deeply, to laugh, to moan in despair, to cry in regret. I cannot continue to use my body to be walked over to make a connection. Feeling every joint in my body tense this morning, used.[22]

What I find meaningful about this passage is the way Moraga marks white women's fluttering by attending to its impact on her own body. People of color rarely have to *do* anything to cause tension in white bodies. Their presence is enough to throw white bodies off-center. People of color understand how their presence alters public spaces, how the texture of the atmosphere noticeably shifts when they enter a room. This is not a free-floating tension. It doesn't simply surround us. It lodges itself more strongly in some bodies than in others. Being mindful of these dynamics has taught me to tune into my own bodily responses as I speak, and to think carefully about white talk's psychological costs for people of color. What must it feel like to hear the word "black"—a word that describes your core identity—stick in the white people's throats? How does it feel to have to listen to the incoherent stuttering and sputtering of white talk?[23] What must it be like to feel white bodies contort in your presence? How painful must it be to politely listen to white people repeatedly try to convince you that you are mistaken about your own feelings and lived experiences? Returning mindfully to the problem of whiteness requires that white people ask ourselves: What must it feel like to recognize, however dimly, our contributions to this pain, anxiety, and anger?

Or, how can I recognize my contributions in ways that focus on the space in between us, on our interactions, and that don't boomerang back to finding ways to restore my own comfort and goodness?

Reni Eddo-Lodge offers additional insight into this awkward choreography of whiteness. Her narrative describes, with painful accuracy, the numbness and disconnection present in white people's slightest bodily responses.

> I'm no longer talking with white people on the topic of race.... I can no longer engage with the gulf of an emotional disconnect that white people display when a person of color articulates their experiences. You can see their eyes shut down and harden. It's like treacle is poured into their ears, blocking up their ear canals. It's like they can no longer hear us.... They've never had to think about what it means, in power terms, to be white, so anytime they're vaguely reminded of this fact, they interpret it as an affront. Their eyes glaze over in boredom or widen in indignation. Their mouths start twitching as they get defensive. Their throats open up as they try to interrupt, inching to talk over you but not really listen because they need to let you know that you've got it wrong.[24]

Eddo-Lodge's ability to read white bodies is unsurprising. Somatic illiteracy is not an option for people of color whose survival depends upon being extremely fluent in the somatic grammars of whiteness. Every twitch, blink, sigh, stammer, shuffle, and contortion offers a glimpse into white people's thoughts. I'm certain that people of color can spot an empty promise, hollow compliment, or a false gesture of kindness long before we speak. Yet, I'd venture a guess that almost all white people are comfortably unaware of the information our movements telegraph. This means that things might be worse. As Sara Ahmed remarks, you "might even will yourself not to notice certain things because noticing them would change your relation to the world."[25] There is knowledge in the racialized body, but white privilege numbs us to its presence. I think we do this because our ignorance has such a huge short-term payoff.

THE PROBLEM WITH WHITE TALK: MORAL, ONTOLOGICAL, AND EPISTEMIC REWARDS

In her essay, "A Phenomenology of Whiteness," Sara Ahmed asks her readers to begin by considering how whiteness involves a form of orientation.[26] So, what's the matter with white talk? Here's the short answer. White talk orients us toward goodness, which distracts us from, rather than engages us with, the heart of the white problem—fear. The long answer is more complicated: white talk has a deep moral, ontological, and epistemological payoff for white people. It permits us to feel as if we are thoughtfully engaging race and racism but allows us to do so from a place of imagined invulnerability, comfort, and safety. I can't use white talk to answer the question "how does it *feel* to be a white problem?" because white talk orients me away from those places that scare me away from places where I am made to feel the weight of my whiteness. White talk is an anesthetizing discourse designed to protect us from pain, but the relief of these utterances is temporary. To answer the question we must peel back, *not* push back, the layers of pain. Pushing back pain only fuels the fire. It agitates us. Peeling back layers of pain creates space for us to attend to these questions with patience and curiosity. To understand why peeling back is better than pushing back, I need to spell out more carefully how white talk bolsters white people's sense of moral goodness, well-meaning white identity, and epistemic authority.

White talk has a strong moral dimension.[27] Barbara Applebaum argues convincingly that its main task is to convince listeners that white speakers are innocent, well-meaning, and good-intentioned people who bear little or no responsibility for the continuing harms of racism. We do this by dividing the world into two kinds of white people—(bad) racist white people and (good) well-meaning white people—and repeatedly offer evidence for our membership in the good group.[28] Goodness is the magnetic north of white talk. It steers our conversations away from those discursive spaces where we feel frightened, anxious, and vulnerable and into spaces that reify our goodness. When I say: *"My ancestors never owned slaves; I have black friends; I grew up in a mixed neighborhood; My uncle is the bigot in the family; or, It's not like I'm part of the Aryan Nation or something,"* I am not making random claims about myself or my extended family. Words are never just words. Words are always doing things.[29] Or, as Robin DiAngelo puts it, the question is *not* "is the claim true or, is the claim false?" Instead we should ask, how does the claim function in the conversation?"[30] To understand this point, it's helpful to distinguish between the literal and the functional meaning of white talk. The claim "I'm not part of the Aryan Nation" is not meant to be taken literally in this context; that is, its function is not to alert listeners to an interesting fact my political alliances, or about whom I exclude from my friendship circles. The content of the utterance may be true, but that's not the point. When spoken in reply to the white problem question, the utterance does something else: it's offered implicitly as evidence of my innocence.

Here's something else to consider. The extreme nature of these examples sets a low bar for moral goodness; it simply requires that we not be moral monsters. When white people make these claims, we grant ourselves permission to flee the unfinished business of racism by placing ourselves in the company of good white people and imagine there is nothing further to say on the subject.[31] We are not part of the problem; we are innocent bystanders.

Focusing exclusively on white moral goodness, as Applebaum argues, makes it challenging to entertain the possibility that our words, actions, body language, thoughts, and beliefs make us complicit in systemic injustices.[32] When you are convinced of your goodness, you feel invulnerable to criticism. The conversation is over.

Next, white talk bolsters a fictitious racial ontology, one that helps maintain the illusion that whiteness is valuable, pure, and unproblematic. White supremacy is held in place by what María Lugones calls a "logic of purity," that is, a "social world [that] is both unified and fragmented, homogenous and hierarchically ordered."[33] The sorting of peoples into so-called "naturally pure groups" is a form of social control. Order demands firm borders between races. There must be no ambiguity and minimal confusion over who does and does not count as a problem. For the fiction of purity to endure, white people must remain ignorant about the origins of the white problem. DuBois's original question, then, is "directed at the ontological core of one's being as in—how does it feel *to be* a problem?"[34] Being a problem is different than having a problem. When I have a problem, an obstacle has been placed in my path. I have a problem when I misplace my office keys or driver's license. To be a problem means that you are, by your very nature, an obstacle. As George Yancy puts it, "within the white imaginary, to be black means to be born an obstacle at the very core of one's being."[35] Charles Mills speaks about the creation of racialized problems in terms of "white mythologies, invented Orients, invented Africans, invented Americas, with correspondingly fabricated populations, countries inhabited by people who never were—Calibans and Tontos, Man Fridays and Sambos," who are part of the "cognitive and moral economy psychically required for conquest, colonization, and enslavement."[36] In the white colonial imagination Africans and black Americans were constructed as essentially childish or brutish. Mexicans were essentially lazy. Jews were imagined to be stingy at their core. Indigenous people were savage, uncivilized. Asians were by nature cunning.

Converting people into problems is a dehumanizing process. It's a short step from being made into a problem to being made into something less than human, into a thing to be feared, managed, targeted, exploited, or destroyed. There is a predictable script that runs through U.S. history that positions and repositions so-called "nonwhite" people as problems to be managed. Consider how the middle passage transformed the Chamba, Wolof, Abron, Fulani, and Bakongo (plural) into a fictional homogenized class "Negroes" or "Africans" (singular)—an identity born as much from the abduction of African peoples from their homelands as from their collective resistance to their new circumstances. In her introduction to the *New York Times Magazine* special issue on the 1619 Project, Nikole Hannah-Jones gives voice to the ontological alchemy of colonization:

> They say our people were born on the water.... The teal eternity of the Atlantic Ocean had severed them so completely from what had once been their home that it was as if nothing had ever existed before, as if everything and everyone they cherished had simply vanished from the earth. They were no longer Mhundu or Akan or Fulani. These men and women from many different nations, all shackled together in the suffocating hull of the ship, they were one people now.[37]

It was the European thirst for land and resources that turned the Quechua, Maya, Anazasi, Pequot, Delaware, Lenape, and Cherokee into "Indians." These fictionalized homogenous categories made it easier to forcibly conscript West African and indigenous bodies into the mission of colonization. When settler colonists needed labor for agriculture and construction, white mythologies reimagined them as beasts of burden whose bodies could "naturally" withstand hard labor, heat, and abuse. If colonial expansion required arable farmland and resources, indigenous peoples and their land management practices were recast as disorderly and wasteful. The new categories "Negro" and "Indian" morphed slowly into "Negro Problem" and the "Indian Problem." Peoples are problematized when their very being is imagined to be defective, deviant, childlike, irresponsible, criminal, immoral, dirty, animalistic, culturally and intellectually inferior, savage, primitive, barbaric, lazy, hypersexual, predatory, violent, slothful, addicted, deceiving, or untrustworthy. And, it is this new imagined being that is understood to be fixed, permanent, and inescapable.

The time-tested problematizing tactics from America's colonial playbook are not confined to the past. In *How Does it Feel to Be a Problem: Being Young and Arab in America*, Moustafa Bayoumi tells the story of Akram, a twenty-one-year-old Palestinian American, who feels the tension between "his own pride in his heritage and his religion, but everywhere he turns—from television shows, movies, news reports, and the occasional customer [at the store where he works]—the culture is droning on that Islam is to be feared and that Arabs are a problem to be dealt with."[38] Most of the time he laughs at how ridiculous the cartoon Arabs look, but under the laughter is "the ache of an identity under siege."[39] When people become problems, their distorted identities can be easily recast for political purposes. The post-9/11 images of Middle Easterners as terrorists endure. Their political currency is so strong that in 2018, the president of the United States asserted, without evidence, that "unknown Middle Easterners" were hiding among the Honduran refugees in a migrant caravan heading toward the U.S.–Mexico border.[40] He folded a new fear into an existing one, and the Honduran refugees became problems by association.

The problem of whiteness cannot be engaged critically by extending this fictionalized-core-defines-the-identity logic to white folks. Recasting the script does not mean re-imagining white people as problems because we are essentially racist-at-core in the same way people of color have been historically represented as lazy, childlike, cunning, or violent at our core. Flipping the script is not the scholarly equivalent of an adolescent back-seat quarrel on a long road trip. It's not . . . *"You're the problem! . . . No, You're the problem! . . . No! YOU'RE the Problem! It's a black problem! No, it's a WHITE problem."* The construction of African, Indigenous, Asian, or Middle Eastern peoples as problems is part and parcel of the process that constructs Europeans as responsible, civilized, human, chaste, clean, trustworthy, citizens, industrious, and moral.[41] They are two sides of the same ontological coin. Positioning some groups as problems invariably places other so-called "civilized" groups in the position to "solve these problems." So, I'm not suggesting that we answer the white problem by flipping the ontological coin in hopes of it landing heads up, making the problem solvers, by nature, the problem. We are not swapping essence for essence here. The white problem is ontologically different from the so-called Indian problem, yellow peril, Mexican problem, Jewish problem, Negro problem, Muslim problem, and immigrant problem. Hunting for buried white essences does not solve the white problem. The question can only be answered by attending to what whiteness does. When the script is flipped, the definition of problem is recast: we shift from attending to the so-called ontological problem of blackness, to understanding *the performative power of whiteness.*[42]

White talk offers a clear illustration of the performative power of whiteness. The conversational detours that characterize white talk reorient our gaze away from unflattering accounts of our white selves. As if any effort to excavate "the feelings that [lie] behind the word *white*," as Thandeka remarks, "were too potent to be faced."[43] The French root (*détour*) means literally to turn away. French speakers tell me that the verb form (*détourner*) can also, fittingly, be translated into English as distort, twist, or misappropriate. To paraphrase James Baldwin, white talk manages white identity by turning the white gaze away from those "disagreeable mirrors" that reflect our whiteness back to us in its plurality. When we turn away, we convince ourselves that we "do not see what we see."[44] María Lugones also implores white women to acknowledge that women of color are "faithful mirrors" that show white women as no other mirror can show us. In her words: "Not that we show you as you *really* are; we just show you as one of the people you are. What we reveal to you is that you are many—something that may itself be frightening to you. But the self we reveal to you is not the one you are eager to know . . . . You block identification with that self because it is not quite consistent with your image of yourself."[45]

I did not fully understand the performative blocking power of whiteness until I read John Langston Gwaltney's *Drylongso: A Self-Portrait of Black*

America. The collected narratives revealed to me a plurality of white selves that I was not eager to know. White selves that were greedy, hateful, arrogant, dishonest, stingy, immodest, unkind, empty, and untrustworthy. These words threw me off-center. The tension between what they saw in white people's character and the picture I had of myself as good-hearted and well-meaning revealed to me the importance of understanding white identity as plural. White folks are neither good nor bad white people. We are good-hearted-greedy-well-meaning-ignorant-lying-immodest-kind-empty-generous-cruel beings.

The performative power of whiteness is also revealed in the tension between white people's reported good deeds and the needs of the communities in which these deeds are done. There is an entire genre of white talk that focuses on white charitability in low-income communities of color but fails to consider how those communities perceive white do-gooders. Most of the time these communities have not asked us for our charity. Sometimes they are frustrated and angry at us for not hearing what they have told us they really need. When outsiders impose our charitable visions onto communities, based on what *they* believe a community needs, and not what residents *know* they need, their deeds become arrogantly missionary. In these contexts, well-meaning whites are not simply "good." We are "good-arrogant-innocent-imperious-well-meaning, and at times misguided. Pausing to consider how members of the community see *us* reveals our plurality. White people block identification with our arrogant or imperious selves because, as Lugones reminds us: "remembering that self fractures you into more than one person. You know a self that is decent and good, and knowing yourself in [that] mirror frightens you with losing your center, your integrity, your oneness." And, "you block identification with that self because you are afraid of plurality."[46] When we respond to the question "how does it feel to be a white problem?" with white talk, we block the possibility of attending to our plurality. Our whitely utterances reinscribe the contours of goodness, rather than reveal our goodness-arrogance-innocence-ignorance. Recasting the script means that white folks have before us the burden of identifying and problematizing whiteness in its plurality by learning to perceive those selves that are not meant to be perceived and understanding how whiteness poses a problem for our collective humanity.[47]

Finally, white talk is an expression of epistemic resistance. I'll have more to say about the epistemic consequences of white talk in my final section; but first, I want to pause to consider a common objection.

OKAY, SO JUST TELL ME WHAT TO SAY!

Okay, I get it. I can't answer the question, "How does it feel to be a problem?" in the fluttering grammar of white talk. I can't use white talk to engage whiteness critically because white talk reorients our attention away from the white problem and toward bolstering our whiteness on moral, ontological, and epistemological grounds. *So, what should I say? How should I have this conversation? Please tell me what to say. I don't want to offend anyone! I feel silenced! I feel trapped! I feel as if everything I say is going to be wrong. I feel like no matter what I say, I'll be called a racist, so why bother? I give up. I can't win.*

I want to make three observations. First, as some readers may have guessed, this objection follows the discursive contours of white talk by steering the conversation back toward white people's goodness and comfort. *I don't want people to think I'm a racist. I don't want to offend anyone, so tell me what to say! I want to avoid discomfort at all costs!* Responding to critical accounts of white talk with "what do *you* want *me* to say?" is boomerang discourse—it repositions white subjects as fixers, missionaries, rescuers, and thus as outside of the critique of whiteness. It fails to engage the performative power of white talk. Further, it suggests that white people rely exclusively on members of oppressed groups for answers rather than trying to figure it out for ourselves. White people alone can fix this nasty racism business if we would just learn to say the right things! As Barbara Applebaum so nicely puts it, these objections "center the question on 'what can I do?', rather than 'what can be done?' and this encourages white moral solipsism, heroism, and narcissism."[48]

There is a strong connection between white privilege, goodness, and rule following. Marilyn Frye once observed that white morality was rule governed: "by believing in rules, by being arbitrators of rules, by understanding agency in terms of the applications of principles to particular situations, whitely people think they preserve their detachment from prejudice, bias, meanness, and so on. Whitely people tend to believe that one preserves one's goodness by being principled, by acting according to rules instead of according to feeling."[49] We take comfort in following rules because rules minimize risk and maintain our illusions of invulnerability. *If I follow the rules of the road, then I'll minimize my risk of accidents; and, I'll be a good driver. If I follow the rules for interacting with people of color, then I'll minimize the risk of being called a racist; and, I'll be a good white person. So, what are the rules? Don't call black people "articulate." Okay. Don't touch black people's hair. Check. Never say I don't think of you as black, Indian, Chinese, etc. Check.* Rules act as insurance against slipping from goodness. *What do you mean I'm prejudiced? I followed the rules. I said all of the things you told me to say!* Rules offer a quick and unreflective path to comfort. It's easier to memorize rules such as "Don't assume that every Spanish speaker is in the country illegally," or "Don't touch black people's hair," than it is to work toward a deep understanding of the history and the politics of uninvited touching.[50] Rules can be used in place of genuine interactions and conversations. Following rules doesn't require a profound change of heart, deep self-examination, or risk taking. It's easier to follow a set of guidelines than it is to interrogate whiteness deeply.

It's interesting how this objection almost always gets framed as a choice between white talk and white silence. White talk is so deeply rooted in our sense of goodness that we assume it is our only voice. It is not. White talk is the sound of insecure goodness masking our deep-seated vulnerability. There are more powerful voices—vulnerable voices—that shake the boundaries of the white self and move us to become mindful of the performances of whiteness. What if we resisted our desire to speak only from the places that comfort us and walked wholeheartedly into what Pema Chödrön refers to as the places that scare you?[51] What if we made a sincere effort to engage our fluttering and move toward settling our bodies? What if we stopped fluttering, touched down, and spent time in uncomfortable spaces?[52] How might we begin thinking about this?

WHITENESS WITH MINIMAL FLUTTERING: "VULNERABILITY-AS-POTENTIAL" AS A NEW POINT OF ENTRY

Quick! Stop fluttering for just a moment! Touch that uncomfortable place inside yourself that makes you want to flee, even if you can only attend to it briefly. Be still. Breathe. Observe. Let's talk about how it feels to be a white problem. Can you talk about your whiteness without falling back into white talk? If you can't that's fine. Don't beat yourself up. Be curious about why white talk springs so quickly from your lips. White talk is comforting for us. Still, can you understand how it skirts the white problem, and how it silences those voices we've been asked to hold in our heads and hearts? Can you grasp how white talk positions white comfort over people of color's lived experiences? Can you acknowledge the ways white talk erases your plurality? Can you recognize how the urge to retreat will close off opportunities for knowledge?

It's time to return to the epistemic dimensions of white talk that I bracketed earlier. I want to say a bit more about why white talk won't answer the question, "how does it feel to be a white problem?" White talk's detours promote *epistemic closure* by confining our discussions to discursive comfort zones where evidence of white innocence has greater epistemic weight than people of color's testimony.[53] White talk is how white folks defend our epistemic home terrain against new knowledge that may unsettle our existing worldview. As such, white talk will not take us into the places that scare us, that is, the places where we can take risks and be epistemically open to seeing ourselves as plural, raw, and contradictory.

White talk closes off alternative paths to knowing. It blocks our entrance to unfamiliar epistemic landscapes. The epistemic closure I have in mind is an expression of willful ignorance. Ignorance (literally, "to ignore") is a central feature of white supremacy and white talk is a means of willfully managing our ignorance in ways that prevent us from feeling vulnerable. Nancy Tuana defines willful ignorance as the condition of "not knowing, and not wanting to know."[54] People with race privilege, she argues, commonly exhibit a "determined ignorance" of the lives, histories, and cultures of those whom we believe to be either inferior or unimportant.[55] Willful ignorance is not a passive expression of ignorance. It is a complex accumulation of acts of repeated negligence and omission. It cannot be explained as a simple gap in our knowledge.[56] That is, it's not the product of missing information, as in: *it's not my fault. I was never taught about the Tulsa Race Massacre, the Indian Removal Act of 1830, or the Chinese Exclusion Act of 1884*. White willful ignorance requires recurrent efforts to resist knowing what is before you. Willful ignorance is actively produced: It is an achievement that must be culturally managed. Managing ignorance requires keeping the habitual detours, dismissals, and denials that characterize white talk in good working order. When we say: *"Why do we need to know about the Sand Creek Massacre? That was all in the past and things are so much better today,"* we put genocide in the past. We opt for epistemic closure. When we say, *"I'm so sick of political correctness, slavery is over! Who cares!"* We refuse to consider how past injustices continue today under different names. White talk is an expression of willful ignorance, but not because the speaker has a gap in her knowledge. Remember: Words *do* things. When we fall back on white talk we *actively* give ourselves permission to not know something important. We opt to dwell in an imagined state of invulnerability, where the cruelties of the past are conveniently severed from both the historical trauma we inherit and our present suffering.

White talk's epistemic effects remain powerful because willful ignorance, in a twisted way, has a huge pay off for white people. Following James Baldwin, Elizabeth Spelman describes how white people remain actively ignorant about people of color's contemporary grievances because we fear that they might be true. It's not simply that we *suspect* that they might be true and choose not to believe them. Her point is more unsettling: "[We] want the claim 'black America's grievances are real' to be false, but we know that if we treat [this claim] as something that could be false, then we would also have to regard it as something that could also be true. Better to ignore [the claim] altogether, given the fearful consequences of its being true. Better not to have thought at all than to have thought and lost."[57] Spelman's argument points to an astonishing conclusion. Not only is the whitely desire to parade oneself as good, pure, and innocent maintained by willful ignorance, but also the costs of this ignorance on the bodies of people of color is so astonishingly enduring that it "drains off the moral capital" we imagine ourselves having accumulated![58] When strengthened by willful ignorance, white peoples' sense of our own goodness collapses into solipsism and narcissism. The scant evidence of goodness that white talk bolsters collapses under the weight of our refusal to consider alternative explanations.

I'm looking for a more courageous path. A way to talk that resists turning our conversations into forums for white goodness or an ignorance management projects. Fear lies at the root of the white problem; but, the conversation itself is not driven by fear—it's driven by white vulnerability in the face of this fear. So, we have a choice. We can either anesthetize our fear with white talk or humbly acknowledge that fear and treat our vulnerability as a source of knowledge. What if we embraced our vulnerability and used it as an entry point into the white problem? What if we replaced white talk with a discourse of vulnerability?

Conventional understandings equate vulnerability with being weak, defenseless, dependent, and susceptible to injury. This sense of vulnerability-as-weakness is not the one I want to use to clear a new path. The vulnerability I have in mind is closer to Erinn Gilson's account of vulnerability-as-potential. On her view, vulnerability is not just what happens to some humans in particular circumstances. It is the basic feature of human existence.[59] In her words:

> Taken . . . as a fundamental state, vulnerability is a condition of potential that makes possible other conditions. Being vulnerable makes it possible for us to suffer, to fall prey to violence and be harmed, but also to fall in love, to learn, to take pleasure and to find comfort in the presence of others, and to experience the simultaneity of these feelings. Vulner*ability* is not just a condition that limits us, but also one that can *enable* us. As potential, vulnerability is a condition of openness, openness to being affected and affecting in turn.[60]

There is a pivotal moment in Lee Muh Wah's *The Color of Fear* that illustrates how vulnerability-as-potential surfaces when we stop fluttering.[61] The film documents a three-day conversation about race among eight men. Halfway through the film Victor (an African American man) and David (a well-meaning white man) have a heated exchange. Over the course of the retreat, David has repeatedly resisted, dismissed, and rejected all the evidence that the six men of color have shared with him about the daily obstacles they face as black, brown, and Asian American men in the United States. In a near-perfect performance of testimonial injustice, David white talks his way out of each and every injustice these men share with him. At some point the conversation breaks down. Victor asks David point-blank why he refuses to hear what they have been telling him. For some reason, David stops fluttering and tearfully replies that he doesn't want to believe that America is like this and that people can be so unkind to one another. He doesn't want to take Spelman's wager. Victor responds, "From here on in, I can work with you." The rest of the conversation is raw, productive, and honest. David lets go of his white talk and makes himself vulnerable to the possibility that others don't share the privileges he experiences as a white man.

Lee Mun Wah once said, "If you accept and acknowledge your mistakes, what I see is your goodness. If you cover up your mistakes with excuses, claiming your goodness, all I see are your faults."[62] It's better to face the pain and suffering than it is to distance yourself from it with objections and excuses. Vulnerability offers us the chance to drop our attachment to comfort and to own our ignorance. We soon learn to recognize fear and discomfort as a source of knowledge and connection, rather than as reason for closure and flight. What if we treated fear, anger, shame, and guilt not as feelings to be squashed, escaped, ignored, or reconfigured favorably, but as genuine sources of knowledge? What if we followed people of color's lead into those discursive spaces where we felt fragile, rather than into the spaces where we felt comfortable? What if we attended to these feelings through our interactions with one another?

My purpose here is not to offer a foolproof template for future discourses of vulnerability. I'm not interested in replacing one set of rules with another. Following Frye, I want us to "act according to feeling."[63] My guess is that our conversations will be shaped by the character of the epistemic communities in which they take place. All that's required is that we carry a genuine curiosity and epistemic openness into these conversations. When we do, alternatives to white talk will emerge. I want to offer the following guidelines as one possible way to begin.

Begin Where You Are, Not Where You Think You Should Be

If you catch yourself falling back into white talk, then mark these moments and be curious about why this pattern persists. The first order of business is not to purge white talk from your discursive repertoire; it is to identify and hold space with the pattern and think about what it sustains. White talk is an emotional artifact of invulnerability, and the rush to extinguish this habit is just another way of restoring our comfort. Instead, follow the white talk back to its source. Ask yourself: What buttons were pushed for me to respond with white talk? What exactly was said to make me feel so unsettled? Name the barriers, detours, and diversions you observe yourself taking. Write them down. Keep talking. Don't beat yourself up. If you don't see the white problem right away, then remind yourself that white talk is part of what makes privilege check proof. There is a reason why we go there when we feel challenged. Don't rush ahead and try to fix yourself. If it helps, do something imaginative and silly: When you hear white talk place an imaginary orange traffic cone next to what you said. Mark it. Don't walk around the cone. Pause. Breathe, and ask yourself, is there a wound my white talk is trying to protect? If you can, describe the vulnerability that triggered your white talk. Remember the phrases you have marked so that when your words repeat themselves you can witness the constellation of markers taking shape. What do these patterns tell you?

Listen Actively with Your Heart, Not Your Head

Listen actively to one another. Don't map out your discursive escape routes and objections while others are talking. Notice what is and is not being said, and how it is expressed. Attend to the tone of one another's words and the gestures used to animate those words. Ask yourself what emotional work your words do and if you repeatedly return to certain themes. White talk is littered with defensiveness . . . I am not . . . I have never . . . I wasn't . . . I don't think . . . but, you can't . . . we can't . . . I won't. Listen for discursive moves that blame people of color for systemic injustice, put racism in the past, or distance yourself from the problem. Be curious about one anothers' stories and observations, and use active language to engage their words. If you are unsure about what someone means, then ask them for clarification. Cultivate a reflective discourse of engagement: *I'm not sure if I understood you correctly. I thought you were saying X. Did I hear you accurately? Why did you find that frustrating? Why does that anger or frighten you? What makes you feel unsafe? Tell us more about that? What do you need from us at this moment?*[64]

Be Mindful of What Makes You Fight, Flee, or Shut Down

Be attentive to what your words and body tell you about race, racism, and whiteness. Each of us has good reasons for why these conversations are difficult. I find it helpful to tune into what my body says to me as I listen and speak. I find that my body expands and relaxes when I listen curiously with an open heart. It constricts, and becomes anxious and unsettled when I try to control the conversation by steering it into places where I feel safe. So, observe how your body feels when you fall back into white talk. Mark the paths each conversation takes. Have you unconsciously changed the topic or shifted the focus? Are people interrupting one another? Where do you direct your gaze when the conversation takes an uncomfortable turn? Where are you pulled? Do you fidget and want to look at your phone? Cultivate an awareness of what makes you feel comfortable or uncomfortable during these conversations. Try writing down the words and gestures that trigger strong feelings. Be honest, authentic, and forgiving. Trust yourself, but recognize that self-trust is slippery. It can easily collapse into attempts to re-center white epistemic authority. Sometimes that happens. Let it go, knowing that when you maintain a healthy curiosity that things become easier.

Take Responsibility for Your Mistakes and Learn from Them

Vulnerability requires letting go of the fear that you'll make mistakes, offend people, and say foolish things. Don't worry. It's likely you will say something that will hurt or be painful to someone. You are human. You will make mistakes, but this is our work. As Sharon Welch remarks, "To move out of our identities as the dominant race, we must learn to fail—because we will, often and embarrassingly and repeatedly. It is not easy to dismantle centuries-long structures of racial oppression."[65] You will feel shame, guilt, anger, but you'll live through the conversation. The important thing is to take responsibility for your mistakes and to be open to talking about them. There is knowledge in our mistakes. Understand that taking responsibility does not mean beating yourself up. Be kind to yourself and others. This is difficult work. Take comfort in your courage and ability to take risks, rather than your ability to get it right.

Treat Discomfort as a Source of Knowledge

Treat anger, fear, and anxiety as natural reactions to moving closer to knowledge. Crafting a discourse of vulnerability requires settling into our discomfort rather than continuing to flutter. You might practice moving toward the places that scare you by making a conscious choice to engage your fears and discomforts in ways that are not aimed at managing your ignorance or merely at protecting yourself from feelings of vulnerability.

Focus on Being Open-Hearted, Kind, and Curious

If white talk maintains the illusion of invulnerability through not knowing, and not wanting to know, then a discourse of vulnerability-as-potential requires cultivating an attitude that is open to knowing. So . . .

Quick. What does it mean to be a white problem? Hmmm . . . that is a really complex and difficult question. I wonder why it makes me uncomfortable. My first inclination is to say, "I'm not the problem!" Why do I become so defensive? Why is that the first place I go? I'm going to mark this response with one of those silly orange traffic cones, so I can come back to it when I feel less threatened. Maybe a pattern will emerge that will tell me something about why the question makes me feel so vulnerable. I've never thought of whiteness as a problem. I wonder if this omission is significant. Perhaps having white privilege means not having to consider the possibility. Maybe white privilege is held in place partially by perceiving people of color as problems. What do you think?

There must be something very big at stake for white people to hang on to white talk so tightly. I can't believe I still do this! It's like the words come out of my mouth before I even realize it! This is telling. What can we learn from this? It's so awkward. I'll admit that the white problem question makes me feel fragile, angry, guilty, and defensive. Do you feel the same way? I am open to exploring what's behind these reactions.

Can you say that again? I want to be sure I understood you clearly. It must be frustrating for people of color to have to listen to white folks continually dodge this topic. What's that like? What does this do to you? Is it painful, exhausting, frightening? Does it wear you down to the point of tears? I'm scared that there is a lot more riding on all of this white problem stuff than I can see right now. What if it's really deep? What if this is our historical inheritance? What if collective white fears and anxieties have been the source of real-life injustices and harm from the start! What if racism really is a white problem! This is immense. What if we took time to dwell together in our anger, fear, and discomfort? What if we listened patiently and carefully to one another's stories and to the connections between these narratives? What if we shared our family histories? Would a more complete picture emerge? Would the problem at least come into focus?

NOTES

1. This chapter is a revised version of Bailey, Alison, "White Talk as a Barrier to Understanding the Problem of Whiteness," which first appeared in *White Self-Criticality Beyond Anti-Racism: What Is It Like to Be a White Problem?*, ed. George Yancy (Lanham, MD: Lexington Books, 2015), 37–57. Copyright © 2015 by Lexington Books. All rights reserved.

2. Alice McIntyre, *Making Meaning of Whiteness: Exploring Racial Identities with White Teachers* (Albany, NY: SUNY Press, 1997).

3. The fact that I understood white talk as an expression of solidarity, rather than a conversational sleight of hand, illustrates perfectly Charles Mills's observation that "white people are able to consistently do the wrong thing while thinking that they are doing the right thing?" Charles W. Mills, *The Racial Contract* (Ithaca, NY: Cornell University Press, 2007), 94.

4. W. E. B. DuBois, *The Souls of Black Folk* (New York: Dover Publications, Inc., 1994), 1.

5. Lerone Bennett, Jr., "The White Problem in America," *Ebony* (August 1965), 29–30.

6. James Baldwin, "White Man's Guilt," in *The Price of the Ticket: Collected Nonfiction 1948–1985* (New York: St. Martin's Press, 1985), 411.

7. Baldwin, "White Man's Guilt," 411.

8. Many thanks to Michael Monihan for clarifying this point.

9. I'm grabbing onto one corner of the white problem here. A complete treatment requires more time. As Charles Mills once said of white ignorance: "It's a big subject. How much time do you have? It's not enough." See, *The Racial Contract*, 13.

10. This is not verbatim. I've tried to capture the basic message of our conversation.

11. Like many white writers, I struggle with questions of voice when I write about race. Sometimes I use the third person plural to refer to white people. This keeps the question of audience open. Other times I place my whiteness front and center. Both strategies run the risk of misinterpretation. Since this chapter is directed primarily, but not exclusively, at white readers, who resist seeing themselves as a problem, I've chosen to speak in the first person singular.

12. Robin DiAngelo, *White Fragility: Why It's So Hard for White People to Talk about Racism* (Boston: Beacon Press, 2018), 2.

13. bell hooks, *Killing Rage: Ending Racism* (New York: Henry Holt, 1995), 46.

14. McIntyre, *Making Meaning of Whiteness*, 46.

15. McIntyre, 46.

16. McIntyre, 46.

17. Elizabeth V. Spelman, *Inessential Woman: Problems of Exclusion in Feminist Thought* (Boston: Beacon Press, 1988), 12.

18. Baldwin, "White Man's Guilt," 411.

19. Barbara Applebaum, *Being White, Being Good: White Complicity, White Moral Responsibility, and Social Justice Pedagogy* (Lanham, MD: Rowman and Littlefield, 2010), 20.

20. Try attending to white talk's affective texture by listening to the examples collected in "White Talk Mashup," Prindle Institute for Ethics, DePauw University (podcast), January 26, 2016, accessed May 8, 2020, https://www.youtube.com/watch?v=TGlyymFQs-U

21. Antiracism trainers use somatic practices to get white people to attend to how racism shows up in our bodies. Lee Mun Wah teaches bodily observation as a central means of understanding conversational dynamics on race. See, Stir Fry Seminars, http://www.stirfryseminars.com/resources/. Sandra Kim's healing from internalized whiteness workshop offers a trauma-informed approach to understanding the impact of colonization on white bodies. See, https://sandrakim.com/about-sandra/. For an affective phenomenological account of fear's impact on bodies see, Sara Ahmed, "The Affective Politics of Fear," in *The Cultural Politics of Emotion* (New York: Routledge, 2014), 62–81.

22. Cherríe L. Moraga and Gloria E. Anzaldúa, eds. *This Bridge Called My Back: Writings by Radical Women of Color*, 3rd edition (San Antonio, TX: Third Woman Press, 2002), xlvi.

23. Eduardo Bonilla-Silva calls attention to the causes of this incomprehensible stuttering—the digressions, pauses, revisions, and tangents that white talk takes. See,

Racism without Racists: Color-Blind Racism and the Persistence of Racial Inequality in America, 4th edition (Lanham, MD: Rowman and Littlefield, 2014), 116.

24. Reni Eddo-Lodge, *Why I'm No Longer Talking to White People about Race* (London: Bloomsbury Press, 2018), x.

25. Sara Ahmed, *Living a Feminist Life*, 28.

26. Sara Ahmed, "A Phenomenology of Whiteness," *Feminist Theory* 8 (2007), 150.

27. My comments are deeply inspired by Applebaum's careful discussion of the connections between whiteness and moral goodness in *Being White, Being Good*. I'm working with her basic argument and observations here.

28. For more on how the good/bad binary works, see Robin DiAngelo, *White Fragility*, 89–99; and, Shannon Sullivan, *Good White People: The Problem with White Middle-Class Anti-Racism* (Albany, NY: SUNY Press, 2014).

29. This is the central idea in John Austin's, *How to Do Things with Words*, 2nd edition (Cambridge, MA: Harvard University Press, 1975).

30. DiAngelo, *White Fragility*, 78.

31. As Applebaum notes, standard accounts of responsibility that tie culpability to actions and chains of causality define responsibility in narrow terms. This makes it difficult to understand how white people perform and sustain whiteness and racism in our everyday ordinary actions. Applebaum does a remarkable job of clarifying the distinction between complicity as a matter of being, and complicity as a matter of doing, and argues for a new conception of responsibility that does not rely so heavily on blame and causal links between individual actions and institutional systems. See *Being White Being Good* (2010). See also Sandra Bartky, "Race, Complicity and Culpable Ignorance," in *Sympathy and Solidarity: And Other Essays* (Lanham, MD: Rowman and Littlefield, 2002).

32. This is a central theme in *Being White, Being Good*.

33. María Lugones, "Purity, Impurity, and Separation," in *Pilgrimages/Perigrinajes: Theorizing Coalition against Multiple Oppressions* (Lanham, MD: Roman and Littlefield, 2007), 127.

34. George Yancy, *Black Bodies, White Gazes: The Continuing Significance of Race* (Lanham, MD: Rowman and Littlefield Publishers, 2008), 86–87.

35. Yancy, *Black Bodies, White Gazes*, 87.

36. Mills, *The Racial Contract*, 19.

37. Nikole Hannah-Jones, "The 1619 Project: Introduction," *The New York Times Magazine*, August 18, 2019, 26.

38. Moustafa Bayoumi, *How Does It Feel to Be a Problem: Being Young and Arab in America* (New York: Penguin Press, 2009), 117.

39. Bayoumi, *How Does It Feel to Be a Problem*, 118.

40. Linda Qiu, "Trump's Evidence-Free Claims about the Migrant Caravan," *New York Times Magazine*, October 22, 2018, https://www.nytimes.com/2018/10/22/us/politics/migrant-caravan-fact-check.html

41. James Baldwin offers the clearest account of how white people project our anxieties and fears onto dark bodies: "I know this, and everyone who's ever tried to live knows this. What I say about you, about someone else, about everybody else, reveals you . . . what I think of you as being, indicated by my own necessities, and

my own psychology, my own fears and desires. I'm not describing you when I talk about you, I'm describing me." The historical invention, in his words, of "the n――" as a placeholder for white anxieties is central to the maintenance of white identity. He remarks, "But you [white folks] still think that the 'n――' is necessary. But he's unnecessary to me." See Baldwin's 1963 KQED interview available: http://www.youtube.com/watch?v=L0L5fciA6AU

42. George Yancy, *Look, A White!: Philosophical Essays on Whiteness* (Philadelphia: Temple University Press, 2012), 3.

43. Thandeka, *Learning to Be White: Money, Race, and God in America* (New York: Continuum, 1999), 4.

44. Baldwin, "White Man's Guilt," 409.

45. María Lugones, "On the Logic of Pluralist Feminism," in *Pilgrimages/Pereginajes: Theorizing Coalition against Multiple Oppression* (Lanham, MD: Rowman and Littlefield, 2003), 72–73.

46. People of color see themselves reflected in white mirrors too. The difference is that survival under white supremacy requires both an awareness of one's plurality, and the ability to move with agility between understandings of how whites perceive you and how you perceive yourself.

47. For a detailed account of "flipping the script" see Yancy, *Look, A White!*, 1–17.

48. Applebaum, *Being White, Being Good*, 5.

49. Marilyn Frye, "White Woman Feminist," in *Willful Virgin: Essays in Feminism* (Freedom, CA: The Crossing Press, 1992), 155.

50. Unwanted touching smacks of ownership and entitlement to another person's humanity. It turns people of color into exotic objects of curiosity. Unwanted touching also references the psychological torment that Africans experienced during slavery—the invasive poking, prodding of auction block inspections. For example, in *The History of Mary Prince: A West Indian Slave Related by Herself*, Mary Prince recalls, "I was soon surrounded by strange men, who examined and handled me in the same manner that a butcher would a calf or lamb he was about to purchase, and who talk about my shape and size in like words—as if I could no more understand their meaning than a dumb beast." Cited in Yancy, *Black Bodies, White Gazes*, 141. Amoja Three Rivers offers examples of these rules in a contemporary context. See her *Cultural Etiquette: A Guide for the Well Intentioned* (Indian Valley, VA: Market Wimmin Press, 1991).

51. Pema Chödrön, *The Places That Scare You: A Guide to Fearlessness in Difficult Times* (Boston: Shambala Press, 2001).

52. Yancy calls this tarrying. In his words, "[t]he unfinished present is where I want whites to tarry (though not permanently remain), to listen, to recognize the complexity and weight of the current existence of white racism, to attempt to understand the ways in which they perpetuate racism, and to begin to think about the incredible difficulty involved in undoing it. Yancy, *Look a White*, 158.

53. Some instances of white talk (i.e., Are you sure they asked you to show your receipt on the way out of the store because you're Latinx?) are testimonial injustices. They harm people of color as knowers and occur "when a prejudice causes a hearer

to give a deflated level of credibility to a speaker's word." Miranda Fricker, *Epistemic Injustice: Power and the Ethics of Knowing* (London: Oxford, 2007), 1.

54. Nancy Tuana, "The Speculum of Ignorance: The Women's Health Movement and Epistemologies of Ignorance," *Hypatia* 21, no. 3 (2006), 1–19.

55. Tuana, "The Speculum of Ignorance," 10.

56. Frye, "On Being White," 118.

57. Spelman, "Managing Ignorance," 121.

58. Spelman, 121. Spelman is drawing on Carolyn Betensky's scholarship here. I've revised the citation to emphasize how ignorance undercuts white people's desire for goodness.

59. Recently scholars have explored this sense of vulnerability as both an alternative to the autonomous, independent subject of liberal philosophy and as a means of exploring the connections between the illusion of invulnerability and violence and oppression. In addition to Applebaum, see, Debora Bergoffen, "February 22, 2001: Toward a Politics of the Vulnerable Body," *Hypatia* 18, no. 1 (2003), 116–34; Judith Butler, *Precarious Life: The Power of Mourning and Violence* (New York: Verso, 2004); Martha A. Fineman, "The Vulnerable Subject: Anchoring Equality in the Human Condition," *Yale Journal of Law and Feminism* 20, no. 1 (2008), 1–23; and, Erinn Gilson, "Vulnerability, Ignorance, and Oppression," *Hypatia* 26, no. 2 (2011), 308–32.

60. Gilson, "Vulnerability, Ignorance, and Oppression," 3.

61. *The Color of Fear*, directed by Lee Mun Wah (Berkeley, CA: StirFry Productions, 1994, DVD.

62. Lee Mun Wah, "The Art of Mindful Inquiry," Stirfry Seminars and Counseling, 2011, http://www.stirfryseminars.com/resources/pdfs/FreeResources_02.24.15.pdf

63. Frye, "White Woman Feminist," 155.

64. My discussion is inspired by Lee Mun Wah, "Nine Healthy Ways to Communicate," Stir Fry Seminars, http://www.stirfryseminars.com/pages/offer.php

65. Sharon Welch, *Sweet Dreams in America: Making Ethics and Spirituality Work* (New York: Routledge 1999), 44. Cited in Ann Russo, *Feminist Accountability: Disrupting Violence and Transforming Power* (New York: New York University Press, 2019), 31.

Chapter 3

Tracking Privilege

Preserving Epistemic Pushback in Feminist and Critical Race Philosophy Classes

There are days when I envy my colleagues who teach a standard Western philosophy curriculum. With the possible exception of discussions about God's existence, most traditional philosophical puzzles do not implicate the self in the deeply emotional ways that courses in feminist and critical race philosophy do.[1] Classroom discussions of race, gender, and their intersections with class/caste, ability, and sexuality use on-the-ground experiences with injustice as their starting point and, as such, have strong psychological and affective dimensions. We know injustice when we feel it. Productive engagement with these topics should call our collective attention to the relationships among knowledge, power, and embodied identity in ways that challenge students' default assumption that knowledge is marked by certainty, universality, and objectivity.

Classrooms are *unlevel knowing fields*: contested terrains where knowledge and ignorance are simultaneously produced and circulate with equal vigor. As Gloria Anzaldúa once noted, "Racism is especially rampant in places and people that produce knowledge."[2] There are constellations of resistances at play here. Dominant groups are accustomed to having an "epistemic home-turf advantage"; that is, we are used to having conversations about racism or sexism in discursive spaces where our perceptions go unchallenged. So, when our epistemic home terrain is under threat, we hold our ground. Consider the white student who is unwilling to hear the testimonies of students of color about the daily injustices they face as anything more than complaining. Members of marginalized groups also resist: we push back against texts and conversations that distort, erase, or fail to acknowledge our experiences. Consider the Latinx student who chooses to be silent or to skip class rather than have another conversation about race and immigration with white students who just want to argue.

I want to focus on one particular node in this constellation of resistant responses. *Privilege-preserving epistemic pushback* is a variety of willful ignorance that dominant groups habitually deploy during conversations that are trying to make social injustices visible. I want to work with, not against, this ground-holding reflex by offering a possible strategy for tracking it productively, with the caveat that resistance can be nuanced. It's not always easy to spot or interpret. I focus on these ground-holding responses because they are pervasive, tenacious, and bear a strong resemblance to critical-thinking practices, and because I believe that their uninterrupted circulation does psychological and epistemic harm to members of marginalized groups.

My discussion begins with two examples from undergraduate feminist and critical race philosophy classrooms with strong applied intersectional content. Privilege-preserving epistemic pushback takes at least two forms. The first strongly resembles critical-thinking practices that encourage students to carefully consider the truth of a particular claim. The second is more sophisticated: it occurs when philosophical concepts are enlisted to fortify this resistance. I argue that this privilege-preserving expression of ignorance is neither a form of skepticism nor an expression of critical thinking. These expressions do a different kind of work. I treat them as *shadow texts*, that is, as texts that run alongside class readings in ways that offer no epistemic friction. I briefly offer a pedagogical exercise designed to help students track shadow texts and to raise questions about the possible harms of letting shadow texts circulate uncritically. In closing, I consider the possibility that shadow texts help track not only the production of ignorance but also the harms of epistemic violence.

DOES THIS HAPPEN WHEN YOU TEACH?

DeEndré walks into class and sits in his usual seat in the back row. We are discussing a section from Claudia Card's "Rape as a Terrorist Institution."[3] DeEndré, who has positioned himself as the class gadfly, busily searches the internet for statistics on sexual assault and domestic violence against boys and men. He finds one, raises his hand, and says: "Men are victims too, according to a recent statistic more men than women are victims of intimate partner violence. It's over 40%!"[4] Armed with new information, he asserts that our discussion would be less biased if we focused more *generally* on intimate partner violence, rather than always focusing on violence against girls and women. Women in the class challenge his response by explaining why gender and race are important to the discussion. They offer more accurate statistics. They tell their stories about how the ever-present threats of sexualized violence affect their daily movements, but he insists that they are reading too much gender into simple episodes of human-on-human violence.

We are discussing institutional racism. Jennifer, a white philosophy major, shares a story about racist graffiti that uses the "n" word. She says the word, animating it with that two-fingered scare-quote gesture to signal that she is mentioning it. I ask her to consider the history of the word and how it might mean something different coming from white mouths. I ask her not to use it. She gives the class a mini lecture on the use–mention distinction, reminding me that it "is a foundational concept in analytic philosophy" and that it's "perfectly acceptable to mention, but not to use the word in philosophical discussions." Sheila, one of two black women in the class, offers a history of the word and how it was used to degrade and discipline black bodies. Jennifer nods in agreement but holds her ground: "Exactly!" she says, "that's what happens when the word is *used*, but I'm just *mentioning* it." Sheila shares how she feels when white folks *mention* the word. She asks Jennifer politely to neither use nor mention it. Jennifer calmly responds that Shelia does not understand the distinction and proceeds to explain it again.

WHAT IS PRIVILEGE-PRESERVING EPISTEMIC PUSHBACK?

Feminist philosophers and critical race theorists will be intimately familiar with these kinds of exchanges. Perhaps your own stories spring to mind as you read them. These responses are not limited to classrooms; one hears them everywhere, but I focus on philosophy classrooms because this is where I spend most of my time engaging them. As part of this engagement, I've thought about how privilege-preserving epistemic pushback functions in academic spaces, and I've wondered aloud about the impact these utterances have when they pass as legitimate philosophical skepticism or critical thinking. To answer this question, I need to say more about the nature and movement of privilege-preserving epistemic pushback.

Feminist epistemologists have long noted the connections between the social location of knowers and a particular social group's understandings of the world. I like Lorraine Code's notion of epistemic terrains because it offers an on-the-ground visual cartography that I find useful when tracking the epistemic social dynamics of the classroom. As Code famously notes, we need to develop

> a new geography of the epistemic terrain, one that is no longer primarily a physical geography, but a population geography that develops qualitative analyses of subjective positions and identities and the sociopolitical structures that produce them. Because differing social positions generate various constructions of reality and afford different perspectives on the world . . . these analyses derive from

a recognition that knowers are always somewhere—and at once limited and enabled by the specificities of their locations.⁵

If knowledge is shaped by a knower's location on a particular social epistemic terrain, and if that terrain is an unlevel knowing field, then it will produce situations where some knowers are epistemically advantaged and others disadvantaged. One species of disadvantage is the structural ignorance that follows from an inability to easily notice certain facts about the world from one's epistemic home terrain: most men struggle to understand why cat-calling women in public places is harassment and not flattery. Most white people struggle to understand how white privilege contributes to our safety, prosperity, and health.

Epistemic home terrains must be constantly and vigilantly guarded and defended. Broadly speaking, privilege-preserving epistemic pushback is a form of worldview protection: a willful resistance to knowing that occurs predictably in discussions that threaten a social group's epistemic home terrain.⁶ Defending that terrain is one way for dominant groups to resist "new material that deeply unsettles the paradigms through which they make sense of the world. When ideologies like the myth of meritocracy or their sense of who they are as a person, are deeply unsettled, students will often fall back on various defense mechanisms to try to maintain order."⁷ In practice, privilege-preserving epistemic pushback is a family of cognitive, affective, nonverbal, and discursive tactics that are used habitually to avoid engaging ideas that threaten us. This resistance, as José Medina argues, offers a form of "cognitive self-protection."⁸ When our sense of self, group identity, core beliefs, and privileged place in the social order is challenged, we adopt defensive postures to resist what we perceive to be destabilizing. Protecting our epistemic terrain requires that we put up barriers made of opinions and prejudices, which are fortified by anger, shame, guilt, indifference, arrogance, jealously, pride, and sometimes silence. These feelings sit in our bodies: our hearts beat faster, our muscles tighten, we scowl, and our minds chatter. Sometimes we shut down completely.

Privilege-preserving epistemic pushback has a strong normative dimension. Terrain-defending habits partially stem from the feeling that others are challenging the basic sense we have of ourselves as good people living in a basically just world. These are not mere disagreements. As Barbara Applebaum observes, they are discursive strategies deployed to protect our sense of both innocence and goodness; this single-pointed focus obscures our complicity in the subtle workings of white racism.⁹ Members of dominant groups are more comfortable discussing social justice from the comfort and safety of our epistemic home terrain, so when we are nudged onto a more critical terrain we become disoriented and unsettled. We defend our epistemic home terrain not only for the sake of maintaining our worldview but also to preserve our perceived entitlement to a racial and gendered comfort that is strongly tied to our sense of being good white people. When our goodness is threatened we respond by redirecting the conversation back to more comfortable turf. We take back the center. If racialized and gendered locations are always epistemic locations, then racialized and gendered (dis)comfort will always yield epistemic discomfort. So, privilege-preserving epistemic pushback is not only a form of cognitive self-protection; it also helps us to maintain an image we have of ourselves as good people or reliable allies.[10]

The lure of being a good white antiracist or a good male feminist, as I discussed in the last chapter, is strongly linked to the desire for ontological wholeness, a form of metaphysical comfort. Robin DiAngelo's account of "white fragility" captures the deep and abiding hold metaphysical comfort has on dominant group members' desire for innocence. White people, she observes, move through social environments in ways that insulate us from race-based anxiety and stress, and this fosters expectations of racial comfort. We have a low tolerance for racial stress. In general, white fragility triggers a constellation of behaviors that work to steer us back to epistemic terrains where we feel whole, comfortable, and good.[11] Consider how white people repeatedly bolster our metaphysical wholeness with stories about our good deeds, merit-based accomplishments, immigration stories, or the long hours we've worked. These narratives keep us whole.

Finally, privilege-preserving epistemic pushback cannot be dismissed as a rare set of responses from a few random individuals who happen to be uncomfortable with social-justice discussions. These responses are patterned and predictable. Their regularity points to their historically deep systemic origins. Like all forms of privilege, these discursive habits are unmarked and circulate subtly. As Beth Berila notes, privilege is the oil in complex systems of domination that help these systems work smoothly. When the works get gummed up, these systems have a "back-up plan that involves built-in, learned reactions that will come flooding in to protect the system of privilege, usually in the form of defensive, so-called resistant reactions. . . . This back-up buffer prevents [us] from really questioning privilege and neatly reroutes [us] back into upholding the system."[12] Consider how easy it is to forecast most non-black people's responses to the Black Lives Matter movement. The words barely leave our lips before the chorus of "I think *all* lives matter!" or "Blue lives matter too" fill the room. So, the pushback I have in mind cannot be attributed exclusively to a few stubborn students who are unwilling to leave their epistemic home terrain. The predictability of these discursive moves signal that these forms of privilege protection are deeply historical and continue to be culturally active.

Predictability, however, does not always translate into visibility. The discursive patterns associated with privilege-preserving epistemic pushback are unmarked, nuanced, and are extremely difficult to spot in philosophy classes because they easily pass as acceptable philosophical engagements. I confess that, in the interest of meeting students halfway, I've sometimes treated this pushback as an objection to an argument; but I feel extremely uneasy about doing so because treating willful ignorance as critical engagement muddies philosophical waters. Philosophy classrooms should be spaces where students learn to engage material carefully and critically, and "I don't buy it! I think you are wrong. You need to convince me!" is a psychological and not a well-reasoned response.[13] Treating privilege-preserving epistemic pushback as a form of critical engagement validates it and allows it to circulate more freely; this, as I'll argue later, does epistemic violence to oppressed groups. For these reasons, we need to be clear about the differences among critical thinking, healthy skepticism, and privilege-preserving epistemic pushback.

CRITICAL THINKING, HEALTHY SKEPTICISM, AND PRIVILEGE-PRESERVING EPISTEMIC PUSHBACK

Philosophers of education have long made the distinction between critical thinking and critical pedagogy. Both literatures appeal to the value of being "critical" in the sense that instructors should cultivate in students a more cautious approach to accepting common beliefs at face value. Both traditions share the concern that learners generally lack the ability to spot inaccurate, misleading, incomplete, or blatantly false claims. They also share a sense that learning a particular set of critical skills has a corrective, humanizing, and liberatory effect. The traditions, however, part ways over their definition of "critical." Nicholas C. Burbules and Rupert Berk's comparison of the traditions provides a useful background for my discussion in the next section. The critical-thinking tradition is concerned primarily with epistemic adequacy. To be critical is to show good judgment in recognizing when arguments are faulty, assertions lack evidence, truth claims appeal to unreliable sources, or concepts are sloppily crafted and applied. For critical thinkers, the problem is that people fail to "examine the assumptions, commitments, and logic of daily life . . . the basic problem is irrational, illogical, and unexamined living."[14] In this tradition sloppy claims can be identified and fixed by learning to apply the tools of formal and informal logic correctly.

Critical pedagogy begins from a different set of assumptions rooted in the neo-Marxian literature on critical theory commonly associated with the Frankfurt School. Here, the critical learner is someone who is empowered and motivated to seek justice and emancipation. Critical pedagogy regards the claims that students make in response to social-justice issues not as propositions to be assessed for their truth value but as expressions of power that function to re-inscribe and perpetuate social inequalities. Its mission is to teach students ways of identifying and mapping how power shapes our understandings of the world. This is the first step toward resisting and transforming social injustices. By interrogating the politics of knowledge production, this tradition also calls into question the uses of the accepted critical-thinking toolkit to determine epistemic adequacy. To extend Audre Lorde's classic metaphor, the tools of the critical-thinking tradition (e.g., validity, soundness, conceptual clarity) cannot dismantle the master's house: they can temporarily beat the master at his own game, but they can never bring about any enduring structural change.[15] They fail because the critical thinker's toolkit is commonly invoked in particular settings, at particular times to reassert power: Those adept with the tools often use them to restore an order that assures their comfort. They can be habitually invoked to defend our epistemic home terrains.

The line between these traditions is not hard and fast, and I concede that there are times when these traditions can work well together to navigate difficult questions. But I'm adamant that philosophical engagements on issues of social justice must simultaneously track the production of knowledge and ignorance. Teaching social-justice issues requires an attentiveness not only to the ways students take up course content but also to the strategies they use to resist it. I neither want to encourage nor silence student resistance. I want to make its operations visible by tracking the movements on the unlevel knowing field.

So, what happens when we treat privilege-preserving epistemic pushback as an expression of healthy skepticism? We can't track its movements. Students routinely justify their resistance by explaining that they are "playing devil's advocate" or that their responses should be taken in the spirit of the healthy skepticism that philosophers are encouraged to adopt as part of our disciplinary best practices. I think this is inaccurate: there is a difference between a lack of agreement and a lack of understanding. The resistance captured by my opening examples is not motivated by a belief that certainty is impossible or that, as a matter of practice, we must suspend judgment on questions of social justice. What's troubling here is not that students enjoy playing the skeptic in philosophy classes. They most certainly do. What's worrisome is that members of dominant groups become habitually skeptical during conversations that threaten our epistemic home terrain. As Gaile Pohlhaus insightfully remarked, "I have seen white students who balked at Descartes' skepticism (and had great trouble understanding how and why anyone would doubt in that way) become perfect Cartesians when it comes to talking about race."[16] Nora Berenstain's scholarship on epistemic exploitation highlights the additional costs of this skepticism on people of color. Dominant groups' default skepticism, she explains, "demand that the victim do the emotionally exhausting work of reliving their experience and defending their interpretation of it in the face of doubt and disbelief. Default skeptical responses also function to erase existing epistemic resources that undermine dominant narratives about the relationship of these experiences to larger structures of oppression."[17]

If the need for worldview protection rather than the quest for certainty is what truly drives privilege-preserving epistemic pushback, then students' doubting reflexes work to obstruct rather than to create knowledge. DeEndré and Jennifer are not merely expressing their doubt; each has an implicit worldview to defend—an epistemic ground to hold—in the face of competing worldviews. Their engagements are aimed at resisting the content of the discussion rather than suspending judgment about the claims being made. Unlike expressions of genuine skepticism that advance classroom discussions by encouraging open-minded, cautious, curious, and engaged doubt, privilege-preserving epistemic pushback is driven by what Medina calls the need for "cognitive self-protection."[18] So I don't think that it accurately describes what is happening here.

We can't track privilege-preserving epistemic pushback if we treat it as an expression of critical thinking either. Critical thinking, when done well, encourages clear, open-minded, cautious, curious, and engaged thinking on difficult issues, but pushback actually fails to do this. Pushback is a defensive reaction, not a critical engagement. Medina's distinction between engagements that are beneficial to knowledge production and the kind that obstruct knowing well makes this clear:

> Resistance can be a good and a bad thing, epistemically speaking. The resistances of your cognitive life keep you grounded. As Wittgenstein would put it, in order to have a real (and not simply a delusional) cognitive life, "we need friction," we need to go "back to the rough ground." But there are also resistances that function as obstacles, as weights that slow us down or preclude us from following (or even having access to) certain paths or pursuing further certain questions, problems, curiosities.[19]

Beneficial epistemic resistance helps us to establish an entry point onto unfamiliar epistemic terrain. It moves the discussion forward productively. In Medina's words, there is a beneficial epistemic friction that prompts us "to be self-critical, to compare and contrast [our] beliefs, to meet justificatory demands, to recognize cognitive gaps, and so on."[20]

DeEndré's engagements offer no beneficial epistemic friction. In fact, they fail by both critical-thinking standards and Medina's criteria. Technically, his response is a red herring. He diverts the focus from the terror of rape culture to the unfairness of how our sexual-violence conversation is framed. He steers it to an epistemic terrain where he feels less fragile. But more importantly, the red herring is not just a logical misstep: it does something. It allows him to neutralize any consideration of how racism and sexism are used to maintain rape culture. His response mirrors the race-neutralizing discursive moves that characterize white talk. You can't focus productively on the racialized/gendered dimensions of sexualized violence when you are operating on epistemic terrain that confines the conversation to broad claims about the violence that happens to people in relationships in general. Epistemic friction is impossible when conversations are pulled onto epistemic terrains where terms such as *white privilege, rape culture,* or *toxic masculinity* have absolutely no hermeneutical currency. So, what's going on here is more than just a logical misstep. DeEndré's resistance has a deeper obstructive nature that Medina (and the critical-pedagogy tradition) find important. His discursive move creates an obstacle to further inquiry. It keeps his affective-cognitive wheels spinning in place by censoring, distracting, dodging, silencing, or "inhibiting the formation of beliefs, the articulation of doubts, the formulation of questions and lines of inquiry."[21]

Jennifer's resistance is more difficult to unpack. It attempts to apply an accepted philosophical concept in an effort to move the conversation forward. Understanding the lack of epistemic friction in this instance requires both an awareness of the discursive dynamics at play and an understanding of how the use–mention distinction is being used. We need to ask: does Jennifer's appeal to the use–mention distinction offer us beneficial epistemic friction, or is it just a case of using the master's tools to defend the master's epistemic home terrain? I'm not suggesting that she uses the philosopher's toolkit maliciously. There is power in mastering the tools of the discipline, and she takes pride in arguing well. I'm just curious as to whether she is pressing the use–mention distinction into the service of a broader strategic refusal to understand (and feel) what Sheila is trying to tell her. One way to explore this possibility is to ask whether these moves create useful points of traction (I like to think of them as toeholds) on unfamiliar epistemic terrain, that is, whether they offer us the beneficial epistemic friction required to know well.

Jennifer understands the distinction between using and mentioning the n-word. She is mindful that her usage picks out the word itself and not the group of people it historically references and degrades.[22] Her usage concerns me for a few reasons. First, the distinction itself is not particularly sensitive to the politics of dehumanizing speech acts. Knowing how the distinction works does not absolve us of the responsibility of choosing to mention those words. She mistakenly thinks that the use–mention distinction is helpful regardless of which words are used/mentioned. Maya Angelou's insight makes this powerfully clear. In a wonderfully candid interview with Dave Chapelle, she explains:

> I believe that a word is a thing. It is non-visible and audible only for the time it's there. It hangs in the air, but I believe it is a thing. I believe it goes into the upholstery, then to the rugs, and into my hair, and into my clothes, and finally even into my body. I believe that words are things and I live on them. I look at the word—the "n" word—which I'm really obliged to call it that because it was created to divest people of their humanity. And, when I see a bottle come from the pharmacy and it says "POISON" and there is a skull and bones, then I know that the content of that thing, the bottle is not that, but the content is poison. If I pour that content into Bavarian crystal, it is still poison.[23]

Angelou's observations suggest that the use–mention distinction is unhelpful here: it neither neutralizes the offensiveness of the word nor does it offer us beneficial epistemic friction. If using the "n" word counts as a ten on a one-to-ten scale of offensiveness, and mentioning it counts as a nine on that scale, then does reducing the harm one step really make it that much better? Use may be more offensive than mention, but the difference is not sufficient to justify uttering the word. The word is poison, and an academic appeal to the distinction does not reduce the damage.[24] So Jennifer's appeal to the distinction does not help us to know well. And if she were to insist that it does, then I'd ask whether philosophical conventions should be privileged over the well-being of students of color in our class.

I'm also curious about the normative dimensions of this move: the use–mention distinction may also be deployed to bolster white folks' desire for innocence and goodness. We might equate our goodness with knowing this distinction. One might imagine a well-meaning white person saying: "I just mentioned the 'n' word. I'm not using it. I know the difference, so I can't be accused of intentionally causing harm. I'm innocent." The appeal functions to redirect our epistemic attention to the white person's intentions and away from the effects of the n-word on students of color in the classroom. When conversations are framed around how someone meant to use the word, the inner life and intentions of the white student become more important than the silencing and constraining effects of its use on the epistemic agency of students of color.

USING "SHADOW TEXTS" TO TRACK PRIVILEGE- PRESERVING EPISTEMIC PUSHBACK

If privilege-preserving epistemic pushback is neither healthy skepticism nor thinking critically, then what is it? How might we engage these responses productively? Are there ways of engaging pushback that offer us at least some beneficial epistemic friction?

It has taken me some time to understand that privilege-preserving epistemic pushback cannot be navigated exclusively with academic philosophy's standard pedagogical playbook. At some point I ditched traditional pedagogies in favor of affectively centered engagements aimed at creating "safe spaces."[25] I thought that establishing conversational ground rules would provide the beneficial epistemic friction necessary to move discussions forward, but these approaches were also flawed. Classroom spaces have never been safe spaces: not everyone feels secure and confident in them. I recognize that classrooms are by nature unsafe spaces, and for a while I thought that these spaces would benefit from pedagogies of discomfort.[26] Discomfort offers the possibility for growth, but it can also play into some students' fragility and make them shut down. And, what we are really asking of students here is not to change the classroom climate to make them feel more comfortable, so they can share their thoughts. We are asking them to be brave enough to open their hearts and to share what they know, even if it's not on the mark. So, it's about inviting them to be brave with the understanding that their courage is what brings the brave space into being. A brave space does not have to be comfortable to be safe.[27] I engage students honestly, in ways that name discomfort by making whiteness, maleness, and heteronormative assumptions visible, decentering them, and rendering them strange. Naming discomfort should not be mistakenly equated with fomenting a hostile environment. At its root, the discomfort comes from inviting members of privileged groups to leave our epistemic home terrains, to muster the courage to sit with discomfort, and to explore the possibility that there is knowledge in understanding how privilege-preserving epistemic pushback functions. This knowledge can be found in cultivating mindfulness around pushback, coupled with active understanding of how resistance maintains ignorance and does epistemic damage. In the end, this focus may offer beneficial epistemic friction.

Good teaching must track simultaneously the social production of knowledge and ignorance. As Nancy Tuana explains, "if we are to fully understand the complex practices of knowledge production and the variety of factors that account for why something is known, we must also understand the practices that account for *not* knowing, that is, for our *lack* of knowledge about a phenomenon."[28] Willful ignorance circulates in even the most progressive spaces. We can make these spaces mindful of ignorance, but never ignorance-free. If privilege-preserving epistemic pushback is an expression of ignorance, then we need a critical philosophical practice for making it visible and tracking it productively. To this end, I'm recommending that we work toward becoming attentive to privilege-preserving epistemic pushback and to use these episodes as points of traction to explore how we cling to ignorance in the service of dodging discomfort. I work with students to cultivate this mindfulness by treating privilege-preserving epistemic pushback neither as a logical misstep nor as healthy skepticism, but as a *shadow text*.

Shadow texts direct our attention to the ways epistemic resistance circulates during classroom discussions. I use the term metaphorically to point to the written and the spoken cognitive-affective content of this discursive resistance. DeEndré's claim that "It's better to talk about intimate partner violence!" is a shadow text. His response shadows the readings in the same way a detective shadows a suspicious person. Good detectives follow their subjects tenaciously without being noticed. The word "shadow" calls to mind the image of something walking closely alongside another thing without engaging it. If Jennifer continues to press philosophical concepts into the service of a broader refusal to understand the dehumanizing history of the n-word, then "I mentioned but didn't use the word 'n———'" is a shadow text. Shadow texts can certainly be understood as reactions to course content, but I prefer to think of them as being called up by deeply affective-cognitive responses to the material. They are deployed protectively. When an idea or comment makes us feel uncomfortable, we stalk the offending claim in an effort to monitor and control its circulation.

Shadow texts do deep epistemic work. By definition, shadows are the product of obstacles. They are dark areas or shapes produced by bodies (obstacles) that come between a light source and a surface. They are disruptive in the sense that they interrupt the movement of light from its source to a surface. Recall Medina's claim that epistemic resistance can "function as an obstacle, as weights that slow us down or preclude us from following (or having access to) certain paths or pursuing further certain questions, problems, and curiosities."[29] *When privilege-preserving epistemic pushback functions as an obstacle, it casts a shadow text.* Shadows are by definition regions of opacity, so shadow texts are regions of epistemic opacity.[30] The discursive detours and distractions signal epistemic closure; they tell listeners, "I'm not going there. You need to convince me." I use the term *shadow text* to focus students' attention on this double meaning.

Treating privilege-preserving epistemic pushback as a shadow text may not always offer the *beneficial epistemic friction* that knowledge-production demands, but it doesn't follow that shadow texts cannot be tracked in pedagogically useful ways. Shadow texts are produced by epistemic obstacles, but the obstacles are not always immovable barriers. Shadow texts provide a useful way to identify and work with privilege-preserving epistemic pushback. Learning to spot shadow texts can offer epistemic friction: They help the class focus on what shadow texts *do*, rather than just on what they *say*. We can ask ourselves, how do shadow texts redirect the conversation? Where do they take us? In this way, shadow texts offer us toeholds—something to grasp that serve as useful points of departure during our conversations—even if the audience remains unmoved in the end.

DeEndré's response offers the clearest example of the shadow-text pedagogy. I've used it with some degree of success to prompt students to become mindful of how privilege-preserving epistemic pushback moves on the unlevel knowing field, although there are always a few learners who respond defensively to the method itself! I begin by writing a question on the board, for example, let's be curious about Card's claim that "rape is a terrorist institution." What do you think she means? Students respond by defining terrorism or by explaining Card's definition. I write all of their responses on the board:

1. The threat of rape is analogous to the threat of terrorism.
2. Rape culture terrorizes women.
3. The threat of rape and the threat of terrorism are completely different!
4. Men are victims, too, according to a recent statistic.

Next, I invite the class to be curious about these responses by asking them to identify which ones communicate resistance. I mark them parenthetically:

1. The threat of rape is analogous to the threat of terrorism.
2. Rape culture terrorizes women.
3. The threat of rape and the threat of terrorism are completely different! [*Resistant Response*]
4. Men are victims, too, according to a recent statistic. [*Resistant Response*]

Next, I ask us to consider how the responses that engage Card's claim directly (1 and 2) differ from the resistant responses (3 and 4). I invite them to think about whether responses 3 and 4 are resistant in the same ways. I try to prompt them to notice how the third response works to resist Card's analogy, and the fourth response works to resist the conversation entirely. Response 3 offers beneficial friction because it engages Card's text in ways that lead to a productive conversation on the psychological impacts of terrorism and rape culture. The last response offers no beneficial epistemic friction: it redirects the discussion to questions about violence against men. Finally, I introduce the term *shadow text*, and ask them to identify which resistant response counts as a shadow text.

1. The threat of rape and the threat of terrorism are completely different! [*Resistant Response to Card's Text*]
2. Men are victims, too, according to a recent statistic. [*Shadow Text*]

The point of this exercise is to make visible the tension between the question and the shadow text. We speculate about why the fourth response "went there," and consider what triggered the resistance to engaging Card's text directly. I invite them to track their own movements in response to the question. I keep the conversation short. We do this exercise together for the next two or three instances of pushback, before I move on to explain epistemic violence. My hope is that students will learn to identify shadow texts themselves, and most of them do eventually understand the basic goal of the practice.

At some point, I ask our class to consider how identifying shadow texts might help us to track the production of ignorance. This requires work. Students will almost always understand ignorance to mean that the speaker is saying something stupid. It's essential for them to understand that tracking ignorance requires that our attention be focused not on a few problem individuals but on learning to identify patterns of resistance and tying ignorance-producing habits to a strategic refusal to understand. We focus on the discursive moves and not the people who make them.

PRIVILEGE-PRESERVING EPISTEMIC PUSHBACK AND EPISTEMIC SILENCING

Until this point, I've focused on how shadow texts might be used to track the social production of ignorance on the unlevel knowing field, but we need to track privilege-preserving epistemic pushback for another reason: its uninterrupted circulation can be psychologically and epistemically damaging.

Psychologically speaking, allowing privilege-preserving epistemic pushback to circulate as if it were healthy skepticism or a critical-thinking practice can create a hostile learning environment. Repeated performances of pushback function as microaggressions: words and behaviors that happen in everyday interactions that "send denigrating messages to specific individuals because of their group membership."[31] In the cases under consideration, privilege-preserving epistemic pushback functions as a form of microaggression called a "microinvalidation," which happens when words or actions are aimed at excluding or denying a person's thoughts or feelings about their lived reality. Consider the impact that DeEndré's *repeated* attempts to neutralize gender has on the women in our classroom who repeatedly and patiently try to counter his "skepticism" with testimony about their lived experience navigating rape culture. The collective effects of his refusal to give uptake to their testimonies is invalidating and has a silencing effect on the classroom climate. There were days when I could prompt no one to respond to his comments. The silence may have been a resistant silence—a tactical refusal to let his pushback continue to wear them down, or it may have been a sign that they had given up, but it was a silence nonetheless. On the one hand, the testimonial agency of the women in class was undermined. They could not get DeEndré to listen. On the other hand, the women's testimonies were heard by many of their peers, who vigorously nodded along in agreement.

Microinvalidations have a collective epistemic impact; they discredit a person's *knowledge* of *her* lived reality, and thus reduce her credibility as a knower. The psychological harms associated with allowing privilege-preserving epistemic pushback to circulate uncritically do epistemic damage because they function as "on-the-ground practices of epistemic silencing."[32] In "Tracking Epistemic Violence, Tracking Epistemic Practices of Silencing," Kristie Dotson uses Gayatri Spivak's definition of epistemic violence as a starting point to explain how members of marginalized groups are regularly silenced or subjected to epistemic violence with respect to giving testimony. Epistemic violence in testimony, she argues, "is a refusal, intentional or unintentional, of an audience to communicatively reciprocate a linguistic exchange owing to . . . any reliable ignorance that, given context, harms another person (or set of persons)."[33] A clear understanding of epistemic violence rests on recognizing a basic feature of linguistic communication. Speakers are always in a relationship of dependence with their audiences. Speakers have little or no control over whether their audience hears them in exactly the ways that they wish to be heard. Successful communication requires reciprocity; it demands both that the audience understand what the speaker is saying and that the speaker's words are taken as they were intended to be taken.[34] This makes speakers vulnerable during linguistic exchanges. Communication commonly fails when the audience's pernicious ignorance (a form of willful ignorance) interferes with these linguistic exchanges.

Dotson uses the linguistic-exchange model to identify two patterns of epistemic violence, both of which rest on invalidating (silencing) the testimonies of members of oppressed groups. The first practice, testimonial quieting, happens when "an audience member fails to identify a speaker as a credible knower" because the speaker is a member of a group that has been historically stereotyped as lacking epistemic credibility.[35] If the speaker is not recognized as a credible knower, then she cannot give testimony. If audiences fail to treat her as a credible source of knowledge, then her testimony will misfire: it will fail to get uptake. DeEndré's gender-neutralizing moves produce testimonial quieting: the women in the class are not treated as knowledgeable about their own lived experiences with sexual violence, and become less vocal as the class goes on.

Dotson's second practice, testimonial smothering, occurs when the speaker self-censors or restricts her remarks because she senses that her audience will be either unable or unwilling to give them appropriate uptake. Testimonial smothering is a practice of coerced silence that exists under any or all of the following related circumstances: (1) the content of the testimony feels unsafe and the speaker may either fall silent or tailor her testimony because she perceives that the audience may find it unintelligible and may form false beliefs about her or her community based on her testimony; (2) the speaker's audience demonstrates a "testimonial incompetence with respect to the content of the testimony of the speaker"; and (3) "the testimonial incompetence must follow from, or appear to follow from, pernicious ignorance."[36] Jennifer and Sheila's exchange touches on all three of Dotson's circumstances. The content of Shelia's testimony is unsafe. In challenging Jennifer's retreat into an established Western philosophical distinction and appealing to her own experience of how the n-word makes her feel, she may be opening herself up to the charge that she can't do philosophy, because she doesn't understand the conceptual apparatus of the discipline. She may fear that the class will think that black women, in general, are not cut out for abstract thought. The exchange illustrates, in Dotson's words, "an epistemic side of colonialism," that has "the devastating effect of the 'disappearing' of knowledge, where local or provincial knowledge is dismissed due to privileging alternative, often Western, epistemic practices."[37] Jennifer's privileging of the use-mention distinction also marks her incompetence with respect to Sheila's testimony: it disappears Sheila's knowledge by cutting her out of the conversation. Jennifer has won the argument but has done so unfairly by retreating to an epistemic terrain where Shelia's concerns about how the use of the word affects her have been erased. Jennifer's desire to make the "n-word" issue into a question about speech acts is ground erasing, and it seems to stem from her pernicious ignorance about racism. It frames the discussion in ways that not only make the history and politics of dehumanizing speech acts irrelevant but also makes it difficult for students of color to offer testimonial evidence of the continued impact of this word on racialized bodies. The conversation becomes a question about speech acts and not about epistemic violence, so the conversation is thus drained of its normative content.

Dotson's mechanism for identifying on-the-ground practices of epistemic silencing is extremely helpful in bringing out the normative epistemic dimensions of my shadow-text pedagogy. Assessing the harms of testimonial quieting and testimonial smothering is a context-dependent exercise, but shadow texts offer helpful ways to track these forms of epistemic violence.[38] If shadow texts are already tracking the production and circulation of ignorance, and if epistemic violence is deeply tied to pernicious ignorance, then it takes very little additional effort to connect privileged groups' epistemic resistance to on-the-ground practices of epistemic silencing. Shadow texts are already tracking the obstacles to knowing, and with a few additional questions we can address instances of epistemic silencing.

We can point to the examples I put up on the board and ask: Whose voices and texts get centered with this move? And, whose voices have you erased? How do these moves meet, or fail to meet, the conditions for epistemic silencing?

Framing privilege-preserving epistemic pushback as a shadow text is pedagogically useful for a number of reasons. First, classrooms are unsafe spaces. Naming and engaging privilege-preserving forms of resistance and discussing the epistemic harms of the pushback turn these epistemic exchanges into teachable moments. I've had some success with helping students to understand that resistance is not always reducible exclusively to isolated incidents of bad behavior, prejudice, or obnoxious interruptions. Engaging epistemic pushback is not just an exercise in keeping conversations on track by steering students back to the issues at hand. I want class members to become aware of the fact that these moves are political and that sometimes they are driven just as much by fear and ignorance as they are by the desire to engage with the text. Something deeper and more complicated is going on here, and it is worth noting and exploring how discursive resistance runs alongside our readings and discussions. Next, acknowledging resistance as a text to be engaged, rather than as an interruption to be managed, can help to diffuse the anger or fear. When resisters' concerns are engaged respectfully, they will feel heard and hopefully will listen more carefully. Initially, shadow texts may not offer the beneficial epistemic friction Medina finds necessary for positive epistemic resistance, but if navigated in the ways I've recommended, they can help to steer classes onto a more active and politically sensitive discursive terrain.

NOTES

1. This chapter contains previously published material reprinted from Alison Bailey, "Tracking Privilege-Preserving Epistemic Pushback in Feminist and Critical Race Philosophy Classes," *Hypatia: A Journal of Feminist Philosophy* 32, no. 4, published by John Wiley & Sons in 2017. Copyright © 2017, Hypatia, Inc. All rights reserved.

2. Gloria Anzaldúa, "Haciendo Caras: Una Entrada," in *Making Face, Making Soul/Haciendo Caras: Creative and Critical Perspectives of Women of Color* (San Francisco: Aunt Lute Foundation Books, 1990), xix.

3. Claudia Card, "Rape as a Terrorist Institution," in *Violence, Terrorism and Justice*, eds. R. G. Frey and Christopher W. Morris (Cambridge, UK: Cambridge University Press, 1991), 296–319.

4. DeEndré was referencing Bert H. Hoff, "U.S. National Survey: More Men than Women Victims of Intimate Partner Violence," *Journal of Aggression* 4, no. 3 (July 2012), 155–63.

5. Lorraine Code, "Incredulity, Experientialism, and the Politics of Knowledge," in *Rhetorical Spaces: Essays on Gendered Locations* (New York: Routledge, 1995), 39.

6. Chandra Talpade Mohanty and Charles Mills also use cartography metaphors. See Mills, "Alternative Epistemologies," in *Blackness Visible: Essays on the Philosophy of Race* (Ithaca, NY: Cornell University Press, 1995), 21–41. And, Mohanty, *Feminism without Borders: Decolonizing Theory, Practicing Solidarity* (Durham, NC: Duke University Press, 2006).

7. Kim A. Case and Elizabeth R. Cole, "Deconstructing Privilege When Students Resist: The Journey Back into the Community of Engaged Learners," in *Deconstructing Privilege: Teaching and Learning as Allies in the Classroom*, ed. Kim A. Case (New York: Routledge, 2013), 34–48. Cited in Beth Berila, *Integrating Mindfulness into Anti-Oppression Pedagogy: Social Justice Pedagogy in Higher Education* (New York: Routledge, 2016), 95.

8. José Medina, *The Epistemology of Resistance: Gender and Racial Oppression, Epistemic Injustice, and Resistant Imaginations* (New York: Oxford University Press, 2015), 5.

9. Barbara Applebaum, *Being White, Being Good: White Complicity, Moral Responsibility, and Social Justice Pedagogy* (Lanham, MD: Rowman and Littlefield, 2010), 184–86.

10. For a complete discussion of white complicity and goodness, see Applebaum (2010).

11. Robin DiAngelo, *White Fragility: Why It Is So Hard for White People to Talk about Racism* (Boston: Beacon, 2018).

12. Berila, *Integrating Mindfulness into Anti-Oppression Pedagogy*, 92.

13. Thanks to Lawrence B. Solum for his clarification of this point.

14. Nicholas Burbules and Rupert Bert, "Critical Thinking and Critical Pedagogy: Relations, Differences, and Limits," in *Critical Theories in Education: Changing Terrains of Knowledge and Politics*, ed. Thomas S. Popekwitz and Lynn Fendler (New York: Routledge, 1999), 46.

15. Audre Lorde, "The Master's Tools Will Never Dismantle the Master's House," in *Sister Outsider: Essays and Speeches* (Berkeley, CA: The Crossing Press, 1984), 112.

16. Gaile Pohlhaus, personal communication, May 12, 2015. See also her, "Discerning the Primary Epistemic Harm in Cases of Testimonial Injustice," *Social Epistemology* 28, no. 2 (2014), 99–114.

17. Nora Berenstain, "Epistemic Exploitation," *Ergo* 3, no. 22 (2016), 571.

18. Medina. *The Epistemology of Resistance*, 5.

19. Medina, 48.

20. Medina, 50.

21. Medina, 50.

22. This problem has received more attention recently. See, Elie Mystal, "If One More White Person Tells Me about the Use-Mention Distinction to Justify Saying the N-Word, I'm Going to Vomit," *Above the Law*, August 30, 2018, https://aboveth elaw.com/2018/08/if-one-more-white-person-tells-me-about-the-use-mention-distinc tion-to-justify-saying-the-n-word-im-going-to-vomit/. And, Randall Kennedy, "How

a Dispute over the N-word Became a Disrupting Farce," *Chronicle of Higher Education*, February 8, 2019, https://www.chronicle.com/article/How-a-Dispute-Over-the-N-Word/245655

23. Maya Angelou. "Iconoclast: Maya Angelou," interview with Dave Chapell, November 30, 2006, video, 22:35, May 1, 2017, https://www.youtube.com/watch?v=okc6COsgzoE

24. Angelou's account of the n-word does not capture the resistant uses of the word among black people. I'm mindful of these instances because there are times when epistemic resistance from students of color can be "world opening." Thanks to María Lugones for reminding me of this point.

25. For helpful discussions and criticisms of safe space pedagogies in philosophy, see Laura Freeman "Creating Safe Spaces: Strategies for Confronting Implicit and Explicit Bias and Stereotype Threat in the Classroom," *APA Newsletter on Feminism and Philosophy* 13, no. 4 (Spring 2014), 3–12. And, George Yancy, "Loving Wisdom and the Effort to Make Philosophy 'Unsafe,'" *Epistemologies Humanities Journal* (2011), http://c961210.r10.cf2.rackcnd.com/wp-content/uploads/2010/12/Essay-Yancy-Loving-Wisdom.pdf

26. I first realized this when two male students repeatedly ignored a sexual assault survivor's testimony. Under the banner of "speaking in a safe space" they continued to appeal to rape myths and "men too" reasoning to dodge questions about their complicity in rape culture. See Megan Boler, *Feeling Power: Emotions in Education* (New York: Routledge, 1999).

27. There is an extensive literature on brave spaces. I'm drawing from Jennifer Bailey and Lennon Flowers, "An Invitation to Brave Space," Interview by Krista Tippett, *On Being*, NPR, October 17, 2019. Transcript, https://onbeing.org/programs/jennifer-bailey-and-lennon-flowers-an-invitation-to-brave-space/

28. Nancy Tuana, "The Speculum of Ignorance: The Women's Health Movement and Epistemologies of Ignorance," *Hypatia* 21, no. 3 (Summer 2006), 9–10.

29. Medina, *The Epistemology of Resistance*, 48.

30. I want to deepen the reader's understanding of obstacles here. Obstacles can be solid and uniform, but the structural nature of privilege-preserving epistemic pushback suggests that these obstacles are sedimented historical objects. They don't suddenly appear. They are the products of centuries of racial and gendered laws, social scripts, visual vocabularies, cultural productions, and political and economic decisions.

31. Derald Wing Sue, *Microaggressions in Everyday Life: Race, Gender, and Sexual Orientation* (Hoboken, NJ: Wiley, 2010), 24.

32. Kristie Dotson, "Tracking Epistemic Violence, Tracking Practices of Silencing," *Hypatia* 26, no. 2 (March 2011), 237.

33. Dotson, "Tracking Epistemic Violence," 238.

34. Jennifer Hornsby, "Disempowered Speech," *Philosophical Topics* 23, no. 2 (1995), 127–47.

35. Dotson, "Tracking Epistemic Violence," 242.

36. Dotson, 244.

37. Dotson, 237.

38. Dotson, 243

Chapter 4

The Weighty Conversation
How White Supremacy Damages White People

The opening pages of Toni Cade Bambara's *The Salt Eaters* begin with a kindhearted query about the pain required to become whole. "Are you sure, sweetheart, that you want to be well? . . . I like to caution folks that's all. . . . No sense in wasting each other's time sweetheart. . . . A lot of weight when you're well. Now, you just hold that thought . . . . Just so you're sure sweetheart, and ready to be healed, 'cause wholeness is no trifling matter."[1] Bambara's words offer guidance about what human beings need to become whole. We are never truly whole until we have the courage to feel and hold the weight of the pain that breaks us. I've taken her wise counsel to heart as I've thought about the damage that white supremacy does to our collective humanity in general, and to white people's humanity in particular.

There is a deep wound at the heart of whiteness that people of color have witnessed, navigated, and written about for a very long time, but that very few white people have examined in any deep, sustained, and meaningful way. I'm not speaking about the *overexposed* side of white dominance as unearned power conferred systemically that I explored in my first chapter. This chapter engages the *underexposed* side of white dominance, the one white people would rather not reckon with because feeling that weight requires a radical vulnerability that is too painful for most of us to bear. Touching that weight means leaving the comforts of whiteness behind and learning to feel what we'd rather not feel. Privilege is designed to be invisible, but it is also designed to feel weightless. More accurately, privilege numbs us to the damage that whiteness does to our humanity. Recall how Peggy McIntosh's compares white privilege to an invisible *and weightless* knapsack. When white people are invited to examine and check our privilege by unpacking that knapsack, our attention and energy is almost always drawn to the more comfortable of the two tasks. When we attend exclusively to making the structures and habits of privilege visible, we do the work of the head and not the heart. It's more comfortable to understand how privilege works than it is to feel what it costs our humanity. Working to make the invisible visible demands a shift in perception, but that shift alone won't heal you.[2] Becoming whole requires the courage to take up and hold space with the weight that breaks you. It calls for emotional vulnerability and risk taking. The wound at the heart of whiteness is much too heavy to endure all at once, but engaging the weight is essential to combating racism. White people's fear of the weight signals our ongoing failure to heal from the damage that white supremacy has done to our collective humanity. This, as David Dean remarks, "maintains the cycle of violence and keeps real racial justice from happening in this country, because of massive defensiveness that makes [white people] unable to stand in genuine solidarity with people of color."[3]

This chapter invites white readers to wade more deeply into the weight of whiteness, to join a weighty conversation about the costs and losses of white supremacy for white people. It invites us not only to see what we'd rather not see but also to feel what we'd rather not feel. I begin with an autobiographical account of the racialized lessons instilled in me as a child during and after the 1967 Newark Race Riots/Rebellions and consider how the wounding marks that installed these lessons remain in my flesh. People of color have invited white folks to the weighty conversation countless times. I briefly engage the content of these generous invitations and consider the obstacles that have kept me, and countless other white people, from joining the conversation. Western epistemic habits that frame knowledge visually make it particularly challenging to feel the weight of whiteness. In the absence of an off-the-shelf weighty epistemology, I offer a vocabulary of weight and gravity. The weight of whiteness can be measured in terms of its costs and losses. Very few white people have taken time to cultivate a felt understanding of the ways whiteness continues to erode our humanity. We are anesthetized to our own brokenness. I offer an account of anesthesia's gravitas and suggest that wading into the weight of whiteness requires that white people cultivate a sensitivity to our own insensitivity, by attending to those moments when we feel the anesthesia pulling us under. We can only feel whiteness's psychological, social, material, moral, epistemic, and historical costs when the anesthesia lifts. My final section argues that white people need to move beyond a simple *understanding* of weight and to *feel* the pain of these costs at the core of our being. The price of belonging—that is, the process of becoming white—is traumatizing. There is a strong overlap between the habits of whiteness and the symptoms of trauma response—the hypervigilance, the emotional numbness, the cognitive dissonance, the avoidance and defensiveness, and the inability to empathize. Becoming mindful of the pain of that trauma is essential to re-humanizing ourselves because, as Bambara reminds us, "wholeness is no trifling matter."

NEWARK LESSONS

When I was six years old, I sat in the second-floor bedroom of our rented home in West Orange, New Jersey and watched Newark burn.[4] There were 159 race riots/rebellions during that long hot summer of 1967, but I could smell the smoke and hear the sirens from this one. I remember expressing concern, as only a six-year-old child can, about the people in Newark whose neighborhoods were on fire. When the National Guard arrived, local television networks interviewed the families who were forced to evacuate their homes. I remember feeling frightened for the children in Newark, but my attention to their suffering was immediately redirected. I was told, "It's not our Newark." The appropriate response to Newark was indifference, not compassion. Newark was everything that whiteness was not. It was urban, mostly nonwhite, poor, crumbling, and destitute. My childhood would continue to be heavily punctuated with cautionary tales from family members, store clerks, and neighbors that either began or ended with the phrase "the Negroes (or Puerto Ricans) from Newark." *Lock the car doors when you drive down Springfield Avenue the Negroes from Newark will approach your car and ask for money. They will rob you. They are not like us. The Negroes from Newark will destroy what we have worked so hard to make. They don't value work. They don't have jobs. The Negroes from Newark drink all day. They live on welfare. Their kids skip school. They don't take care of their things.* As I grew older the lessons became more gendered. *Don't get your ears pierced... you'll look like a Puerto Rican from Newark. You don't want to get pregnant or end up like one of those Puerto Rican or black girls in Newark. Sometimes young girls who go to Newark end up in the gutter without their underwear. Don't say hello, don't make eye contact, keep walking. The Negroes and Puerto Ricans are moving from Newark to West Orange! They are getting closer!*

On the fiftieth anniversary of the Newark Uprising, I asked my father if he remembered anything about that long hot summer. I wanted to know if the events were still in his body. For the longest time he told me that he could not remember anything, but when I asked again and he said, "Well, I remember that Mr. Sloan knew the Essex County chief of police well, and that he had arranged for three county policemen to guard the front entrance to the Park that week. We were worried that the barbarians were at the gate." Barbarians. Fear. That's what he remembers.

My parents moved from Evanston, Illinois, a very white suburb of Chicago, to West Orange two years earlier. My father wanted to live closer to his extended family and was excited to find a rental property in Llewellyn Park. Llewellyn Park was the second planned suburban community in the United States. In 1853, Llewellyn Solomon Haskell, a New

York businessman purchased one hundred acres on the southern slope of the Watchung Mountains and set out to create a suburban community of country estates for the families of nineteenth-century industrial entrepreneurs. By the mid-1960s the gated community's glory days had faded and the residents consisted of the elderly grandchildren of these founding captains of American industry—the Chubb, Edison, Sloan, and Colgate families. This meant there were very few children to play with in the neighborhood. When my sister and I saw children playing in the public playground outside Park's entrance, we pestered our mother to take us there. One day she gave in and drove us to the playground. The community outside the park was predominantly white working-class and black. My sister and I ran to join the children on the swings, stopping periodically to glance back at my mother, who sat alone nervously smoking a Kent cigarette on the wooden park bench. She fidgeted with her handbag and looked compulsively at her watch. She never picked up the book she brought to read. Her eyes remained fixed on her daughters as they played. Her lack of ease was intelligible. Without uttering a word, my mother's body told me everything I needed to know. The Newark lessons were being telegraphed through her demeanor and movements.[5] After thirty minutes, she announced that it was time to leave. During our family dinner we told our father about the day at the park. His angry response provided the missing soundtrack to my mother's discomfort that afternoon. *Why did you take the girls to that park? Where did you ever get such an idea? It's not safe to go to that park!? Don't you EVER take them there again!*

Two years later we moved to my father's hometown, ten miles west of the Park. The black and brown faces all but vanished and the Newark lessons were amended with anti-Semitic lessons. *I hope that you are not getting serious with that Jewish boy. Do you have to get a job at that Jewish bakery? New York Jews stick to their own kind. They are stingy and untrustworthy. They won't pay you well.* I folded these lessons into the Newark lessons. To be white was to be non-Jewish. As the amended Newark lessons continued, the false promise of whiteness slowly took hold of my being. Bit by bit, day by day, I learned, what Lillian Smith describes as "the dance that cripples [sic] the human spirit." In her words, "step by step . . . [t]hese ceremonials in honor of white supremacy, performed from babyhood, slip from the conscious mind down deep into muscles and glands and become difficult to tear out."[6] George Yancy describes these ceremonials as the clicks that install white identities. In his words, "Not only are the white bodies that initiate the clicks performing their white identities though them; the clicks themselves install white identities, hail white identities, and solidify white identities."[7]

White identity is a form of sedimented trauma numbed by privilege. Etymologically, the word trauma means "to wound," so the wounding clicks are also traumatizing clicks. They have an impact. They have weight. They are part of my flesh, my thoughts, and my nervous system. These descriptions have helped me conceptualize how the neatly layered community messages about the value of whiteness slowly eroded my humanity. The Newark lessons' wounding clicks were not installed painlessly. Each click left a deep, fragile, and painful mark that has never quite healed. As the marks multiplied, the lessons formed a tangled constellation—a coherent yet damaged way of being that continues to orient my gaze, influence my cognitive habits, structure my understandings of the world, and shape the rhythms of my breath. For most of my life, my energy has been directed toward protecting this wound. I now understand that my efforts would have been better spent making sacred that pain so that I might heal from it.

Assessing the damage of whiteness is a dangerous act. My body is white, but whiteness is also in my body, and this is the hardest truth of all. Through her interviews with white people, Thandeka observes how white children learn to be white through their interactions with the white adults in their lives, who discipline and punish them when they express compassion for people of color, befriend or date people who are not white, or respond to racial injustice with empathy and righteous anger. In her words, white children realize "that the content of their own white racial identity was not, at core, feelings of racial supremacy, but rather, feelings of emotional defeat. They had learned at an early age that if they did not conform to the racial expectations of their caretakers, they would be emotionally abandoned."[8] Thandeka's words have helped me to understand how the phrase "it's not our Newark" functioned to whiten me. My six-year-old heart gravitated toward feeling empathy for the children in Newark who were now living in a militarized zone. There was humanity in my initial response, but my childhood fears and tears were quickly re-directed. I had to, in Thandeka's words, "cognitively forget what I had affectively experienced."[9] If the children in Newark could be abandoned, then I might be abandoned too. The conditions of love and belonging would be extended to me only if the Newark lessons were permitted to take root in my young being. The lessons were painfully wounding and I had to contort myself to make the pain stop.[10] This was the price of belonging. There is a brokenness that springs from the tension between feeling and forgetting, which in Lillian Smith's words, "split my body from my mind and both from my soul."[11] Compliance, distance, and indifference were how I learned to protect the wound. If I wanted to belong, I had to forget—better to be broken and belong, than to be whole and abandoned, or so it seemed at the time.

The Newark lessons are not part of my past. They are part of my flesh. They are my flesh. As Claudia Rankine remarks, "you can't put the past behind you. It's buried in you; it's turned your flesh into its own cupboard. Not everything remembered is useful, but it all comes from the world to be stored in you."[12] This is what trauma does. The body keeps the score.[13]

And so, I learned that the price of belonging required cultivating the habits I needed to live in an *unsettled* white body—a fleshy cupboard filled with racialized fear, suspicion, guilt, anger, shame, anxiety, and distrust of black and brown bodies. It's no surprise that the Newark lessons created habits that I was told would keep me safe: hypervigilance, dissociation, disconnection, distancing, indifference, an inflated sense of self-worth, opportunityand resource hoarding, a false sense of invulnerability, historical amnesia, the inability to hear and believe people of color's testimonies, a flattering ancestral narrative, and endless diversion strategies (e.g., white talk, white tears, white fragility, assertions of color blindness, privilege-preserving epistemic pushback, silencing, victim blaming, and other strategic refusals to feel). In retrospect, what's most chilling is that my broken body did not feel unsettled. It did not feel heavy because the habits I developed in response to the Newark lessons were numbing and dissociative habits. They made the damage feel weightless. I was incapable of feeling how my humanity had slowly been bargained away in the name of belonging.

HISTORICAL INVITATIONS TO THE WEIGHTY CONVERSATION

People of color are tired of bearing the weight of America's historical baggage alone and have, for centuries invited white folks to join the weighty conversation. There is an entire "literature of white exposure," in African American literary and scholarly traditions that addresses the costs of whiteness for white people.[14] The literature includes generous invitations to share the weight, to take it up, and to feel its costs. Harriet Jacobs testifies from her "own experience and observation, that slavery is a curse to the whites as well as to the blacks. It makes the white fathers cruel and sensual; the sons violent and licentious; it contaminates the daughters, and makes the wives wretched."[15] Frederick Douglass's *Narrative*, describes slavery's effects on Sophia Auld, his mistress. He recalls how her "cheerful eye, under the influence of slavery, eventually became red with rage; that voice made all of sweet accord, changed to one of harsh and horrid discord; and that angelic face gave place to that of a demon. Thus, slavery is the enemy of both the slave and the slaveholder."[16] W. E. B. DuBois notes how slavery's legacy and white supremacist cultural values damage white Americans—"To be a master is not to be a man; it makes one something other, something less than fully human."[17] He points to an "especially deep and festering wound in the collective psyche of white America."[18] James Baldwin eloquently describes the disfiguring process of becoming white: "White men—from Norway . . . became white in America: by slaughtering the cattle, poisoning the wells, torching the houses, massacring Native Americans, and raping Black women. This moral erosion has made it quite impossible for those who think of themselves as white in this country to have any moral authority at all—privately, or publicly."[19] Barbara Smith invites white women to consider "how racism distorts and lessens your own lives as white women—that racism affects your chances for survival, too, and that it is very definitely your issue."[20] George Yancy's "Dear White America" letter begins with "a weighty request," an invitation to listen with love to those parts of our white selves that might cause us pain and terror.[21] His invitation is a "gift is that is heavy to bear," because holding the gift means being "open to a kind of death."[22] He asks white people "to linger with the gravitas of their own whiteness and the history of whiteness . . . to feel the weight of their responsibility for the perpetuation of white power, hegemony, and privilege."[23] Gloria Anzaldúa boldly observes how "[p]eople who practice racism—everyone who is white in the U.S. are victims of their own ideology and are impoverished by it."[24] The invitation writers' arms have grown tired from bearing this weight alone. They have been kind, patient, and generous with white people. Yet, the stack of invitations remains largely unopened and unanswered. How can this be?

BARRIERS TO THE WEIGHTY CONVERSATION

The weighty conversation begins when white people find the courage to embrace the profound discomfort we feel in response to the invitation. It asks us to be curious about why we continue to avoid the conversation. Like Eula Biss, "I have written and erased hundreds of sentences here, trying and failing to articulate something that I can sense, but cannot speak. Like a bad loan, the kind where the payments increase over time, the price of whiteness remains hidden behind its promises."[25] My own desire for comfort and security prompted me to plan my entrance into the conversation very carefully. White minds like to plan. Rule following and planning offer a false sense of security. I drew up mental guidelines that I thought would make the conversation run more smoothly. I now realize that I was searching for a comfortable way into the weight, a way to lighten my engagement with it without poking the wound. I now recognize that white supremacist culture, like computer malware, had choreographed my entrance into the weighty conversation before I could say a word.

Kenneth Jones and Tema Okun concisely summarize the attitudes and habits that characterize white supremacist culture.[26] White supremacist culture values perfectionism, a sense of urgency, defensiveness, objectivity, paternalism, power hoarding, either/or thinking, and individualism. It is characterized by the worship of the written word, the belief that there is one correct way to do something, that quantity is more important than quality, and that numerical growth defines progress. White supremacist culture fears open conflict. It feels entitled to comfort. White minds generate a closed-system thinking that is marked by dualism, hierarchy, and mechanistic thinking.[27] White minds believe that strict adherence to the Western scientific method yields unerring truths. White minds break down things into components, to understand how they are ordered and how they function. You don't have to be white to have a white mind. White ways of knowing have a gravitas that shapes conversations before they begin. So, I'm not surprised to discover the many ways that Lillian Smith's dance that breaks the human spirit had quietly choreographed my entrance into the weighty conversation.

Perfection. I assumed there was a safe way to join the conversation, so I searched for a painless path free of messy pitfalls.[28] I over-armored myself by trying to anticipate every mistake and objection in advance. I worried that people of color might hear the story of my Newark lessons as an attempt to evoke pity, center white trauma, or escape responsibility. I was concerned that walking into the weight might trigger narratives of confession or solicitations for forgiveness. I told myself that the conversation was impossible, that any response to the invitation would shift my white attention from collective action to personal transformation projects (either/or thinking). I took to heart people of color's concerns about the ease with which weighty conversations might be easily enlisted in the service of color-blind understandings of racialized damage, violence, and trauma. In hindsight, these were scholarly ways of protecting the wound. There is always the risk that weighty conversations will take these directions. There is no perfect or painless way to open the stack of weighty invitations. You just have to start opening them, one at a time, with grateful attention to the lessons they contain, and the understanding that there will be more lessons in your fumbled and imperfect responses.

I fear open conflict. I felt white fragility's uncomfortable tug. The weighty conversation feels dangerous: what if it re-centers whiteness! I'm afraid that the claim "white supremacy damages white people too!" sounds too much like white talk, that it closely resembles those discursive patterns white people habitually use to dodge uncomfortable conversations—"white people suffer *too*!" Don't assume that similar-sounding claims do similar discursive work. Claims ending with what I hear as "the snarky too," mark psychological discomfort and signal a strategic refusal to hear what's been said. So, I'm asking white readers to hear "the too" in the claim "white supremacy damages white people too" not as the snarky too that takes back the center, but as 'the too' that acknowledges that white people need to begin our healing work closer to home. As Resmaa Menakem puts it, "white Americans as a group do not get to make their own historical intergenerational trauma the center of national attention. That trauma is real, and white Americans need to acknowledge it, face it, and mend it."[29] We can't get free until we clean up our own house. We don't have a right to comfort here because our comfort is tied to others' suffering. The weighty conversation contains the pain of our personal, family, and national histories. We have a choice about whether to feel that pain in ways that promote healing and wholeness or ways that promote numbness and comfort.

Objectivity. I encountered some surprising epistemic barriers as I opened the invitations. Western epistemology favors visual and cognitive accounts of knowledge over somatic, affective, auditory, and tactile understandings of the world.[30] Post-Enlightenment ways of knowing pull our sites of understanding upward toward the eyes and the head, and away from the feelings we hold in our hearts, guts, and limbs.[31] We fumble the weight when we describe white privilege exclusively in the language of visibility. McIntosh's knapsack is not weightless because it is empty—it is filled with passports, blank checks, and other obstacle-removing tools. It just *feels* weightless because white supremacy structures the world so that white people have, generation after generation, been anesthetized to privilege's contorting weight. Privilege is anesthesia: it keeps us from feeling whiteness's costs and losses. In other words, white people are more comfortable framing white supremacy in terms of what privilege does *for* us than we are thinking about what it does *to* us. As Joy James explains, white folks secretly want to have it both ways, they "want the benefits of whiteness, but they want them to come with no costs."[32] So, most white people take up the question of race privilege halfway: we learn to see the structures that benefit us but refuse to feel the damage they do to us. We have, in José Medina's words, become "insensitive to our own insensitivity."[33]

The weighty conversation is painful by necessity. At some point I realized that my desire to control the conversation was more about protecting the wound at the heart of whiteness than it was about healing it. My planning, perfectionism, flights to objectivity, latent fragility, and tendency to check out when things got real wasn't helping anyone. As Rachel Cargle explains, "Silencing happens when, for white people hearing the truth is too much; when the truth hangs so painfully heavy on their shoulders that they'd rather get rid of the weight, than face the issues head on."[34] When white people cling to our discomfort, people of color are silenced. When we manage the conversation too closely, or spend most of the time in our heads, we don't show up for people of color in ways that are useful and supportive. The weighty conversation is not about restoring white comfort. It's about exposing and feeling the pain of the wound at the heart of whiteness long enough to restore our humanity. It requires the courage to pause and to feel white supremacy's gravitas even though every cell in our bodies recoils from the task. *Weight? What weight? Seriously, I don't feel any weight. I don't even know what you're talking about. I just don't feel anything. There is nothing there. You must be imagining it. If the weight is so heavy and if its gravitational pull is so strong, then why can't I feel it?*[35] Here is a short answer: It's no accident that the knapsack feels weightless to white people. Resistance to the weighty conversation is so tightly woven into the structure and habits of white supremacist culture that even our most sincere attempts to join the conversation are eclipsed by our latent desire to protect the wound. So, don't assume that the weight is not there because you can't feel it. Assume that it's there and be curious about *why* you can't feel it.

WADING INTO THE WEIGHT: A TOKEN TO CARRY INTO THE CONVERSATION

I have something for you. A token to carry into the weighty conversation to remind you of its urgency—something to grasp when you feel the urge to drop the weight. Imagine a delicately engraved stone. It reads: *White supremacy banks on white people's fear of the weighty conversation. As long as we are numb to the weight of whiteness in our own being the violence will continue.* White supremacy does not want white people to feel its weight because if we realized its true costs; that is, if the price of whiteness were tangible, if it were presented to us as an actual bill, then it would dawn on us that the racial contract is really a suicide pact.[36]

White fragility prevents white people from taking up the weight of whiteness too quickly. Pushing white people into the weighty conversation will certainly prompt most of us to quickly exchange the engraved token for the comforts of ignorance. It's better to wade into the weight gradually, engaging it as a weightlifter steadily increases the weight she adds to her bar. This pace accommodates white fragility, but I'm not convinced this is a bad thing. Slow and steady journeys are not necessarily comfortable ones and wading mindfully into the weight helps to cultivate a sensitivity to the damage. When we enter the weighty conversation gradually with curiosity and compassion, instead of fear and defensiveness, everything shifts. We make space for reflection, anger, and tears.

I began feeling the weight of whiteness by observing its imprint on the world around me. "Sometimes," Sara Ahmed observes, "you have to watch someone else disappear before you become aware of your own disappearance. Sometimes you have to witness the violence directed toward another before you can witness the violence directed toward yourself."[37] Consider how we get a sense of a vehicle's weight by attending to the depth of the tire tracks it makes on a snowy road. Imprints are reflections. They mirror the vehicles' weight back to us, as if to say, something heavy has been here. It has altered the landscape. Similarly, we can attend to white supremacy's imprint on people of color's lives by focusing on the weight of whiteness in their worlds, as if to say, something wounding has been here. It is has altered the community.

People of color feel the weight of whiteness every . . . single . . . fucking . . . day. Frantz Fanon felt the weight when he "had to meet the white man's eyes," and that "unfamiliar weight burdened [him]."[38] Breonna Taylor felt the weight when three Louisville police officers battered down her apartment door and shot her eight times. Marc Peebles felt the weight when three white women in his neighborhood called the police after he started an urban farm in his Detroit neighborhood. Lolade Siyonbola felt the weight when she woke up from a nap in her Yale dorm common room and had to respond to a barrage of questions from campus police about what she was doing there. George Floyd felt the weight as a Minneapolis police officer squeezed the last breath from his body in front of a crowd of people pleading with the officer to stop. The weight crushed Serena Williams as she went into labor with her first child. Money, fame, and knowledge were not enough to get the hospital staff to believe her when she told them something was wrong. Charlene Teters, an indigenous Spokane artist, felt whiteness's weight the afternoon she took her children to a University of Illinois basketball game. She heard them cover their discomfort with laughter during the cartoon Indian mascot's half-time dance. The weight expressed itself as cultural insensitivity and indifference. White sports fans identified more strongly with their cartoon Indian mascot than with their fellow indigenous students.[39] The weight shadows black, brown, and indigenous bodies when they shop, pass through airport security, register to vote, sign leases, wait for their friends at coffee shops, or make bank deposits. Its gravitas presses against their bodies in the form microaggressions, unwanted sexual attention, violence, and public harassment.

If you listen carefully, you can hear the weight in the timber of white voices as they respond to these incidents with indifference. *What did she expect? Well, they shouldn't have . . . He should have known that. . . .* The weight of whiteness accumulates in dark bodies, weathering them, and making hearts fragile.[40] It's the weight of trauma. It causes "white people fatigue syndrome."[41] The weight, as Ahmed remarks, gathers "like things in a bag, but the bag is your body, so that you feel like you are carrying more and more weight. The past becomes heavy . . . . At the time, each time, something happens. You are thrown. . . . You begin to feel a pressure, this relentless assault on the senses; a body in touch with a world can become a body that fears the world."[42] Sometimes you cope with the violence and the pain by numbing yourself or cultivating an unhealthy indifference. There is growing medical evidence that people of color's higher rates of post-traumatic stress disorder (PTSD) can be legitimately traced to racialized trauma, those ongoing individual and collective harms resulting from-exposure and repeated re-exposure to race-based stressors.[43] Aurora Levins Morales describes this historical trauma as "a big backpack full of rocks we haul around on our backs. It slows us down, tires us out, and skews our aim."[44]

I encourage white readers to understand, first and foremost, that the comfort we receive from avoiding the weighty conversation comes at an extremely high price for black, indigenous, and all people of color. Reluctance to feel, name, and engage this weight is an expression of power because the weight of whiteness has never been spread evenly across the population. No matter how horrible it feels to wake up to the pain of the weight, no matter how nauseous, angry, depressed, frustrated, or guilty we feel when we touch that deep festering wound at the heart of whiteness, it will *never* match the pain people of color feel on a daily basis simply because white folks lack the courage to heal ourselves. As white allies, it is our responsibility to restore our humanity by attending to the weight that white supremacy does not want us to feel. This means not only having the courage to empathetically witness whiteness's weight on people of color's lives, but also realizing that witnessing the weight alone, and at a distance, makes us permanent spectators. Weighty conversations are not spectator sports. It is too easy for well-meaning white people to train our attention *exclusively* on white supremacy's impact on communities of color and to use this as a righteous way of dodging the weighty conversation. It's easier to go with righteous anger and empathy than to engage the depths of our own anesthetized pain.[45] Empathetic witnessing slides too quickly into the missionary desire to repair and rescue. To be clear, I'm not suggesting that white people completely avoid empathetic engagement with the examples I've given. I'm arguing that we won't be able to fully feel the weight of our whiteness if our curiosity does not extend beyond the worlds where we feel most comfortable. The weighty conversation requires, in Peter Levine's words, a gradual "descent into the parts of our being that are alien, that we might prefer not to deal with."[46] So, we don't get to excuse ourselves from the weighty conversation on the grounds that we are too busy focusing on the weight's impact on brown, indigenous, and black bodies. Self-repair is an essential part of world repair. This is a collective project.

So, if you can't feel the weight of whiteness in your own white body at this moment, then can you at least attend to its imprint on people of color's lives and communities? I'm not asking white people to witness the weight from a comfortable distance. I'm asking whether you can *feel* that crushing weight without continually lifting yourself from people of color's testimonies. If you can, then it's time to wade more deeply.

MEASURING THE WEIGHT OF WHITENESS IN TERMS OF COST AND LOSS

The weight that interests me is *not* the onerous weight described in "The White Man's Burden," Rudyard Kipling's hymn to U.S. imperialism.[47] The weight is not the burden of empires. Neither is it the burden of *noblesse oblige*; the weight white people feel obliged to carry because we suspect that we have a self-appointed duty to help the so-called "less fortunate." The weighty conversation invites white people to attend to a different kind of weight: the kind that impoverishes us by preventing the full expression of our humanity. The weight is measured in terms of those whitely habits that sever our connections with one another. I'll have more to say about whiteness's costs in a later section. For clarity's sake, I want to identify the costs and losses upfront, so readers can keep the damage in mind as we wade into the weight. The costs and losses of white supremacy are at root psychological. These include a false sense of entitlement, hypervigilance, resource and opportunity hoarding, a distorted racialized perception of the world, unwanted racial biases, diminished creativity, a damaged moral compass, difficulty sustaining relationships with people of color, a distorted sense of safety and danger, historical amnesia, and the erasure of our own ethnic and cultural ancestries.

I think of these costs and losses as the collateral damage of white supremacy. Collateral damage is secondary damage, a form of injury and devastation that moves sideways from its intended targets. As Tim Wise observes, white people had

> better understand that [white supremacy] is a system that is every bit as capable of hurting and killing us. We are not the first targets. No. We are not the intended targets. We are perhaps the collateral damage of this system, but damage nonetheless. And, if we don't want that to continue. If we want to be free of the risk, in which we ourselves are now placed, then we need to care about it not as an act of altruism or self-concern, but as an act of liberation and this is our job, and this is our duty irrespective of our guilt.[48]

Invitations to the weighty conversation summon white people to take up relational understandings of how the violence done to communities of color relies on white people being psychologically, morally, materially, spiritually, and epistemically disfigured enough to allow that violence to continue. As Thomas DeWolf puts it: "We are both imprisoned by the past. I talk about black people being in maximum-security prison and white people being in minimum-security prison and that's the big difference, but we don't usually talk about the trauma of white people. You can't put us in prison without imprisoning yourself. Whatever boundaries and stipulations you put on us to remain in power, you have to change yourself to maintain that order."[49] Attending to the collateral damage of white supremacy helps us to recognize its broad-spectrum toxicity. We come to understand how our desire to protect rather than to heal the festering wound at the heart of whiteness is what allows the violence to continue. Yet, there is no off-the-shelf weighty epistemology that accurately captures the felt knowledge contained in the weight of whiteness. So, in its place, I offer a weighty vocabulary, one that both measures the weight of whiteness in terms of psychological, social, material, moral, epistemic, and historical costs and losses, and explores white people's strategic refusal sensitize ourselves to how whiteness's gravitational pull works to protect the wound.

WEIGHT, GRAVITAS, AND THE LOSS OF HUMANITY

White supremacy's costs and losses are best expressed in the *language of weight* and the *language of racial gravity*.[50] I begin with the weight. An object's weight is measured in units (e.g., kilos, pounds, carats). The weight of whiteness is measured in costs and losses to our collective humanity. This claim requires unpacking. The words "loss," "destruction," and "separation" share a common etymological root. The Old English word for loss (*los*) means ruin or destruction, and the Proto-Germanic word *lausa*, comes from *leu*—"to loosen, divide, or cut apart.[51] Humanity names those qualities that make us human, such as our ability to love, to be emotionally present for one another, to empathize or sympathize with one another's plight, to respond to another person's suffering with kindness, to be considerate, tolerant, benevolent, and compassionate. Human beings are wired for connection. Our relationships and interdependent nature are the seat of our humanity. Anything that servers or loosens that connection takes a piece of our humanity with it. People who are homeless are a telling barometer of our humanity. Our humanity is eroded when we avert our gaze and walk past them while quietly justifying our indifference. Our inner voice tells us . . . *There is nothing to be done here. They must have made bad choices. They alone are responsible for their condition. Anyway, there are shelters to help them. I'd rather donate to the mission than give them money directly. I don't trust them to spend it wisely. They are probably addicted.* Our humanity fades when we respond to the news of another school shooting by *thinking*, "this is so horrible," but not *feeling* outraged to the point where tears, anger, and grief consume our being. When we are in touch with our humanity, our *felt* response to the steady increase of mass violence in America should not be acclimation, it should be righteous anger, compassion, and mourning. Our humanity evaporates when we detach ourselves from the ebb and flow of life, become disconnected from our histories and communities, or treat animals and natural world as inert matter for public consumption. We lose our humanity when we decide whose lives matter. We are all part of one another, so when we damage, break, or sever that sacred bond of human connection, we not only harm others; we also damage that part of ourselves that makes us human. James Baldwin captured this Faustian bargain best when he wrote that "the price of the ticket, is our moral being, our humanity."[52] George Yancy echoes these costs when he says that white peoples' failure to tarry with their whiteness "comes as an ugly and terrible price—you live a diminished and truncated life of what it means to be truly human, and we are reminded constantly that our humanity does not matter."[53] Broken connections feel heavy. Consider the weight of a broken heart, lost friendship, the passing of a loved one, or the loss of one's community after a move. That's the texture of weight I want us to feel. The weight of loss is not a dead weight: it's a present, vibrant, and active emptiness.

The weight of whiteness also can be expressed in the *language of gravity*; that is, in those psychological, material, and cultural forces that stoke our fears and pull our attention away from the weighty conversation. White supremacy culture has what Marcus Anthony Hunter calls a "racial gravity," which functions in the same way that gravity affects matter in the natural world. When it rains, my basement leaks and rainwater is pulled to the lowest point of the cellar. Like my leaky basement, interlocking systems of oppression have a social and psychological gravitational pull. "Racial gravity is a feeling. It is the invisible hand organizing us all. Racial gravity . . . pulls bodies into formation."[54] Whiteness has gravitas: it instinctively draws us into social scripts and habits that preserve our comfort and sense of belonging. In her memoir, Serena Jones shares a childhood story that illustrates the gravitational pull of belonging. Her father, a minister and civil rights activist, promises to take Serena and her friends swimming before her birthday party. When he discovers that the local public pool is closed, he offers to drive to the public pool in Lake Highlands, an African American part of Dallas. Without thinking, she blurts out: "Oh gross! I don't want to swim with black people." Her father pulls over, and trembling with rage, says, "you have no idea how horrible what you said is!" He gives his daughter a choice. She can either go to the pool and have birthday parties every year or skip the pool and never have another birthday party again. She senses her friends' discomfort about swimming at Lake Highlands and replies, "I never want to have another birthday party again!" The gravitational pull of belonging with her friends is stronger than the social justice messages she received from her parents and church.[55] Sensitizing ourselves to racial gravitas offers an opening, a space to break from what Ann Russo calls "the numbness that comes with our witnessing, experience, and being complicit in systemic trauma and violence."[56]

Whiteness's weight and gravity work in tandem. When white people feel fragile, hurt, or uncomfortable, the gravitational force of whiteness floods in to ease the pain of the trauma wound. It pulls us toward comfort, silence, safety, and suburbs. The weighty conversation asks us to resist these gravitational forces and to remain present with the weight long enough to feel its contorting effects. Becoming sensitized to the weight is at once an act of resistance and the first step toward re-establishing human connections and thus restoring our own humanity. The weighty conversation can lead us on a path to wholeness, connection, healing, reconciliation, and liberation, but only if we have the courage to walk into those places that feel most heavy.

Faithful but Disagreeable Scales

James Baldwin offered white people an unpalatable truth when he observed that his skin color must "operate as a most disagreeable mirror, and that a great deal of one's energy is expended in reassuring white Americans that they do not see what they see."[57] White supremacy relies on white ignorance and distraction to function smoothly. So, it hands us a more flattering mirror—the Evil Queen's mirror from the Snow White story—"Mirror, Mirror in my hand, who is the fairest in the land?" This mirror reflects only those selves that we *want* to see—the good white self, the reliable white ally, the innocent white self, and the white savior. It is the Queen's mirror that hangs on the wall of the master's house. It has a strong and vain gravitational pull. Once it catches our gaze, it is agonizingly difficult to look away. Who wants to trade a flattering mirror for a disagreeable mirror, one that reflects back to you the many white selves you'd rather not know?

When I teach Baldwin's essay, white students frequently think that he is claiming that disagreeable mirrors reflect an unflattering essentialist truth about white people's character. They insist that Baldwin characterizes white folks as people who are truly rotten to the core but who live under the mistaken impression that they are good. They suggest that gazing into the disagreeable mirror blows our "good white people" cover.[58] This is not Baldwin's view, but racial gravity pulls them toward this interpretation. The good white person/bad white person binary is one way that white supremacy culture pulls white reflections toward unified accounts of the white self as either essentially good or bad. The Queen's mirror reduces the plurality of white selves to an imagined unified white self. This move is designed to obscure the unflattering and damaged selves that we'd rather not know. The gravitational pull toward a unified good self or bad white self is what desensitizes us to the weight. We cannot feel the weight of whiteness if we continue to believe that the unified self is the only self we have. To touch the weight, we have to understand white selves as plural, and for this, we need a more complex mirror.

María Lugones offers white women a *faith mirror,* one that resists the gravitational pull toward either a good or a bad unified white self. Faithful mirrors reflect back to us the *many selves that we are.* Women of color, she explains, are faithful mirrors: "Not that we show you as you *really* are; we just show you as one of the many people that you are. What we reveal to you is that you are many—something that may in itself be frightening to you. But the self we reveal to you is also one that you are not eager to know, for reasons that one may conjecture."[59] Faithful mirrors reveal our plurality; they uncover *some* of the selves white people are not eager to know. White people may be decent, helpful, and fair, but we are at once greedy, defensive, entitled, controlling, cruel, fragile, ignorant, and arrogant. The language of plurality curdles the good/bad white person dichotomy. White plural selves are neither good nor bad. We are good-greedy-ignorant-innocent-complicit-fragile-cruel-helpful-controlling-kind-entitled-humble-arrogant, etc. The gravitational pull of whiteness blocks identification with the unflattering selves because "remembering [those unflattering selves] fractures you into more than one person. You know a self that is decent and good, and knowing yourself in our mirror frightens you with losing your center, you integrity, your oneness."[60] We fear the weight, so we "block those selves that are unflattering, painful, *and heavy.*"[61] The Queen's mirror edits our multiplicity in favorable ways that highlight only those parts of our self that we are comfortable acknowledging. We are Good!-(*greedy*)-Innocent!-(*ignorant*)-Helpful!-(*controlling*)-Kind!-(*entitled*)-Humble!-(*arrogant*), etc.

The weighty conversation invites us to resist the gravitational pull of these goodness-preserving edits, and to feel our plurality, so we can become sensitized to the brokenness that our plurality reveals. We cannot heal from the damaging weight of whiteness if we continue to retreat to a unified comfortable self that is numb to the wound.

At some point I realized that these faithful but disagreeable mirrors do double duty as *faithful but disagreeable scales.* Mirrors reveal those selves and lived realities that white people would rather not *see.* Scales reveal the weight that white folks would rather not *feel.* When you are numb to the weight, you imagine yourself a whole, weightless, and unbroken being.[62] We can't feel our brokenness if unflattering selves are repeatedly edited out for comfort. Returning to Baldwin, we might say that skin color operates as a disagreeable scale, and that a great deal of people of color's energy is directed at reassuring white people that we should be feeling the brokenness of our disconnection that goodness and privilege mask. I know that scales measure mass and not affect, but, in the absence of a weighty ontology, the metaphor usefully redirects our attention toward what is felt.

Joseph Brandt offers a clear example of how skin color operates as a faithful but disagreeable scale. He recalls a moment during an anti-racism workshop when an African American woman called everyone's attention to white participants' habit of retreating to their heads when group discussions became uncomfortable. She remarked,

> You people really don't give a damn! But it's not that you don't want to. You just don't know how to. You don't know how you feel! Your heads have been cut off from your guts, and you've lost touch with your own feelings. Sure, you can empathize with the feelings of others, with the pain of other people's oppression, but you can't feel the pain of your own oppression and brokenness. You have been anesthetized to the agony of the destruction inside of yourselves. If you could see and feel the effects of racism on your own people, you would not be able to tolerate it. You would not be able to control your anger. . . . But you white people have lost your ability to feel. The best you can do is to understand with your minds, with no response from your emotions.[63]

I sat with the unnamed speaker's words for a very long time, recalling how the Newark lessons slowly pulled my head from my heart, soul, and gut. How heartbreaking not to be able to feel the pain of my own brokenness. The best I could do was understand it with my mind. And, so I did. I spent at least fifteen years trying to think my way out of whiteness, only to realize that I had picked up the white problem from the wrong end.[64] White supremacy can't be dismantled by retreating to our heads because racism lives in our bodies. If I wanted to heal the disconnections between my head and heart I needed to make a greater effort to wade into the weight more deeply. Remember, wholeness is not a trifling matter. It demanded that I step onto that faithful but disagreeable scale and make peace with the fact that I have been numb to the agony of the destruction inside of me. If the weight was so heavy, then why could I not feel my own brokenness?

The Gravitational Pull of Anesthesia

Anesthesia has its own gravitas—it pulls you under. It severs connections. It blocks sensations.[65] It pulls us apart. Anesthesia is an essential part of the master's tool kit. I did not quite understand the connection between anesthesia and my own brokenness until I read Mab Segrest's account of the "anesthesia of power."[66] Pharmaceutical examples offer the clearest account of how anesthesia dulls the senses and severs human connection. In *Born to Belonging: Writings on Spirit and Justice,* Segrest examines a passage from the Civil War diaries of Mary Boykin Miller Chestnut, a self-described white southern woman, slave mistress, and vehement supporter of the confederate cause.[67] Her diary recounts a moment when she witnessed a "mad woman" being forcibly separated from her husband and children at a slave auction. Chestnut writes,

> Of course, she was mad, or she would not have given her grief words in that public place. Her keepers were along. What she said was rational enough, pathetic, at times heart-rendering. It excited me so that I quietly took opium. It enables me to retain every particle of mind or sense or brains I have, and so quiets my nerves that I can calmly reason and take rational views of things otherwise maddening.[68]

Chestnut's words bring to light the connections between anesthesia, the dehumanization of black bodies, and the loss of her humanity. The auction unsettles her. She takes opium to settle her body in order to take "a rational view of things," which is a nice way of saying that she blocks the sensory evidence of slavery's inherent cruelty. She takes refuge in her head. Today Chestnut's "excitement" might be characterized as a secondary trauma response. What's chilling here is not just that she takes the opium; it's that she equates anesthesia with knowledge. In a twisted epistemic reframing of the tragic event, she understands her secondary trauma response as an obstacle to, rather than a source of, knowing. As Segrest remarks, "people don't need to respond to what they pretend they don't know, and they don't know what they can't feel."[69] The faithful but disagreeable scale reveals to Chestnut a self that she is not eager to feel, so she numbs herself to the weight. She disconnects from the horror before her, as if to say, "I don't want to see this. I don't want to feel this."

Be still with this scene for a moment. Where does it pull you? Do you say to yourself, *well, you've chosen a really extreme example! She was a slave owner who took opium, so that's a pretty exceptional case. And, it happened over a hundred and fifty years ago.* True, the case is dramatic in its cruelty, but I lead with it because it offers a straight-forward example of the relationship between anesthesia and the loss of our humanity. Chestnut's response to the slave auction is neither unique nor exceptional. In *Watching Slavery: Witness Reports and Travel Texts*, Joe Lockard analyzes witness texts and traveler's reports of slave auctions and everyday life under American slavery. He writes, "The common observations of nausea and dissociation reported by witnesses who had never seen a slave auction can be understood as an unmediated encounter with raw capital valuation and formation. Sometimes the sight was so alienating as to be hallucinatory."[70] So, if your first response was to treat Chestnut's response as an historical anomaly, then the anesthesia is still with you. You looked away, and in the second it took you to formulate a response, your humanity fell away. You stepped off the scale. You moved from your heart to your head. You temporally distanced yourself from the event. You moved from a feeling being to a thinking being. You surrendered to the gravitational pull of whiteness and released the weight. And, so I ask you, what is your opium? What kind of person do you become when you choose anesthesia over compassion?

The ties between anesthesia and inhumanity are not relics of the past. On June 14, 2018, Attorney General Jeff Sessions stood at a lectern before a crowded room of people in Fort Wayne, Indiana and defended the Trump administration's decision to forcibly separate immigrant children from their parents. He began, "I would cite to you the Apostle Paul and his clear and wise command in Romans 13, to obey the laws of the government because God has ordained the government for his purposes."[71] Session's opium was not pharmaceutical. It was partisan and scriptural. He quietly recited the passage he needed to take a rational view of things otherwise maddening. Perhaps he knew that he could not simultaneously maintain his allegiance to the administration and feel compassion for the immigrant families who were being publicly and irreversibly traumatized. His allegiance (desire to belong) cost him his humanity. What kind of leaders do we become when we choose numbness over connection? How much do you have to contort yourself in order to see a person in need as a problem and not a human being?

Sit with this scene for a moment. Where does it pull you? Did you dismiss his words because you imagined that Sessions's behavior could be explained away as the deeds of a cold-hearted man following the president's orders? Did you make excuses for his behavior? Perhaps you think that only heartless people anesthetize themselves. If so, the anesthesia is still at work in you. You have averted your gaze from the trauma-inducing policy on our southern border. You looked away for a second, and in the time it took you to jump from your heart to your head, your humanity evaporated. Anesthesia is not the product of heartlessness. Heartlessness is the product of anesthesia. You focused on Session's brokenness and overlooked your own. You stepped off the scale and released the weight.

Most instances of anesthesia are more subtle than the scenes I've put before you. The everyday anesthetizing habits of white people appear as inattention, lack of interest, or indifference to the experiences, concerns, needs, and feelings of people of color. Anesthesia can be broadly understood as anything that allows white folks to look away, stop listening, disconnect, dissociate, distract ourselves, or otherwise break the connections we have with one another. Most white people are so hooked into our whiteness that we don't know how to live in our white bodies without anesthesia. It predictably kicks in when people of color share their painful life experiences with us. We anesthetize ourselves when we blame them for the injustices and violence they suffer and for "making us" feel guilty about that injustice. We desensitize our hearts when we fail to be fully present for people of color when we are in one another's company. White talk, white fragility, and white defensiveness are anesthesia, and so is ignorance. Segregation is anesthesia because it breaks human connections geographically and spatially. We anesthetize ourselves when we confine our lives to white spaces in order to avoid the discomfort of moving through places where our whiteness feels raw and exposed. We anesthetize when we relegate racial violence to the past or talk over it loudly with stories about how it's so much better than it used to be. The color-blind mantra "I don't see color, we are all the same," numbs us to the truth that race is one of the first things we notice about a person; and, when we are honest with ourselves, we have to admit that we do not treat everyone equally. Color blindness, as José Medina observes, "involves being affectively numbed to the racial aspects of social experience." The "distinctive kind of affective numbness underlying racial insensitivity may consist in feeling indifference and apathy as a result of a cultivated lack of interest in the members of a social group and their predicament."[72] We anesthetize ourselves when are convinced that some people's lives, neighborhoods, culture, history, faith, education, health, and well-being matter more than others. The myth of meritocracy makes white people unresponsive to the reality that people of color work three times as hard to get half as far. Collectively, the anesthetizing habits of whiteness mean that white people move through the world on a dull emotional register, half-awake, uncurious, and oblivious to the fact that our insensitivity contributes to people of color's continued suffering. And so, I ask you again dear reader—what is your opium?

The problem is not that white people feel nothing at all. It is that we are unable endure the pain of our own brokenness once the anesthesia lifts. Lee Mun Wah's *If These Halls Could Talk* offers a vivid illustration of the ties between the everyday habits of whiteness and anesthesia. There is a moment in the documentary when Will Amado Syldor Severino (an African American student) works to get Leif Mattern (a white student) to feel how central anesthesia is to his whiteness.

Will: What gets me is that you can shut down like that, ya know? And how when you talk about your experiences [as a white man] that you only talk about what you *can't* do and what you *don't* feel. Ya know, "I don't feel this way. I've never felt that way," but you feel something, so why don't you talk about that? Why don't you talk about what you *do* feel?

Leif: .... for me, as me ... *not* as a white person, but as me ...

Will: No! You *as a white person ... a white man.*

Leif: ... as a white male I tried to open up, and then I was shut down, and I'm angry about that ... and I felt like I was so open, and I wanted to feel that hurt, and now I'm shut down, and I don't know how to open back up again.

Will: But, you are not shut down, that's what I'm trying to say. You are not shut down. This is who you are as a [white] person. This is who you are. You are numb. You have lost a piece of yourself as a human being. You cannot connect with me because you are not fully human enough to connect with me. You are not shut down. This is what you are feeling. You are *feeling* numb. That's why I keep talking about the hurt. What does it feel like when the emotion you feel is numbness?[73]

At the close of the exchange, Lee Mun Wah observes:

> And what I'm also hearing . . . and what might be very difficult to hear is, what's it like to be white and out of control? What's it like to be white and to not know! [Will] told [the group] a story, and some part of you, as I watch you listening . . . you're still thinking about [yourself]! "I'm a gay man, I know." "I'm a woman, I know." But I cried when I heard him. Because it didn't make sense, [for enslaved Africans to be treated as property and not as people]. It means that somehow you can't figure it all up [in your head]. I just cried. I don't know how to understand it. Why are you so caught up with how to do it? . . . . Why aren't you crying? Because I see white people do this all the time in my workshops. [Imitating white people: *"Thank you, I have a question. What year did that happen? . . ."*] So, I want you to consider: Why are [people of color] crying and you're just thinking about yourself. [74]

Wading into the weight of whiteness encourages us to cultivate a sensitivity to our own insensitivity gradually. One way to do this is to become mindful of the moments when whiteness pulls us apart. There is a gap between a racialized stimulus (i.e., when white guilt and fragility are triggered) and our response to that stimulus (i.e., defensiveness, numbness, dissociation). The more we work toward learning to stop, pause, and hold space in that gap, the more sensitized we become to the weight. Once I began thinking about whiteness as anesthesia, I began to notice how tightly our numbing behavior is woven into American mainstream culture. Police violence, gun violence, the calculated circulation of false information, and our jaw-dropping indifference to human suffering has become background noise for most Americans. On top of that, as Brené Brown observes, "we are the most addicted, we are the most medicated, obese, [busy], and in debt adult cohort in human history. We're numbing . . . we just stay so busy that the truth of our lives can't catch up."[75] Yet, I remain hopeful. I'm banking on the fact that with tons of work and attention that the anesthesia will eventually lift, and that we will be able to feel what white supremacy has cost us. Perhaps the feeling will slowly emerge "like an earthquake beneath us," and we will be offered the opportunity to rewrite the story of who we are. I'm hopeful the tremors have begun even as I type these words.[76]

UNDERSTANDING WHAT WHITE SUPREMACY COSTS WHITE PEOPLE

White anesthesia is an artifact of centuries of dissociation, indifference, and segregation. Recovering our humanity requires not only that we *understand* the price of the ticket but also that we learn to *feel* its costs and losses. A great challenge lies at the heart of this observation. A handful of white anti-racist scholars and activists have offered their personal accounts of what white supremacy has cost them.[77] The habits of white anesthesia linger in our bones and make it difficult to name the damage. So, I start by naming them. Bringing voice to the damage allows me to feel the history that continues to rattle in my bones. What do you feel as you read this? Which parts of the story I've been telling make you feel light? And, which parts make you feel heavy?

The Psychological Weight: The Costs of Entitlement, Fear, and Hypervigilance

The weight of whiteness is at root psychological. Most white people are unaware of the subtle ways we sustain our brokenness and disconnection. There is a white form of emptiness that is difficult to put into words. When we numb our connections to others, we treat some lives as more valuable and worthy of protection than others. When we foster connections primarily with other white people, we risk directing our empathy and compassion to those lives alone. Believing that some cultures are more valuable than others nurtures a false sense of pride and cultural superiority. We become prone to over-valuing European aesthetic, political, scientific, and cultural accomplishments and measuring indigenous and non-Western cultural expressions against European standards. Devaluing or destroying another groups' culture is the first step toward acting violently toward them. This disconnection and devaluation, in turn, foster a distorted sense of entitlement. We feel authorized to take an unfair share of resources, opportunities, and other people's time, so much so that when our access to social goods is restricted, we feel as if we've been treated unjustly. Consider how claims such as "a Mexican took my job," or "a Chinese student took my seat in the Harvard law school first-year class," presuppose an imagined rightful ownership of these opportunities. Our false sense of entitlement not only fosters selfishness and arrogance; it also fuels the psychological condition that Robin Di'Angelo calls white fragility. We feel entitled to racial comfort; that is, freedom from feeling psychologically fragile or anxious around matters of race.[78] We fear coming face-to-face with people of color because these encounters force us to feel the many selves we would rather not feel. We fear that people of colors' experiences, histories, and words will erode a worldview that is favorable to us. We fear racial retaliation.

Fear and entitlement are a toxic combination. They give rise to hypervigilance, a form of attending that eats us away from the inside. The clicks that installed my Newark lessons did not teach me to interact with people of color in healthy and sensible ways. They taught me to be vigilant, to regard brown and black bodies with suspicion, to casually monitor them as potential threats. As Becky Thompson and Veronica T. Watson argue, "People of color are made into strangers by the act of policing whiteness, and whiteness becomes ever more anxious though its hypervigilant attempts to identify those who should not be part of the body, the community, of whiteness."[79] Ghassan Hage treats hypervigilance as a species of paranoia—a "pathological form of fear based on an excessively fragile conception of the self as constantly threatened," even when no threat exists. He associates white paranoia with a fear of "losing its 'civilized' [white] identity that propelled the colonial project and gave rise to the nation in the first place."[80] People of color are hypervigilant by necessity because navigating white worlds safely has always required an elevated vigilance, which white people usually misread as shiftiness. There is a difference between being on guard because your history is saturated with white terror, and harboring questionable beliefs about people of color's so-called criminal nature. Consider how much energy and attention hypervigilance drains from our collective being, and how it severs human connection at first glance. This is a part of myself that I'd rather not feel.

The Social Weight: Diminished and Strained Interpersonal Relationships and Alliances

Hypervigilance and entitlement produce an anxiety and exhaustion that makes social relationships with people of color challenging to form and sustain. Racism drives an unnecessary wedge between friends, family, community members, co-workers, and neighbors. It produces a social anxiety that pulls us to self-segregate when we eat, work, worship, or gather as a community. I'm saddened by the ways my Newark lessons continue to impact cross-racial friendships.[81] I recently had a conversation with a white friend about the awkward dynamics such friendships. She began, "I consider Jasmine to be my closest friend. We can be having a great time together, and suddenly something shifts, and I *never* know what made things sour. I've just come to accept that I'm going to mess up now and again, and that I'll never completely understand what causes a painful turn." I've also experienced this. My childhood understanding of friendship was nourished through my interactions with other white children. Interracial friendships are more nuanced and require a different texture of care. I recall playing with my friend Lucinda's ten-year-old niece at their home one summer. We got along well. So, I mailed her a fun card the following week. As a child, I loved getting mail and I thought she might too. My card was returned with "no such address" handwritten on the envelope. The address was correct, so I blamed the post office and let it go. To this day, I wonder whether I committed some white-woman social faux pas—a touch that lingered too long, a hug that was jarring, an inappropriate comment? In hindsight, I believe the family was probably protecting their daughter from a white woman who tried to get too friendly too quickly. Sometimes it's necessary for people of color to sever relationships to protect themselves and their families from whiteness. I can't help but feel that my own interactions with Lucinda's niece would have been different if I'd been able to form friendships with people of color as a child.

Attempts to heal from the Newark lessons have also cost me the trust of a few extended family members and neighbors. I find it painful to connect with relatives whose long-standing racism and anti-Semitism have been fortified by Fox News and alt-Right radio. One of my cousins has traded this hunting rifle for a semiautomatic weapon, and it takes a great amount of energy to talk with him. Childhood memories of our summers playing together are not strong enough to sustain the connections, which rupture with each news cycle and each toxic remark, designed to bait me. Relationships with white neighbors and acquaintances are also fragile. Because I'm white, a few of my neighbors assume that they can safely share their hopes about "what kind of a family" will be moving into the house on the corner. A white woman at the post office, whom I've never met, openly shares with me how those "Hindu Indians" complained about her Christmas tree in the lobby, and she had to take it down. As I pay for my stamps, she tells me how "they are ruining everything that is good in this town." She assumes that because I'm white, I'll agree with her.

The Material Weight: Looting, Hoarding, and the Intricate Trap of Safety

White supremacy asks white people to place our identities as consumers and accumulators over our responsibilities as citizens, workers, and neighbors. This impulse can't be explained away as a general survival instinct. Survival is a cooperative effort.[82] My hunch was confirmed during a recent class discussion. After listening to four white women justify their hypervigilance, Renee, a black queer student, said, "I'm sick of white folks thinking that we want to take their stuff. We don't want your stuff! It's nasty! We got our own stuff." The impulse to hoard is a response to feeling empty and insecure. Accumulation offers us temporary relief from what we'd rather not feel. There is a history here. Richard Wright once remarked on white people's "constant outward-looking, their mania for radios, cars, and a thousand other trinkets, made them dream and fix their eyes upon the trash of life, made it impossible for them to learn a language that could have taught them to speak of what was in theirs or other's hearts. The words of their souls were the syllables of popular songs."[83] Our emptiness and sense of entitlement pull us to hoard opportunities, resources, and emotional attention. We take more than our fair share of education dollars, healthcare resources, well-paying jobs, tax credits, second chances, government bail outs, homes in nice neighborhoods, clean water, healthy food, congressional seats, and people of color's time. This great white wanting is a product of European colonization, a habit that most likely comes from centuries of taking indigenous land, taking labor, taking resources, taking knowledge, taking bodies, taking . . . taking . . . taking what was never ours to take. As Aurora Levins Morales observes, systems of privilege

> are constructed on fear of scarcity an insatiable hunger for more wealth, more power, more imaginary guarantees, and they depend on the ability of the privileged to ignore the huge social consequences of inequality, to dehumanize or ignore the people destroyed by the pursuit of excess. They are built on the belief that no one else will look out for us, that narrow self-interest is just common sense, that social equality and reciprocity will impoverish rather than enrich our lives.[84]

This "infinite piracy" is linked directly to ecological disaster:

> It's heartbreaking that there are so many people who cling to the sinking ship of infinite piracy, unable to imagine a society of reciprocity, respect, and mutual care that would meet the needs of all, including themselves. They would rather accelerate their looting, hoping to amass as much wealth as possible before the ship founders, even though that ship is our entire world and no amount of ownership will keep them from drowning.[85]

We fear our colonial debt will be called in, but in the meantime, we continue to fill our lives with stuff to anesthetize the pain of our emptiness. What are the costs of taking more than your share? What do hoarding and accumulation do to human connection? What do we lose when we fix our attention on the trash of life?

The false promise of whiteness contains an intricate trap of imagined safety. The lessons that taught me to see people of color as threats and urban spaces as dangerous also taught me to trust white people and to equate suburban spaces with safety. This particular lesson has unspoken risks for white girls and women. The cautionary tales I heard about sexually aggressive black and Puerto Rican men concealed from me the statistical reality that two-thirds of all sexual assaults against girls and women are committed by people they know. If people self-segregate along racial lines, then sexual violence is more likely to be intra-racial.[86] My Newark lessons turned boys and men of color into decoys. If they were the aggressors, then white boys and men's sexually aggressive behavior was somehow excusable, not predatory at all. This put me in harm's way more times than I'm comfortable recounting. It was white neighbors and family friends who groped and grabbed. It was the husband of the family I babysat for regularly who asked questions that made me freeze during the car ride home. It was white boys and men who pushed sexual encounters past my comfort zone, followed me around, showed up unexpectedly, and badgered me for my phone number. It was white men who, seeing me alone, sat themselves down uninvited and chatted me up. My own protective instincts were directed at the wrong targets and this cost me dearly. This intricate trap of safety continues to disorient my attention. Sometimes I'm unable to tell whether I'm in genuine danger, being played, or being protected. I've made the costly mistake of trusting predators, and fearing those who, as it turns out, had my best interests and safety at heart. This part of myself is extremely painful to feel.

Historically, white workers have taken refuge in a false sense of material safety. Critical historians have extensively documented capitalism's habit of stoking the white working-class fears about immigrants and nonwhite U.S. ethnic populations taking their jobs in order to push them to accept longer hours, less pay, reduced benefits, and unsafe working conditions.[87] Poor and underemployed whites continue to hope that the one percent (who kind of look like them) will share their bounty in exchange for loyalty. Capitalism will never deliver on this false promise, because the promise will never serve their bottom line. Yet poor white workers repeatedly trust that their employers will protect their jobs and keep their workplaces safe, so they fail to form alliances with working-class people of color, or recent immigrants, to retain their access to these social goods. Lyndon B. Johnson's off-the-cuff response to some racist graffiti captures the costs of these fractured alliances perfectly. "I'll tell you what's at the bottom of this," he once told a young staffer, "If you can convince the lowest white man he's better than the best colored man, he won't notice you're picking his pocket. Hell, give him somebody to look down on, and he'll empty his pockets for you."[88] What are the material costs of placing our trust and safety in the hands of predators and con men who repeatedly exploit us generation after generation?

The Moral and Epistemic Weight: The Costs of Perceiving and Judging Wrongly

CharlesMills offers a clear account of how white supremacy teaches white people to make sense of the world inaccurately, while simultaneously assuring us that our shared misperceptions are accurate. "Whites," he says, "experience genuine difficulties in recognizing certain behavior patterns as racist, so that quite apart from questions of motivation and bad faith they will be morally handicapped [*sic*] simply from the conceptual point of view in seeing and doing the right thing."[89] White numbness and ignorance are expressed as implicit bias, testimonial injustice, and micro- and macro-aggressions. Perceiving the world wrongly increases the odds that we will make inaccurate moral judgments. The Newark lessons made me morally ambivalent at best and morally confused at the worst. There was a disorienting tension between my Sunday School lessons, which taught me to follow the golden rule; and, my Newark lessons, which asked me to conform to the social expectations of my white upper-middle-class community—an awkward and unsettling strain between "do unto others" and "not our Newark."

The Newark lessons did not soften my heart; they thickened my moral skin, forcing me to navigate the world with a broken moral compass. If we perceive the world wrongly, then we will feel the world wrongly. This makes us prone to misjudging other people's actions and intentions. As José Medina notes, "disagreement is often not just about what is there to see, but rather, about what the appropriate way to feel about what one sees is; that is, it is not just a disagreement about beliefs, but a disagreement about feelings and emotions."[90] Consider how white school teachers and administrators perceive young black girls as more adult-like, sexually mature, and in need of less nurturing and protection. This phenomenon, sometimes called "adultification," or "age compression," leads black girls and young women to be disciplined more severely and frequently for small infractions.[91] Age compression cost Tamir Rice his life. Tamir was twelve, but when the police arrived at the park, they reported seeing a twenty-one-year-old. The summer of 2018 was filled with white moral misjudgments. A white woman, who the internet christened "Permit Patty," called the police to report an eight-year-old black girl selling bottled water in front of her home "without a permit." Her actions were criminalized in a way that no white kid's lemonade stands would ever be. White kids selling lemonade are cute. They are entrepreneurs, not lawbreakers. Black kids are troublesome unlawful peddlers. Later that summer, a white man in North Carolina called the police on a black woman and her family who were swimming at their neighborhood community pool. White families are neighbors. Black families are gate crashers. As Mills argues, white people continue to make inaccurate moral judgments, while continuing to assure themselves that their judgments are accurate. The sad part is that these racialized double standards *feel* like justice to us. For most white people, it "makes sense" to hold people of color's everyday actions to a more draconian set of standards. *Well, she looked like an unlawful peddler. They just seemed like they didn't belong to the swim club.* The fear that twists white moral compasses cultivates in white people a high intolerance for people of colors' everyday activities, which we justify, because we imagine that they keep us safe and protect our entitlements. What are the costs of making moral judgments with a damaged moral compass?

The Weight of Historical Amnesia: The Costs of Varnished Histories and Buried Ancestries

Historical amnesia is a tactic for anesthetizing ourselves to the past. The self-congratulatory heritage that passes for American history keeps us from feeling the violence of colonization at the root of the American democratic experiment. When we wall ourselves off from understanding the indigenous, African, Asian, Mexican, and other non-European histories of North America we opt for a weightless history. We avoid telling what John Hope Franklin has on many occasions referred to as the "the unvarnished truth" about America.[92] When I share with students historically accurate accounts of Plymouth Plantation or the settlements at Jamestown and Salem they bristle. *We can't teach that in our schools! Students would never be proud to be American if they knew that!* Precisely. If we taught American history as it really happened, the weight would be too much. I understand not wanting to traumatize young school children with stories of how the men of Plymouth Plantation dismembered the Wampanoag chief Metacom (King Phillip), hung his body parts from trees, and put his head on a pike at the entrance of the Colony where it remained for twenty years. Students' responses to those unpolished truths are telling. Rather than integrate this new information into an unvarnished history, they rush to restore the unified narratives of their childhood. The tension between the ideals of democracy and violence that brought our republic into being are too difficult for them to parse, and so, they return to the Queen's mirror.

Signs of trauma are evident in white people's unwillingness to engage this tension honestly. Deep down inside we sense that the truth is too heavy to bear. I myself didn't realize how numb I'd become to the traumas of colonization until one day, for some reason, I found myself staring at Andrew Jackson's face on a twenty-dollar bill. I was struck by how uncritically his image circulates. I wondered what members of the Cherokee, Seminole, or Creek nations feel when they pull a twenty from their wallet to pay for groceries or gas only to be met with the face of the person who orchestrated genocidal military campaigns against their ancestors.[93] Historical amnesia permits white people to lift our white psyches from the terrors of colonization. What does this institutionalized forgetting cost us? What does it say about our democratic values and ideals?

Ancestral amnesia moves predictably in the well-worn tracks left by our weightless narratives of freedom and progress. The racial contract requires that we trade our ancestries for the empty promises of whiteness. Through the generations my German, English, Welsh, Irish, Scottish, and Dutch ancestral stories, traditions, games, prayers, daily rituals, languages, and folkways were replaced with empty commercial rituals. As a child we did not read from my great grandfather's German Bible. We did not wait for Sinterklaas or observe St. Stephen's Day. We exchanged store-bought gifts, watched Christmas movies, and hung cheap decorations. This created in me a great wanting for an authentic and nourishing identity.[94] These losses prompted me to romanticize and consume the cultures of my Jewish, Italian, and Polish friends who lived in homes where their grandparents' traditions were visible and vibrant. They had Passover Seders. Their extended families still spoke Italian, German, Yiddish, Polish, and Czech. I sought refuge in their families, homes, and rituals in hopes of filling my emptiness. My countless efforts to assimilate into cultures that were not my own never filled me. They were poorly veiled attempts to recover what whiteness gradually removed from my ancestors over the generations. When whiteness is marked by an absence of culture, then what European Americans face is, in David Roediger's words, "not merely that whiteness is oppressive and false; it is that *nothing but* oppressive and false . . . a terrifying attempt to build an identity based on what one isn't and on whom one can hold back."[95]

There will be more costs and losses. The racial contract was initially drafted to contain and control indigenous, African, Chinese, and Mexican bodies, but once the machinery of domination is fully operational, it can be easily redirected to control us as well. We learn that black, brown, indigenous, and immigrant bodies don't matter, or that they matter less, but we fail to understand that, from the perspective of those in power, our lives really don't matter either. When images of welfare and social services are tied to black and brown faces (and now undocumented immigrants), programs such as Temporary Assistance for Needy Families, Housing Assistance, and Supplemental Nutrition Assistance Programs get cut. These forms of government assistance are used primarily by underemployed whites, so they suffer when these programs are cutback. The militarization of city police forces, "justified" as a response to the perceived growing gun violence in poor black and brown neighborhoods, can be easily redirected to the suburbs. Mass shootings now target suburban majority-white public schools, outdoor concerts, churches, synagogues, and college campuses. Whiteness does not protect us from the cut-and-run capitalism that continues to move manufacturing jobs overseas. The so-called "war on drugs" did not protect white people from the opioid epidemic. Predatory lending practices are now widespread. The systems designed to control people of color's lives don't stay closed: They can be re-oriented to acquire new targets at any time.

I've recently come to understand how my Newark lessons serve as a renewable resource for white supremacy. My fears have been easily redirected toward new targets in unexpected ways. I first realized this on a flight from Washington, D.C. to Chicago, shortly after the 2016 presidential election. The new administration had just issued Executive Order 13769, which suspended people from majority Muslim countries from entering the United States. I took my seat next to a woman wearing a hijab and a pair of bright green athletic shoes. While we were waiting to take off, she started fiddling with the timer app on her phone, running it from three minutes to zero over and over again. Out of nowhere I felt a gut-wrenching fear. How does the colonized mind make sense of a Muslim with a stopwatch? Muslim . . . timer . . . bomb! I sat with a truly paralyzing fear until the flight attendant announced our departure. The Homeland Security catch phrase "if you see something, say something," made an uninvited appearance in my thoughts. I considered pressing the flight attendant call button, when she stowed her phone and put on her headphones. Now, I should mention that I was partnered with an Iranian man for five years and socialized regularly with members of the local Middle-Eastern community. But, my Newark lessons were strong enough to break that connection and pair it with a new target. What's it like to live in a body where the state can hijack your fears and direct them toward violent ends?

FEELING WHAT WHITE SUPREMACY AND PRIVILEGE COST US

At this point white readers may think to themselves—*Finally! We've named the costs and losses of whiteness for white folks! The collateral damage of white supremacy is now intelligible! The weighty conversation is over. It took some doing, but we eventually got to the bottom of how white supremacy damages us. White people lose our humanity because the psychological, social, material, epistemic, moral, historical weight severs our heads from our hearts. It's so obvious to me now.* If you think that the conversation ends here, then the anesthesia is still at work in you. You've waded into the weight, but only up to the point where you can *understand* your own brokenness. The weighty conversation asks more of us. It asks us to *feel the weight of your own brokenness*. When we focus too closely on understanding the damage, we risk making the weighty conversation more about our brokenness than about our healing and collective liberation. We've lost sight of Toni Cade Bambara's kindhearted observation—there's "a lot of weight when you're well." It's not enough to know the weight is there. We must hold space with that weight from here on out. We must, every day, for the rest of our lives, work diligently at restoring and maintaining our humanity and this requires knowing that the wound at the heart of whiteness is a trauma wound and learning to feel that wound.

The Trauma Wound at the Heart of Whiteness

I did not feel the weight of my own whiteness until I began to treat the wound at the heart of whiteness as a secondary trauma wound. Just because you can't feel the pain it doesn't mean that it's not there. Your body keeps track of it whether you realize it or not. The word "trauma" comes from the ancient Greek word τραύμα, meaning to wound, hurt, or damage the body. Trauma's damage is relational: it is the chronic disruption of connectedness. It can displace social engagement behaviors with defensive reactions (fight or flight) and immobilization (freeze or dissociate). "Trauma," as Deb Dana explains, "compromises our ability to engage with others by replacing patterns of connection with patterns or protection. If unresolved, these early adaptive survival responses become habitual autonomic patterns."[96]

The ways we learn to move through the world—turning inward, slowing our movements, backing down, backing away, moving toward one another, and isolating ourselves—are all guided by the autonomic nervous system."[97] The Newark lessons replaced neurological patterns of connection with patterns of protection, and these continue to keep me "imprisoned in experiences of disconnection."[98] It comes as no surprise that white people's anesthetizing habits are a trauma response, a way of insulating ourselves against feelings that may be too overwhelming for our autonomic nervous system to handle. People with trauma histories commonly experience "more intense, extreme autonomic responses, which affect their ability to regulate and feel safe in relationships."[99] Our autonomic responses have been adapted in the service of survival. This means that white supremacy has a firm hand in shaping how white bodies and bodies of color respond physiologically to one another. It explains why white guts tighten when we walk past people on the street who are visibly Muslim or African American; why we startle easily when a person of color walks into the room unexpectedly; and why our attention is drawn to our car door locks when we drive through brown or black neighborhoods. Complex systems of domination, in Shannon Sullivan's words, "help constitute the body's muscle fibers, chemical production, digestive processes, genomic markers and more."[100]

I'd long suspected that costs and losses of whiteness had a curious correspondence to the features of trauma response exposure. I was unable to fully grasp this until I read Becky Thompson and Veronica T. Watson's "Theorizing White Racial Trauma and its Remedies." According to the authors,

> At the heart of racism are attempts of the perpetrators to deny knowledge of themselves as violent aggressors, morally destitute, even barbaric. In the United States, whiteness has rarely had to confront the image and knowledge of itself.

Instead, it has worked hard to repress and discredit that history, *which has continued the silence and deepened the trauma rather than opening avenues of accountability and healing.* . . . Rather than stay present to feel the pain of brutalized bodies and psyches, and then act from that knowledge, most white people deny, justify, and then reproduce the very violence that was the source of their own dis-ease.[101]

The authors reference Laura van Dernoot Lipsky's research to explain the correspondences between the costs and losses of white supremacy for white people and secondary trauma symptoms. Her research on trauma stewardship lists sixteen warning signs of trauma overexposure.[102] Ten of these resonate with the habitual behaviors of white supremacist culture that I outlined earlier. They include (1) hypervigilance; (2) an inability to embrace complexity (i.e., reducing pluralist selves to singular selves; reducing complex historical and ancestral narratives to unified flattering narratives); (3) minimizing (i.e., undervaluing people of color's experiences with racism); (4) an inability to listen and deliberate avoidance (i.e., white talk, strategic refusals to understand or feel the weight); (5) dissociative moments (i.e., anesthesia's gravitas); (6) a sense of persecution; (7) guilt, fear, anger and cynicism; (8) an inability to empathize; (9) numbing and addiction; and, (10) grandiosity (i.e., white people's tendency to make it all about us). "These secondary trauma symptoms," as Thompson and Watson observe, "have an eerie resonance with what can happen to white people as part of a racist society."[103] They conclude: "What van Deroot Lipsky describes as the coping mechanisms that alleviate the pain of 'staying in touch with the heart that was breaking,' look a lot like normative white culture in the United States."[104] As I suspected, the habits of whiteness are coping mechanisms. They keep us from feeling the pain of our own brokenness. It comes as no surprise that shutting down, disconnecting, and numbing are trauma responses; but, when we check out or shut down we can't heal. So, how do we engage the wound at the heart of whiteness in ways that promote healing over anesthesia?

The Soul Nerves of White Folks: White Supremacy and Trauma Exposure

If the costs and losses of white supremacy share common features with trauma exposure, then recent literature on trauma offers sage advice for healing.[105] What if we treated the habits of white supremacy as the product of trauma exposure? In his book *My Grandmother's Hands: Racialized Trauma and the Pathway to Mending Our Hearts and Bodies*, Resmaa Menakem observes that white supremacy doesn't live in our heads, it lives and breathes in our bodies, so it would be better to call it *white-body supremacy*. White-body supremacy has become part of American bodies regardless of race because everyone breathes in the same toxic messages about whiteness daily, to the point where these messages change our brains, organs, and nervous systems. He explains:

> Our bodies have a form of knowledge that is different from our cognitive brains. This knowledge is typically experienced as a felt sense of constriction or expansion, pain or ease, energy or numbness. This knowledge often gets stored in our bodies as wordless stories about what is safe and what is dangerous. The body is where we fear, hope, and react; where we constrict or release, and where we reflexively fight, flee, or freeze. If we are to upend the *status quo* of white-body supremacy, we must begin with our bodies.[106]

When we start in the body, we learn that some of the deepest emotions we feel—love, fear, anger, shame, grief, hope, and disgust—are in reaction to phenomena in the world. These reactions involve the activation of a complex network of nerves that connect the brainstem, the pharynx, heart, lungs, stomach, internal organs, and spine. Neuroscientists call this complex system the *vagus nerve*, but Menakem poetically re-names it the *soul nerve* because it is connected directly to the region of the brain that does not depend primarily on logical reasoning to navigate the world. The soul nerve functions to maintain a state of balance between our bodies' active energy (mobilizing it to respond to what threatens our safety) and its resting energy (recovering, feeling settled, and grounded).[107] The soul nerve is the reptilian region of the human brain: it only understands survival and protection. It does not respond to threats by pausing to think them through and weighing possible options. It proactively issues survival directives that pull our bodies toward what makes us feel safe and away from what may harm us. When faced with a potential threat, our bodies will respond in a number of ways. We may fight, flee, freeze, befriend, or fawn. These are the only responses on the lizard brain's menu. White-body supremacy functions most powerfully in this reptilian part of our brains. It hijacks the *soul nerve* and reframes common human fears along racial lines. There is a sense in which, following DuBois, the souls of white folks are animated by what I've come to think of as the *soul nerve of white folks*. This is why most white bodies turn inward, fall silent, or make ourselves less noticeable when we share confined spaces with people of color. This is why the pace of my step quickens when I walk past a group of young Latinx men waiting for their bus. My Newark lessons have paired basic reptilian brain functions to the presence of black and brown male bodies, and as the old saying among neuroscientists goes: neurons that fire together wire together.

Trauma creates unsettled bodies. There is a difference between living in an unsettled body that you have to continually anesthetize and living in a settled body that you can feel. The difference lies in how we respond to the pain at the heart of whiteness. Menakem's description of white-body supremacy has helped me to feel the connections between the habits of whiteness and the trauma wound at the heart of whiteness. His distinction between clean pain and dirty pain, in particular, has helped me to isolate and feel a particular texture of pain that white people need to engage, in order to live in our whiteness with minimal anesthesia. I reach for his distinction when I feel myself being pulled under. In his words,

> Clean pain is the pain that mends and can build your capacity for growth. It's the pain you experience when you know, exactly, what you need to say or do; when you really, really don't want to say or do it; and when you do it anyway. It's also the pain you experience when you have no idea what to do; when you're scared or worried about what might happen; and when you step forward anyway with honesty and vulnerability.[108]

Clean pain exposes us to felt knowledge. Clean pain hurts to the point of tears, but wading slowly through the pain is the quickest path toward wholeness. Clean pain wakes us up. The experience of moving into clean pain is unpleasant, but in the end it gives us a sense of expansion and openness. Sandra Kim compares clean pain to that tingling-numb feeling you get when you begin to move after sitting in a contorted position for too long.[109] You may not realize that your foot has fallen asleep, but your movement makes you suddenly aware that the circulation to your leg has been cut off long enough for you to lose feeling. So, you are faced with a choice. You can re-contort yourself in hopes of postponing the pain that comes with un-contorting yourself; but, this is a false refuge. You can also take a deep breath, unfold yourself slowly, and patiently breathe through the discomfort you feel as the blood returns to your foot. You might wiggle your toes to move things along, or temporarily pause and re-contort yourself to enjoy a moment of relief. Eventually, you realize that re-contorting only prolongs the pain. So, you move into a full-on unfolding stretch. It's uncomfortable, but eventually the pins and needles stop buzzing and the feeling returns. This is what clean pain feels like. Clean pain offers a liberatory promise: once we move through the pain we no longer need to manage it with the anesthesia of re-contortion. Audre Lorde's revision of Descartes' *cogito* captures this—"I feel therefore I can be free."[110] Clean pain pulls you back into your body. It forces you to stop, observe, breathe, and settle. It teaches you to hold space with what you've been taught not to feel.

Dirty pain offers no such promise. It is, in Menakem's words, "the pain of avoidance, blame, and denial."[111] Dirty pain does more damage in the long run because it requires constant anesthesia to settle our discomfort. Living in an unsettled body, like remaining in a contorted position, is not a path to healing. Think about it. We have a choice between two unpleasant responses to the weighty invitation. We can either settle our bodies by moving through the tingly discomfort of clean pain or cling stubbornly to dirty pain by managing it with endless doses of anesthesia. Consider how messed up this is. White people prefer the false comfort of endless anesthetized contortion over the sensitized movement of liberation. Dirty pain feels safe to us; but, this is not healing; it is addiction. Most white people live our entire lives stuck in endless cycles of dirty pain and anesthesia. Something touches that deep and festering wound and we reach for the nearest thing to numb it. Soon the anesthesia wears off and the wound's rawness returns, so we anesthetize ourselves over, and over, and over again so that we can maintain the illusion of a settled body.[112] The anesthetized body is a not settled body. It moves fictitiously through the world on a less vibrant emotional register. There is a difference between feeling calm because you have metabolized your (clean) pain and have begun to feel whole and unbroken, and feeling calm because you have numbed yourself to the point where you feel absolutely nothing at all. Here's the sad part about living your entire life in a fully anesthetized body. You can't selectively numb the emotions you don't want to feel. Neurologically speaking, there is no local anesthesia. It's an all or nothing deal: You either feel everything or feel nothing. When you anesthetize pain and anxiety, you also anesthetize love and joy.[113] And, here's the tragic part—white people have anesthetized our bodies for so long that we truly believe we are comfortable and safe in our numbness. Anything that disrupts our numbness feels like a threat.

Let us return to Toni Cade Bambara's kindhearted query about the pain required to become whole. White people will never be able to feel the weight of whiteness until we have the courage to choose clean pain over dirty pain. If white people are sincerely committed to spending time on those disagreeable but faithful scales, then we must resist the urge to re-contort ourselves by choosing to metabolize the pain, learn from the discomfort, and work toward mending the trauma in our being. When the body metabolizes clean pain, "it can then settle; more room for growth is created in the central nervous system; and the self becomes freer and more capable, because it now has access to energy that was previously protected, bound, and constricted."[114] Metabolizing clean pain helps our bodies, and the bodies around us, feel more settled. Collectively we become more whole when we have the courage to sit with the pain and feel what comes up for us. I say "more whole," because I don't think that white people can ever be fully whole under white supremacy. The very act of keeping an eye on wholeness, however, may leave us in a better place. Wellness may not always look like wholeness, but I want white people to work toward wellness, even if we fall short of complete wholeness. We will never feel complete, then, until we find the courage to hold space with the weight of the pain that breaks us. The cure for the pain is in the pain. And, as it turns out, the pain of white supremacy is generations deep. We inherit the pain of those who came before us.

NOTES

1. Toni Cade Bambara, *The Salt Eaters* (New York: Vintage Books, 1980), 3–5, 10.

2. McIntosh acknowledges the weight but foregrounds the visible: "We need more understanding of the ways in which white privilege damages white people, for these are not the same ways that it damages the victimized." See, "White Privilege and Male Privilege: A Personal Account of Coming to See Correspondences through Work in Women's Studies," in *The Feminist Philosophy Reader*, eds. Alison Bailey and Chris J. Cuomo (New York: McGraw Hill, 2008), 67.

3. David Dean, "Healing the Dominant Group: Breaking the Cycle of Violence," *White Awake* (blog), August 31, 2016, https://whiteawake.org/2016/08/31/healing-the-dominant-group-breaking-the-cycle-of-violence/

4. This chapter contains previously published material reprinted from Alison Bailey, "Newark Lessons: A Response to George Yancy's Backlash," *Philosophy Today* 62, no. 4, published by DePaul University in 2018. https://doi.org/10.5840/philtoday2018624245. Copyright © DePaul University.

5. The Newark lessons were not directed at me alone, the black and Puerto Rican families who shared the playground surely felt my mother's vigilance. See Layla Saad, "I Need to Talk to Spiritual White Women about White Supremacy (Part One)," *Layla F. Saad* (blog) August 17, 2017, http://laylafsaad.com/poetry-prose/white-women-white-supremacy-1

6. Lillian Smith, *Killers of the Dream* (New York: W.W. Norton and Company, 1961), 91.

7. George Yancy, *Look, a White!: Philosophical Essays on Whiteness* (Philadelphia: Temple University Press, 2012), 30.

8. Thandeka, "Whites: Made in America: Advancing American Philosophers' Discourse on Race," *The Pluralist* 13, no. 1 (Spring 2018), 31.

9. Thandeka, "Whites: Made in America," 31.

10. The language of suturing and contortion point to the same problem. George Yancy uses the language of suturing to capture the degree to which white people are unwilling to be vulnerable. "Being un-sutured, he says, is not just to remain open to be wounded, but it is also to cultivate the practice of remaining with the open wound itself, of tarrying with the pain of the opening itself, an incision, as it were." I use the language of contortion and unfolding because I want to highlight the role anesthesia plays in protecting the wound. The image of living a contorted existence also keeps readers attention focused on connections between the weight of discomfort, pain, and

a refusal to move. See Yancy, "Introduction: Unsutured," in *White Self-Criticality beyond Anti-racism: How Does It Feel to Be a White Problem?*, ed. George Yancy (Lanham, MD: Lexington Books, 2015), xvii.

11. Smith, *Killers of the Dream*, 27.

12. Claudia Rankine, *Citizen: An American Lyric* (Minneapolis, MN: Greywolf Press, 2014), 63.

13. See, Bessel Van der Kolk, *The Body Keeps the Score: Brain, Mind, and Body in the Healing of Trauma* (New York: Penguin Books, 2015).

14. Veronica T. Watson, *The Souls of White Folk: African American Writers Theorize Whiteness* (Jackson, MS: University Press of Mississippi, 2013), 3–14.

15. Harriet A. Jacobs, *Incidents in the Life of a Slave Girl: Written by Herself* (Cambridge, MA: Harvard University Press, 2000), 52.

16. Frederick Douglass, *Narrative of the Life of Frederick Douglass* (New York: Dover Publications, 1995), 33.

17. William Edward Burghardt DuBois, *Black Reconstruction in America: Toward a History of the Part Which Black Folk Play in the Attempt to Reconstruct Democracy in American, 1860–1880* (New York: Routledge, 2017), 475.

18. Watson, *The Souls of White Folk*, 53.

19. James Baldwin, "On Being White and Other Lies," *Essence* (April 1984), 90–92.

20. Barbara Smith, "Racism and Women's Studies," *Frontiers: A Journal of Women's Studies* 5, no. 1 (Spring 1980), 49.

21. George Yancy, *Backlash: What Happens When We Talk Honestly about Racism in America* (Lanham, MD: Rowman and Littlefield, 2018), 19.

22. Yancy, *Backlash*, 19, 69.

23. George Yancy, *Black Bodies, White Gazes: The Continuing Significance of Race in America* (Lanham, MD: Rowman and Littlefield, 2017), 120.

24. Gloria Anzaldúa, *Making Face, Making Soul: Haciendo Caras* (San Francisco, Aunt Lute Books, 1990), xix.

25. Eula Biss, "White Debt: Reckoning with What is Owed—And What Can Never Be Repaid—for Race Privilege," *New York Times*, December 5, 2015, https://www.nytimes.com/2015/12/06/magazine/white-debt.html

26. Kenneth Jones and Tema Okun, "White Supremacy Culture," in *Dismantling Racism: 2016 Workbook* (dRworks Books, 2016), 28–35, https://resourcegeneration.org/wp-content/uploads/2018/01/2016-dRworks-workbook.pdf

27. Ann Wilson Schaef, *Native Wisdom for White Minds: Daily Reflections Inspired by the Native Peoples of the World* (New York: One World Balentine Books, 1995), 1–6.

28. Lisa Tessman remarks, we "had better have both some pretty good reasons for persisting in the project and some decent idea of how to avoid likely pitfalls." See, *Burdened Virtues: Virtue Ethics for Liberatory Struggles* (New York: Oxford, 2005), 34.

29. Resmaa Menakem, *My Grandmother's Hands: Racialized Trauma and the Pathway to Mending Our Hearts and Bodies* (Las Vegas, NV: Central Recovery Press, 2017), 268–69.

30. This is not true of some African epistemologies. See Oyèrónkẹ́ Oyěwùmí, *The Invention of Woman: Making an African Sense of Western Gender Discourses*

(St. Paul, MN: University of Minnesota Press, 1997); and José Medina's remarks on epistemic insensitivity in *The Epistemology of Resistance: Gender and Racial Oppression, Epistemic Injustice, and Resistant Imaginations* (New York: Oxford University Press, 2015), xi–xii, 14, 18, 21.

31. For a deeply useful account of non-cognitive sources of embodied knowledge and the problem with thinking our way out of racism see Shannon Sullivan's *The Physiology of Sexist and Racist Oppression* (New York: Oxford University Press, 2015).

32. Joy James, "Contort Yourself: Music, Whiteness, and the Politics of Disorientation," in *White Self-Criticality: How Does it Feel to Be a White Problem?*, ed. George Yancy (Lanham: MD: Lexington Books, 2015), 211.

33. José Medina, "Color Blindness, Meta-Ignorance, and the Racial Imagination," *Critical Philosophy of Race* 1, no. 1 (2013), 45. Insensitivity is a core theme in his *The Epistemology of Resistance* (2015).

34. Rachel Cargle, "When White People Are Uncomfortable, Black People are Silenced," *Harper's Bazaar*, January 9, 2019, https://www.harpersbazaar.com/culture/politics/a25747603/silencing-black-voices/

35. José Medina raises an important point about white people's claim that they can't see what's before them: "But what does this "blindness" involve? Is it a pretend blindness in which one denies what one sees, or a genuine blindness resulting from having been trained not to see? And what does this alleged blindness tell us of the subject who proclaims it and of the culture that promulgates it?" See, "Color Blindness, Meta-Ignorance, and the Racial Imagination," 43. Sullivan extends Medina's insight: "Is affective numbness a pretend numbness in which a person denies what she feels, or a genuine numbness resulting from being trained not to feel?" See *The Physiology of Sexist and Racist Oppression*, 158.

36. Charles Mills, *The Racial Contract* (Ithaca, NY: Cornell University Press, 1997).

37. Sara Ahmed, "Snap," *Feminist Killjoys* (blog). May 21, 2017, https://feministkilljoys.com/2017/05/21/snap/

38. Franz Fanon, *Black Skin, White Masks* (London: Pluto Press, 1986), 110–11.

39. *In Whose Honor?: American Indian Mascots in Sports*, dir. Jay Rosenstein, New Day Films, 1997 [5:00–5:56].

40. The term "weathering," was coined by Dr. Arline Geronimus. See, Gene Demby, "Making the Case That Discrimination Is Bad for Your Health," *The Code Switch Podcast*, National Public Radio, January 14, 2018.

41. bell hooks, "Representing Whiteness," in *Black Looks: Race and Representation* (New York: Routledge, 2014), 177.

42. Sara Ahmed, *Living A Feminist Life* (Durham, NC: Duke University Press, 2017), 23. Ahmed's remarks are about sexual harassment, but her observations apply to racialized microaggressions and macroaggressions.

43. For a primer see, "What Is the Psychological Impact of Racism?" *HuffPost Live* (May 21, 2013), https://www.youtube.com/watch?v=lDlzVNH4Skc

44. Aurora Levins Morales, *Medicine Stories: Essays for Radicals* (Durham, NC: Duke University Press, 2019), 13.

45. Francis E. Kendall, *Understanding White Privilege: Creating Pathways to Authentic Relationships across Race* (New York: Routledge, 2006), 37.

46. Peter Levine, *In an Unspoken Voice: How the Body Releases Trauma and Restores Goodness* (Berkeley, CA: North Atlantic Books, 2010), 291.

47. Rudyard Kipling, *Poems* (New York: Alfred Knopf, 2007), 96–99.

48. Tim Wise, "The Pathology of Privilege: Racism, White Denial and the Costs of Inequality," filmed 2008 at Mt. Holyoke College, South Hadley, MA, video [50:52], https://www.youtube.com/watch?v=t4mVaLvpsXs

49. Thomas Norman DeWolf and Sharon Morgan, *Gather at the Table: The Healing Journey of a Daughter of Slavery and a Son of the Slave Trade* (Boston: Beacon Press, 2012), 199.

50. I use gravitas to capture the activity inherent in weighty pull, not dignity or seriousness. For additional scholarly treatment of the weight see: Eric Arnesen, "Whiteness and the Historian's Imagination," *International Labor and Working-Class History* 60, no. 60 (October 2001), 3–32; Chris Crass, *Towards a Collective Liberation: Anti-Racist Organizing, Feminist Praxis, and Movement Strategy* (Oakland, CA: PM Press, 2013); Ann Russo, *Feminist Accountability: Disrupting Violence and Transforming Power* (New York: NYU Press, 2018); Zeus Leonardo, "Tropics of Whiteness: Metaphor and the Literary Turn in Whiteness Studies," *Whiteness and Education* 1, no. 1 (2016), 3–14; and, George Yancy, "The Violent Weight of Whiteness: The Existential and Psychic Price Paid by Black Male Bodies," in *The Oxford Handbook of Philosophy of Race*, ed. Naomi Zack (London: Oxford University Press, 2017), 587–97; and, Yancy, *Backlash* (2018).

51. Online Etymology Dictionary, "Lose (v.)," https://www.etymonline.com/word/lose#etymonline_v_12441

52. James Baldwin, "On Being White and Other Lies," *Essence* (April 1984), 91.

53. Yancy, *Backlash*, 57.

54. Marcus Anthony Hunter, "Racial Physics or a Theory for Everything that Happened," *Ethnic and Racial Studies* 40, no. 8 (2017), 1173–83.

55. Serene Jones, *Call It Grace: Finding Meaning in a Fractured World* (New York: Viking, 2019), 90.

56. Ann Russo, *Feminist Accountability: Disrupting Violence and Transforming Power*, 21–22.

57. James Baldwin, "White Man's Guilt," in *The Price of the Ticket: Collected Nonfiction 1948–1985* (New York, St. Martin's Press, 1985), 409.

58. My point is not to reduce people of color to the function of reliable mirrors for the purposes of white consciousness raising. The shift is not from "what do I think about me" to "what do you think about me." It is about the interactions between us and what these reveal about race.

59. María Lugones, *Pilgrimages/Peregrinajes: Theorizing Coalitions Against Multiple Oppressions* (Lanham, MD: Rowman and Littlefield, 2003), 72.

60. Lugones, *Pilgrimages/Peregrinajes*, 73.

61. Lugones, 73. My italics.

62. I fully appreciate that disagreeable mirrors also reflect the weighty costs of whiteness. I introduce the disagreeable scale as a tidy way to tie Baldwin and

Lugones's implicit insights into a weighty vocabulary. I want to focus on the weight and worry that mixed metaphors about heavy mirrors and weighty reflections might confuse even the most careful reader.

63. Joseph R. Brandt, *Dismantling Racism: The Continuing Challenge to White America* (Minneapolis, MN: Ausburger Books, 1991), 55.

64. See my, "Despising an Identity They Taught Me to Claim: Exploring a Dilemma of White Privilege Awareness," in *Whiteness: Feminist Philosophical Narratives*, eds. Chris J. Cuomo and Kim Q. Hall (Totowa, NJ: Rowman and Littlefield, 1999), 85–107.

65. The etymological roots of anesthesia come from the Greek *anaisthēsia*, meaning a "want of feeling or perception, lack of sensation (to pleasure or pain)." See, "Anesthesia," *Online Etymology Dictionary*, https://www.etymonline.com/word/anesthesia

66. Mab Segrest, "Of Soul and White Folks," in *Born to Belonging: Writings on Spirit and Justice* (New Brunswick: Rutgers University Press, 2002), 162.

67. My summary follows Kendall's reading of Segrest. See, *Understanding White Privilege*, 33–34.

68. Mary Boykin Chestnut, *A Diary from Dixie*, 25–26, quoted in Segrest, "Of Soul and White Folks," 165–66.

69. Segrest, "Of Soul and White Folks," 162.

70. Joe Lockard, *Watching Slavery: Witness Texts and Travel Reports*, 2nd edition (New York: Peter Lang, 2008), xxxi.

71. The passage is Romans 13:1: "Let everyone be subject to the governing authorities, for there is no authority except that which God has established. The authorities that exist have been established by God." The passage has been used historically as an indisputable order for Christians to obey state authority. It was used to justify Southern slavery and the Fugitive Slave act. Lincoln Mullen, "The Fight to Define Romans 13," *The Atlantic*, June 15, 2018, https://www.theatlantic.com/ideas/archive/2018/06/romans-13/562916/

72. Medina, "Color Blindness, Meta-Ignorance and the Racial Imagination," 49.

73. "The Numbness," *If These Halls Could Talk*, directed by Lee Mun Wah (Berkley, CA: Stir Fry Productions, 2014), DVD.

74. "The Numbness" [1:04:30].

75. Brené Brown, "The Price of Invulnerability," TEDx Talk, Kansas City, 12 October 2010, http://www.TEDxKC.org/

76. I wrote this section before the CoVid-19 pandemic and the killing of Breonna Taylor and George Floyd. Serena Jones, "On Grace." Interview by Krista Tippett, *On Being*, NPR, December 5, 2019, https://onbeing.org/programs/serene-jones-on-grace/

77. See Beth Berila, *Integrating Mindfulness into Anti-Oppression Pedagogy: Social Justice in Higher Education* (New York: Routledge, 2016), 97–100; Francis E. Kendall, *Understanding White Privilege*, 19–40; Tim Wise, *White Like Me: Reflections on Race from a Privileged Son* (Brooklyn: Soft Skull Press, 2005), 119–50; Paul Kivel, "The Costs of Racism to White People," (2002), www.paulkivel.com; Becky Thompson and Veronica T. Watson, "Theorizing White Racial Trauma

and its Remedies," in *The Construction of Whiteness: An Interdisciplinary Analysis of Race Formation and the Meaning of White Identity*, eds. Stephen Middleton, David R. Roediger, and Donald M. Shaffer (Jackson: University Press of Mississippi, 2016), 234–55. See also, Diane J. Goodman, *Promoting Diversity and Social Justice: Educating People from Privileged Groups*, 2nd edition (New York: Routledge, 2011), 84–101.

78. Robin DiAngelo, *White Fragility: Why It's So Hard for White People to Talk about Racism* (Boston: Beacon, 2018), 2.

79. Thompson and Watson, "Theorizing White Racial Trauma and Its Memories," 237.

80. Hage Ghassan, *Against Paranoid Nationalism: Searching for Hope in a Shrinking Society* (North Melbourne, Australia: Pluto Press, 2003), 4.

81. For an account of how white children's close childhood friendships with black adults changes with age see Wendell Berry's powerful, yet overlooked, account of his childhood in Kentucky. *The Hidden Wound* (Berkeley: Counterpoint, 2010), especially Chapters 7–9.

82. Humans are hardwired for sharing and community. In many indigenous cultures stinginess, hoarding and accumulating more than you need is an embarrassment. As a New Guinea elder put it, "I am a big man. See these shells? They are valuable in our culture. I could have trunks of them . . . but then I wouldn't be a big man. A big man gives away what he has and shares with others." Ann Wilson Schaef, *Native Wisdom for White Minds*, 8 January entry.

83. Richard Wright, "The Man Who Went to Chicago," in *Eight Men*, introduction by Paul Gilroy (New York: Harper Perennial, 1996), 214.

84. Morales, *Medicine Stories*, 4.

85. Morales, 177.

86. This is not true for sexual violence against indigenous girls and women who report that 8 in 10 rapes or assaults were perpetrated by white men. See, the National Institute for Justice, "Five Things about Violence against American Indian and Alaskan Native Women and Men," https://nij.gov/five-things/Pages/violence-against-american-indian-and-alaska-native-women-and-men.aspx#five

87. See, DuBois, *Black Reconstruction in America* (2017), David R. Roediger, *The Wages of Whiteness: Race and the Making of The American Working Class* (London: Verso, 1991), and George Lipsitz, *The Possessive Investment in Whiteness: How White People Profit from Identity Politics* (Philadelphia: Temple University Press, 2006).

88. Bill Moyers, "What a Real President Was Like," *The Washington Post*, November 13, 1988. W.E.B. DuBois describes this as the "public and psychological wage of whiteness."

89. Mills, *The Racial Contract*, 85.

90. Medina, *Epistemologies of Resistance*, 49.

91. See, Rebecca Epstein, Jamilia J. Blake, and Thalia González, *Girlhood Interrupted: The Erasure of Black Girls' Childhood* (Washington, DC: Georgetown Law, Center on Policy and Inequality, 2019), https://www.law.georgetown.edu/poverty-inequality-center/wp-content/uploads/sites/14/2017/08/girlhood-interrupted.pdf. And,

Monique Morris, "Why Are Black Girls More Likely to Be Punished in School? *TED Radio Hour*, National Public Radio, March 29, 2019, https://www.npr.org/templates/transcript/transcript.php?storyId=707191363

92. I've been unable to trace this quote to a single source. John Hope Franklin's imperative "We've got to tell the unvarnished truth," appears near the entrance to the Museum of African American History and Culture in Washington, D.C.

93. David E. Stannard summarizes the gruesome details of Jackson's monstrous acts against indigenous people: "Then, in 1828 Andrew Jackson was elected President. The same Andrew Jackson who once had written that 'the whole Cherokee Nation ought to be scourged.' The same Andrew Jackson who had led troops against peaceful Indian encampments, calling the Indians 'savage dogs.' And boasting that 'I have on all occasions preserved the scalps of my killed.' The same Andrew Jackson who had supervised the mutilation of 800 or so Creek Indian corpses—the bodies of men, women, and children that he and his men had massacred—cutting off their noses to count and preserve a record of the dead, slicing log strips of flesh from their bodies to tan and turn into bridle reins." *American Holocaust: The Conquest of the New World* (New York: Oxford, 1992), 121.

94. Christian Lander puts it bluntly: "As a white person, you're just desperate to find something else to grab onto. You're jealous! Pretty much every white person I grew up with wished they'd grown up in, you know, an ethnic home that gave them a second language. White culture is *Family Ties* and Led Zeppelin and Guns N' Roses—like, this is white culture. This is all we have." Lander cited in Hau Hsu, "The End of White America?," *The Atlantic*, January/February 2009, https://www.theatlantic.com/magazine/archive/2009/01/the-end-of-white-america/307208/

95. Roediger, *The Wages of Whiteness*, 13.

96. Deb Dana, *The Polyvagal Theory in Therapy: Engaging the Rhythm of Regulation* (New York: W.W. Norton and Company, 2011), xviii.

97. Polyvagal theory was first introduced by Stephen W. Porges in his *The Polyvagal Theory: Neurophysiological Foundations of Emotions, Attachment, Communication, Self-Regulation* (New York: W.W. Norton and Company, 2011). My summary follows Deb Dana's more accessible introduction to Porges's scholarship.

98. Dana, *The Polyvagal Theory in Therapy*, 49.

99. Dana, xvii.

100. Sullivan, *Physiology of Sexist and Racist Oppression*, 17. On Sullivan's account, the "unconscious habits" of whiteness are fully biological and physiological. They reside in the body and nowhere else. Space restrictions prevent me from fully engaging Sullivan's remarkable and extensive treatment of the hardwired habits of whiteness, though much of what I say about the autonomic nervous system affirms her basic insights about how the body takes up whiteness.

101. Thompson and Watson, "Theorizing White Racial Trauma," in *The Construction of Whiteness: An Interdisciplinary Analysis of Race Formation and the Meaning of White Identity*, eds. Stephen Middleton, David R. Roediger, and Donald M. Shaffer (Jackson, MS: University of Mississippi Press, 2016), 234 and 236. My italics.

102. Lipsky's full list includes feeling helpless and hopeless, a sense that one can never do enough, hypervigilance, diminished creativity, inability to embrace

complexity, minimizing, chronic exhaustion, the inability to listen/deliberate avoidance, dissociative moments, sense of persecution, guilt, fear, anger and cynicism, the inability to empathize/numbing, addictions, and grandiosity (or an inflated sense of importance). Laura van Dernoot Lipsky with Connie Burk. *Trauma Stewardship: An Everyday Guide to Caring for Self While Caring for Others* (San Francisco: Berrett-Koeler, 2009), 41–91.

103. Thompson and Watson, "Theorizing White Racial Trauma," 236.

104. Lipsky cited in Thompson and Watson, 236.

105. Polyvagal theory offers a concise neurological understanding of trauma wounding. When applied to questions of race it accounts for many of the behaviors associated white brokenness (i.e., hypervigilance, anesthesia, and dissociation). At this point in my discussion I'm reluctant clutter my argument with additional conceptual tools, so I'll speak generally about healing, pain and trauma wounds in ways that engage whitely behaviors without too much reference to neurological conditions that regulate them. For the basics of polyvagal theory see Porges (2011), and Dana, (2011).

106. Menakem, *My Grandmother's Hands*, 5–6.

107. Menakem's account of white-body supremacy follows the basic premises of polyvagal theory.

108. Menakem, 19–20. My account is a condensed summary of Menakem's basic explanation.

109. Sandra Kim uses this metaphor to call attention to the ways that white supremacy puts white people into contorted positions and how the pain of moving out of those positions prompts us to fold back up into ourselves. Healing from Internalized Whiteness Three-Day Training, Washington, D.C., January 16–19, 2019, https://everydayfeminism.com/healing-from-internalized-whiteness/

110. Audre Lorde, "Poetry is not a Luxury," in *Sister Outsider: Essays and Speeches* (Berkeley, CA: The Crossing Press, 1984), 33.

111. Menakem, *My Grandmother's Hands*, 20.

112. As Segrest observes, "the affective void from which feelings and perceptions have been blocked in oneself and cast onto Others is the space where addictions arise." See, "Of Soul and White Folks," 169.

113. Brené Brown, *The Gifts of Imperfection: Let Go of Who You Think You're Supposed to Be and Embrace Who You Are* (Center City, MN: Hazelden, 2010), 72–73.

114. Menakem, *My Grandmother's Hands*, 20.

Chapter 5

Inheriting the Weight of Whiteness

I confess to having more than a mild addiction to those public television ancestry programs. There is a nervous excitement as Henry Louis Gates, Jr., host of the popular PBS series *Finding Your Roots*, asks guests to open their family history scrapbooks. They turn the pages and stare into their great-grandfather's eyes for the first time. Their eyes tear up as they touch the names of their furthest back ancestors on slave schedules or trace the boundaries of family farms on settlement maps. The series is an intoxicating blend of celebrity biography and forgotten history. Excavating lost ancestries taps into a basic human drive to know who we are, where our people came from, how we got there, and what we inherit from those who came before us. Our ancestries are fragile. Our family stories usually fade within a generation or two. This explains the wonder guests feel when their forebearer's worlds come softly into focus. *How could I not have known this? How could such an incredible story have been lost?* What I love about Gates's interview style is the way he lets the newly discovered information sink in before asking his guests how they *feel* in response to the legacies blooming before them. Genealogy contains a powerful alchemy. The process of retrieving ancestral worlds from obscurity is strangely settling. There is a wholeness that comes from knowing that we are part of a greater story than we realized. Even the most painful revelations feel healing. The past may not be the one we were seeking. It might not match the stories our grandparents shared with us. It may complicate and confuse our basic understandings of American history; but, at least we have a rudimentary picture of the people who crafted the world into which we were born. Our ancestor's lives reach up through us in unexpected ways. They are part of our fleshy cupboards. Their deeds remain in our bones and knowing this changes us.

I'm intimately familiar with these feelings. Five years before he moved, my father entrusted to me the family heirlooms his parents and their ancestors cherished for at least five generations. Among the furniture, china, and silverware, were boxes of letters, keepsakes, photographs, linens, pewter candle holders, portraits, tintypes, scrapbooks, land deeds, Bibles, and marriage announcements. "Perhaps," he said, "you can make sense of all of this." He yearned for me to put names to the hands through which these treasured objects had passed and to tell the stories they held. Our ancestors ate from these spoons. They left their bread dough to rise in this bowl. They carefully unfolded, read, and refolded these letters and returned them to the painted toleware box I held in my hands. Young girls' hands lovingly stitched family names and dates into the registers of their embroidered schoolgirl samplers. They glued photos into scrapbooks and annotated them in crisp white ink. At some point these everyday objects became heirlooms.

I answered my father's request with two books tracing his maternal and paternal family lines back to the Dutch, English, Welsh, and German colonization of North America.[1] His maternal line runs directly back to the seventeenth century Dutch and English colonization of lower Manhattan and the farmlands of Middlesex and Monmouth County, New Jersey. His paternal line reaches back to the Massachusetts Bay Colony and early English settlements at Haddam, Middletown, Hartford, and Wethersfield, Connecticut. During my research I began to feel how the weight of whiteness predated my childhood Newark lessons; it was as much a part of my inheritance as those treasured heirlooms. My ancestors were among the original signatories of the racial contract. Their deeds and decisions contributed to the transformation of what many indigenous people call Turtle Island (North America) into what my people arrogantly called the "New World"—from a raceless state of nature to a highly regulated racialized polity.[2] Piecing together my ancestry was like witnessing eleven generations carefully negotiate and construct the systemic conditions from which all immigrants from the British Isles and Europe would eventually benefit. What did it take for my ancestors to become white? And, what brutal measures and social practices did they use to maintain their whiteness over the generations?

Colonization requires amnesia and numbing. As Alexis Shotwell explains, "we become who we are in part through what we know and what we are made (or made able) to forget . . . a central feature of white settler colonial subjectivity is forgetting; we live whiteness in part as active ignorance and forgetting."[3] Our family trees are shaped as much by what we have inherited as they are by what has been forgotten or erased. The process of belonging often demands an orchestrated forgetting. We contort ourselves to fit comfortably into communities, families, and social norms that will benefit and protect us. This requires a conscious silencing and forgetting of those parts of ourselves (our native languages, customs, traditions, and habits) that block paths to belonging. Filling in the gaps in our family tree rarely restores these losses. The problem here is not that there is a gap in our family history, which can be easily back filled by dumping more dates, census data, and photos into our pedigrees. Collecting facts can help us piece together the contours of these ancestral puzzles, but they lack feeling and depth. As Warren Read notes, data points offer us a "picture posed and taken under the best light with the subject carefully still . . . they capture a moment in time, often when things are at their best and most presentable."[4] This ignorance about our ancestral pasts is not benign; it is actively produced; and, as I will argue, excavating your family's past honestly and critically offers us one way of disrupting the anesthesia of power I spoke of in the last chapter. Remembering the past involves more than excavating names, dates, events, and places. It requires that we sit with the feelings that surface for us when we stumble into the horrors of colonization that are part of our family histories. These are opportunities to make tangible the inhumanity we inherit.

This chapter continues the weighty conversation I began in the last chapter. It invites people with white ancestries—especially those of us with settler colonial pedigrees—to hold space with the discomfort, pain, and messiness of the weight we inherit from our ancestors.[5] I begin with a brief history of genealogy as a social practice. Next, I offer Henry Louis Gates's interview with Ben Affleck as a cautionary tale about the costs and losses sustained by white people's strategic refusal to re-member, and hold space with our forgotten ancestral wounds. Whiteness has a strong gravitational pull on our family pedigrees. It draws our family narratives toward comfort and innocence. It compels us to edit out unsavory ancestors and drop family histories into those glorious colonial master narratives designed to numb us to the violence of colonization. Genealogy does more than excavate lost pedigrees. It can be used medicinally in ways that recognize "the power of history to provide those healing stories that can restore the humanity of the traumatized."[6] Medicinal approaches to genealogy offer us a powerful antidote to ancestral amnesia. I introduce a practice I call "holding space with your ancestors," as a means of affectively engaging parts of our ancestral pasts that we'd rather forget. The principal aim of this chapter, however, is to hold space with my own ancestors. My family lines run through some of the more visible atrocities of American colonization: The Pequot Wars, King Phillip's War, the Wethersfield Witch Panic, and the colonization and ensuing slave trade in New Jersey and lower Manhattan. In particular, I want to hold space with my Morgan and Van Wickle ancestors, who, in 1818, engineered a plan to sell over 137+ free, bonded, and enslaved people of African descent into permanent slavery in the south. My desire to hold space with these ancestors is rooted in a feeling I cannot seem to shake. The wound at the heart of whiteness is generations deep. It is a weight heavy enough to break me, a weight that my ancestors numbed for generations, and a weight I've inherited from them in desensitized forms.

HOW THE GRAVITATIONAL PULL OF WHITENESS SHAPES PEDIGREE

I'm not unfamiliar with the history of European genealogy. The desire to piece back together your family tree is more than existential; it is historically intertwined with wealth preservation and social status. Pedigree documents belonging: it traces family bloodlines in order to record valuable relationships and to bury unsavory ones. Preserving whiteness has a strong influence on most white people's approach to family tree construction. Active ignorance and forgetting work silently in the stories we share about our family heritage. In *Family Trees: A History of Genealogy in America*, François Weil explains how genealogy, as practiced in Europe and the British Isles, was originally the prerogative of kings and princes. The importance of lineage was later recognized by lesser nobles as a way to lay claim to lands and establish political authority. The commercial bourgeois of medieval cities imitated this practice as a way to bolster their family's political standing and identify suitable marriage partners for their children. By the late fifteenth and early sixteenth centuries, Europe experienced a two-century genealogical growth spurt fueled by the nobility's need for pedigrees to establish and defend their social and economic status against those who would challenge their membership in the privileged class. Predictably, settler colonists from these regions brought this status-centered genealogical consciousness to North American along with their appetite for wealth and opportunity.[7]

Genealogy is a promiscuous social practice. Like all history, family history is an act of interpretation. The ancestries we construct are a potent mix of autobiography, pride, patriotism, memory, legend, data, and the historical imagination. Pedigrees are fragile things. Family stories yield easily to the gravitational pull of power and historical amnesia. When tied to social capital, pedigree can be used to bolster social status, preserve wealth across generations, and to find suitable marriage partners. Colonial pedigrees are wielded skillfully to re-inscribe boundaries between pedigreed old money and rootless new money.[8] And, these class divisions were not confined to white families. After emancipation, even "colored aristocracy" drew up family pedigrees to distinguish themselves from less established black families. They claimed prominent African ancestors and notable indigenous and white forbears for the purposes of fortifying their social status.[9]

Pedigree also serves a moral function: it is often used to instill pride in the family name or to shame ill-behaved descendants into living up to ancestral standards of education, faith, and achievement. When tied to nostalgia and patriotism, pedigrees bend to fit comfortably into colonial master narratives populated with freedom-seeking pilgrims, resilient pioneers, and brave patriots. Historical amnesia conveniently brackets the genocide, torture, environmental destruction, looting, and violence fueling these narratives of courage and progress. When energized by the rising science of evolutionary biology in the 1870s, family lineage projects took a sharp eugenic turn. In Francesca Morgan's words, "Late-nineteenth-century genealogists altered their own practices to express more restrictive race and class distinctions.... [G]enealogy came increasingly to accommodate the new science-based racisms—placing 'Anglo-Saxons' above others—that accompanied educated Americans' escalating confidence in heredity," and to explain falsely perceived intellectual and behavioral differences among the races.[10] Hereditary organizations, like the Daughters of the American Revolution (DAR) and the General Society of Mayflower Descendants solidified a national upper class that brought together the capital, power, and resources of "the white West with the white East, and the white North, with the white South."[11] Historically speaking then, pedigree construction has always worked to maintain social prestige, power, and wealth. Achieving these ends requires that family trees to be pruned carefully.

A CAUTIONARY TALE: BEN AFFLECK'S ANESTHETIZED PEDIGREE

The previous chapter drew on Resmaa Menakem's account of *white-body supremacy* to connect the costs of whiteness with the trauma wound at the heart of whiteness. It claimed that white people's choice to live with the dirty pain of ignorance, forgetting, and erasure confines us to living in unsettled bodies. The anesthetized body is an *artificially* settled body, a body that chooses addiction to repeated numbing over the clean pain of wholeness and liberation. The same can be said about the *anesthetized pedigree*.

Genealogy is not immune to the contorting habits of closure and protection. The same forces that disfigure our humanity also distort our ancestral narratives. If there is trauma in our bodies, trauma in our families, and trauma in our communities, then there is a good chance that we will find trauma in our pedigrees. There will be branches of our family tree we don't want to feel. We contort when we unearth evidence that our ancestors, like all people, were complicated and sometimes cruel beings. We choose the dirty pain of avoidance and denial when we prune our family trees to fit comfortably into colonial master narratives. Consider how the histories of violent conquest are overwritten with tales of courageous ancestors leaving their homelands and traveling to new worlds in search of freedom and wealth, and the sacrifices they made to put down roots on colonized soil.[12] Colonial master narratives re-direct our genealogical gaze toward family histories that foreground our ancestors goodness, fortitude, accomplishment, and sacrifice. When told independently of their historical contexts, these narratives embrace a willful ignorance—a strategic refusal to understand the complexity of our ancestral life worlds. And so, I begin with a cautionary tale about the costs of ancestral amnesia and the dangers of the anesthetized pedigree.

In 2015, Henry Louis Gates, Jr. interviewed Ben Affleck for an episode of his popular public television series. During their conversation Gates reveals to Affleck that his third great-grandfather, Benjamin Cole, owned a large cotton farm which the family ran with slave labor. The Hollywood megastar's response to this unwelcome news offers a stunning example of the relationship between white discomfort and the lure of the anesthetized pedigree. Their conversation begins innocently enough. Gates invites Affleck to share anything he might know about his family's deep roots in Savannah, Georgia. Affleck is surprised to hear that he has any southern ancestry at all. So, Gates introduces Affleck to his Cole family ancestors, and later in their conversation, he shares a copy of the slave schedule from the 1850 Census. In his trademark style, Gates invites Affleck to read aloud the line that lists Benjamin Cole as the owner of twenty-five enslaved people. He repeats this fact back to Affleck, taking care to place this unsettling information in its historical context—owning twenty-five enslaved people places the Cole family among the top ten percent of elite southern planters. Affleck's direct ancestors owned people and Gates is curious to hear how Affleck feels about this. A deleted portion of the interview offers some insight.

Affleck: God. It gives me kind of a sagging feeling to see . . . a biological relationship to that. But, you know, there it is, part of our history.
Gates: But consider the irony . . . . Your mom went back fighting for the rights of black people in Mississippi, 100 years later. That's amazing. [13]

Initially, Affleck appears to react to the news with a sense of wonder, but once it sinks in, he insists that their conversation about the Cole family be deleted from the episode. Affleck describes the weight he inherits from Cole "as kind of sagging feeling," but the weight quickly shifts to a guilt-laced fear. In the long run the news unsettles him. It provokes a crisis, a not-so-subtle shift in how he holds the family history in his embodied memory. Affleck could have walked into the uncomfortable truth about his ancestry; he could have held space with his ancestors, and treated the news as an opportunity to feel through the complexities of the Cole family's life in the context of America's plantation economy. He could have asked: *What brought my Cole ancestors to Georgia? Who called that land home before they cleared and farmed it? What are the names of the twenty-five people my ancestors enslaved? Where are their descendants today?* Instead, he chose anesthesia over knowledge, demanding that Gates remove all slavery references from the episode. Perhaps he was worried that this inconvenient truth would tarnish his celebrity status. He later tells reporters, "I didn't want any television show about my family to include a guy who owned slaves. I was embarrassed. The very thought left a bad taste in my mouth."[14]

Affleck's attachment to white comfort has additional costs. As Sara Ahmed observes, the "availability of comfort for some bodies may depend upon the labor of others and the burden of constant concealment."[15] Honoring Affleck's *post-hoc* editing request places Gates's scholarly integrity and PBS's reputation as a source of accurate historical programming at risk. To accommodate Affleck's request, the network has no choice but to postpone the third season of the program.[16] When the Affleck episode airs, historical truth takes a back seat to white comfort. PBS viewers are presented with a sanitized pedigree that echoes colonial master narratives. No slave owners here, just an ancestor interested in Spiritualism and a Revolutionary War veteran.[17] And why should we surprised? Colonization requires that colonizers forget how we traded our humanity for the chance to seek our fortunes. White people have always overwritten our unflattering histories with tales of glory. Isn't that the version of American history most of us were taught?

Affleck's anesthetized pedigree serves as a cautionary tale. It makes visible the connections between white fragility and ancestral amnesia. The good news is that Affleck is not completely numb; he feels something—"a sagging feeling." Weight makes things sag. It makes hearts grow heavy. He eventually regrets his decision. The bad news is that, rather than tasting the bitter legacy of American slavery, he demands a palate cleanser. Shannon Sullivan's account of the inherited habits of whiteness has helped me to understand how the anesthesia Cole needed to run his cotton plantation continues to circulate in Affleck's body. In her chapter, "Demonizing White Ancestors," she describes how good white people's tendency to distance ourselves from our ancestral slave holders works to sever us from unsavory ancestors and questions of accountability. She cautions against this habit.

"If white people no longer distance themselves from white slaveholders by treating them as monsters and themselves as angels, they will be better able to see *how their ancestors' damnable acts live on in their own lives*."[18] Distancing ourselves from unsavory ancestors anesthetizes us to the weight we inherit. It breaks our human connections to our family pasts. "Attempting to distance oneself from white slaveholders, as if they were completely different from white people today, is an attempt to cover over the ways that the lives and habits of contemporary white people and white slaveholders are similar."[19] The anesthesia Cole needed, in order to numb his humanity to the point where purchasing human beings and working them to death made sense, still circulates in Affleck's body. The pull toward comfort is a contemporary expression of the anesthesia Cole required to make his fortune in the cotton market. It's a failure to understand how the Cole family lost their humanity in pursuit of their fortune. It's a refusal to consider the connections between the anesthesia Cole needed to break the human connection between himself and the people he enslaved, and the anesthesia Affleck needs to sever the connection between himself and his slave-owning ancestors. Affleck's entitlement to comfort, then, is doubly numbing: he is numb both to his family's slave-owning past and to the fact that his pull toward comfort shifts the burden of constant concealment onto Professor Gates and the PBS staff.

When robbed of their historical context and complexity, our ancestries become barriers to healing. Covering up the past does not make us whole; it makes us restless and numb. It presses us into becoming the guardians of painful secrets. Secrets, like lies, have their own weight and the weight continues to keep us sick as a nation. There are better ways of engaging the wound at the heart of whiteness. The weighty conversation can lead us down a path toward healing, reconciliation, and collective liberation, but we must have the courage to enter the uncomfortably heavy spaces in our ancestral lines without contorting. We must summon the courage to do genealogy without anesthesia.

GENEALOGY WITHOUT ANESTHESIA

Practicing genealogy without anesthesia provides a deeply personal response to the weighty invitation. The practice asks us to return to the scene of our ancestral crimes with open and curious heart because, in Alice Walker's words, "the world cannot be healed in the abstract. . . . . Healing begins where the wound was made."[20] All healing begins with a diagnosis. We have a diagnosis. There is a wound at the heart of whiteness that we inherit from our ancestors, a wound we continue to self-medicate with our ignorance, forgetting, editing, dissociation, distancing, accumulating, and consuming. When left untreated the pain persists. Untransformed pain is transmitted pain—our own suffering and trauma are blown through other people's bodies. Practicing ancestry without anesthesia is an act of historical and psychological recovery: it's not enough to simply excavate the past; we must also hold space with the feelings that come up for us along the way.

Weil's history does not discuss resistant genealogical practices, and to be fair this is not his project. However, there is an emerging literature which suggests that genealogy can play a strong role in recovering our humanity. Remember: genealogy is a promiscuous social practice; it need not yield to the gravitational pull of whiteness. There are resistant genealogies that engage ancestral pasts in ways that disrupt the anesthesia of power. "Genealogy," as Catherine Nash notes, "has been mobilized in different historical and geographical contexts and by different social groups, and across a spectrum of agendas from naturalizing the elite transfer of power and property to the use of genealogy as a radical recovery of historical knowledge by subordinated groups."[21] Genealogy is not just about pedigree, it can also function as an "archeology of the psyche that will eventually lead to an understanding of the soul wound or historical trauma."[22]

THE MEDICINAL VALUE OF FAMILY GENEALOGY

Aurora Levins Morales's "The Historian as Curandera" offers an inspiring account of history's healing power. Her approach encourages me to consider how genealogy's medicinal power might be used to counter the anesthetized pedigree. Morales's motives are transparent. Her interest in history "lies in its medicinal uses, in the power of history to provide those healing stories that can restore the humanity of the traumatized, and not for any inherent interest in the past for its own sake."[23] The stories we tell about the past are never neutral. "In their writing," Morales explains, "I chose to make myself visible [not only] as a historian with an agenda, but also as a subject of this history and one of the traumatized seeking to recover herself."[24] Her *curandera historian* facilitates the process of unforgetting. She makes absences and omissions visible. She shifts the historical landscape by centering the experiences of those at the margins of history and gives voice to the questions emerging from those locations. She identifies contradictions in fact patterns. She expands her understanding of evidence beyond the written word and attends to the agency of the oppressed. The curandera historian resists simple and ahistorical accounts of people as one-hundred-percent good, evil, complicit, or resistant. People are complex. So, we must tell their stories in a language that acknowledges how ambiguity and contradiction are part and parcel of the fabric of life. She asks readers to resist equating rigor with objectivity and invites us to show ourselves in these stories by talking and writing openly and honestly about the personal and emotional stakes we have in telling them. She encourages us to cross borders and to leave the official texts, disciplines, databases, and locations where we feel most at home. Morales's account inspires me to imagine a parallel archetype, a *curandera genealogist*; that is, the family historian that takes these guiding principles to heart as she pieces together the forgotten worlds her ancestors once inhabited and uses them in the service of broader community healing projects.

The genealogist's healing touch is strongly felt in Joy DeGruy's *Post-Traumatic Slave Syndrome: America's Legacy of Enduring Injury and Healing*. Her book is not specifically about genealogy, but her insights resonate deeply with the medicinal family histories I'm after here. DeGruy offers a clear appreciation of the knowledge to be gained from naming and feeling the pain black people inherit from the traumas of slavery and colonization. She focuses on the ways the descendants of enslaved Africans continue to "bear the burden of [their] ancestry, to some degree," and how the legacy of slavery and anti-black violence "remains etched into [their] souls."[25] She unpacks the psychological damage that holding secrets does to their collective humanity and, following James Baldwin, recognizes how knowing your history (including your family history) is essential to psychological, emotional, and physical well-being. Her work attends carefully to "how children of the African diaspora" can heal from the multi-generational trauma carried forward from the trafficking, torture, and enslavement of black bodies into the present. DeGruy extends her own version of the weighty invitation by asking her readers to consider how each of them carries these ancestral wounds within them. In her words, the cycles of oppression that the wounds of colonization set in motion

> leave scars on the victims and victors alike, scars that embed themselves in our collective psyches and are passed down through generations, robbing us of our humanity . . . .[C]laiming our humanity will require much work from all of us. Those who have been the victims of years, decades, and centuries of oppression must heal from injuries received first-hand, as well as those passed down through the ages. Those who have been the perpetrators of these unspeakable crimes, and those who continue to benefit from those crimes, have to honestly confront their deeds and heal from the psychic wounds that come with being the cause and beneficiaries of such great pain and suffering.[26]

What's important about this passage is how DeGruy ties the restoration of our *common* humanity to our *collective* healing. The words "recovery" and "restoration" are rich with possibility in both genealogical and medicinal contexts. Recovery refers to the process of reclaiming possession or control of something that has been lost, forgotten, erased, or stolen. Restoration is an act of repairing, fixing, mending, and revitalizing—a way to nurture back to life what has been damaged. Healing may begin where the wound was made, but our *collective* recovery cannot happen if the descendants of the colonized work steadfastly toward their wholeness, while the descendants of the colonizers remain comfortably indifferent to the suffering our ancestors caused and sustained and the scars that we inherit from them.[27] People of color have repeatedly invited white people to engage our historical and ancestral pasts honestly with attention to the ways colonization has eroded our humanity. Sadly, these patient requests remain buried in the bottomless stack of unopened invitations to the weighty conversation.

I'm trying to get in touch with the scars in my own being as I sift through these invitations. Since the 2016 election I've had a bone-deep feeling that coincides historically with shameless cruelty of our times. In the same breath I say to myself—*This is not who we are. Wait, this is who we've always been, white people have just been anesthetized to most of the violence behind nation building.* The visible rise of white supremacy in our nation provides us with the occasion to reckon with the residual collective historical trauma we all carry in our bodies. Serena Jones captures this persistent feeling.

> [O]ne of the characteristics of trauma is the deep human desire to repress it and to not deal with the story of the harms that have happened. But the truth of the matter is . . . that the harm haunts you, haunts your dreams as an individual, haunts your collective unconscious as a society, until you tell the story, until you face the truth of the horrors that have happened. And I think what is happening in our nation today is, all of the harms of the past have come up to claim us, all at once, and they're not going to let us go until we [reckon] with them.[28]

The connection between recovering our historical/ancestral past and recovering our humanity is tangible. Marginalized communities are more attentive to the shapes these haunting harms take inour being. They are more likely to contextualize their family histories in relation to power frameworks. The weight of the past is solidly present in their family narratives from the beginning and is treated as a source of knowledge. In West African traditions, the act of recovering the past is captured visually in the Sankofa adinkra, the symbol of a highly stylized bird whose head turns backward toward the past, while its feet face forward.[29] She carries a precious egg in her mouth. In the Twi language of Ghana, the word "Sankofa" translates literally into "it is not taboo to fetch what is at risk of being left behind," and figuratively as "go back and get it." The symbol is popular among African American historians and genealogists.

This is not my heritage to claim, but I'm inspired by the direct simplicity with which the Sankofa communicates African American people's focused determination to actively take back what has been lost, to learn from the past, and to bring forward from it what is good.[30] This humility and perseverance is absent in most white people's genealogy projects. Few consider Morales's wise counsel about the importance of making absences and omissions (like race) visible, leaving official texts, centering marginalized voices, embracing contradictions, and resisting oversimplified accounts of our ancestor's moral character. Instead, we prioritize filling in the empty branches on our family trees over fleshing out the communities that nourished those trees. As Christine Sleeter observes, "White genealogists tracing individual ancestors, used the past only as a background context in which to locate their ancestors within a traditional narrative that minimizes racism. Black genealogists linked their family's story with a larger narrative of navigating and challenging racial oppression."[31] Something must shift. What if we approached genealogy medicinally, in ways that make the felt legacy of whiteness tangible in our bodies? What if white people became curious about what it took for our ancestors to become white? What if we considered how we inherit the habits that maintain our whiteness? What if we acknowledged the ways our attachments to the anesthesia of power have prevented us from accessing the fully raw account of our heritage? What if we treated genealogy as a healing practice that puts us in touch with the slow erosion of our ancestors' humanity? If Ben Affleck's ancestral amnesia offers a cautionary tale, then medicinal genealogies offer a hopeful antidote.

MEDICINAL WHITE GENEALOGIES

I finished the genealogy for my father's maternal line in time for the Christmas holiday and sent copies of the book to my relatives. They enjoyed learning about the family history, but when they read about the 1818 Van Wickle and Morgan slave scandal, they got quiet. *Why do you have to make our family tree so heavy?* I wanted to give voice to the forgotten and unfelt parts of our lineage, to shine light on the dark corners of our pedigree that were hiding in plain view. I was so focused on excavating the story that I'd completely lost track of its contorting power—it disrupted our family narrative. Some people were not happy about this.

Genealogy has the power to make the historical personal. There is an affective difference between knowing generally about slavery, the genocide of indigenous peoples, and racialized violence, and knowing the names, locations, and details connecting your ancestors to these horrifying projects. The weight we inherit as descendants feels heavier than the weight we take on as nonfamily historians or spectators. A handful of white people know this in our hearts. A few white anti-racist activists, community leaders, and critical genealogists have opened the weighty invitation and committed themselves to holding space with their ancestors long enough to feel the inconvenient truths resting among the branches of their family trees.[32] I've come to think of these undertakings as *medicinal white genealogies*. The medicinal value of genealogy lies in its courage to hold the weight that reaches up to claim you. Healing requires more than just excavating what feels weighty; it asks us to hold space with what we discover long enough to feel what has been lost, to feel what it has cost us. White medicinal genealogies are sparked by crisis and curiosity. I'm not the first white person to feel my people's ancestral weight reach up, tap me on the shoulder, and motion to me to return to those places my ancestors inhabited, to retrieve what has been forgotten, and bring forth what is good. Sometimes our ancestry catapults us unexpectedly into worlds that don't fit comfortably into the stories we inherit. The weight feels crushing at first.

Warren Read felt the weight when he plugged his mother's maiden name "Dondino," and "Minnesota" into a search engine and read something about a rape and the lynching of three black circus workers in Duluth, Minnesota. An odd feeling crept through his body. He clicked on the link and began reading a newspaper article about his great-grandfather's role in the 1920 lynching of Elmer Jackson, Elias Clayton, and Isaac McGhie. His gut knotted. His hands began to shake. He wondered if the deep-seated emotional fears that prompted Louis Dondino to incite the riot that led to a triple lynching on that warm evening of June 15 were still with him. "It's horrifying to own," he says, "but the spores of my forefathers are in the soil that feeds me, like a dormant fungus lying in wait, and they keep appearing, breaking through in spite of what my heart and my memory are telling me."[33] Read's book, *The Lyncher in Me* chronicles his search for redemption in the face of his family history. He researches Duluth history, the Dondino family, and the events leading up to that muggy summer evening. One day he stumbles across a news story about a group of Duluth citizens working to build a memorial at the site of the tragedy. He contacts them. It turns out they are looking for information about his family. They invite Read to deliver the keynote speech at the memorial dedication. He describes the feelings that come up for him as he stands before the crowd on the day of the ceremony:

> And, I embraced for the first time, the significance of this spot, my place on this hallowed ground. My heart broke. In front of me I saw the men, those helpless boys kicked, beaten and dragged unmercifully. . . . And I felt the pull—from

eighty-three years away. I felt the powerful pull of the mob, and its ugliness was overwhelming.

. . . And , I pictured my great-grandfather in my place gazing at the jail just as I was, only sneering, shouting encouragement . . . the images were unrelenting.[34]

It feels unsteady, treading across the ground of an old wound decades after the injury. When we shake our family trees we can't avoid shaking the branches entangled in adjacent family trees. Read reconstructs his great-grandfather's life in Duluth, and when the pieces fall into place, he reconstructs the life of Elmer Jackson, the only lynching victim to leave a paper trail leading to family origins in Pennytown, a freedman's settlement Saline County, Missouri. He returns to the Jackson family home sites in Topeka where Elmer was raised, and to the Pennytown settlement where Elmer spent his childhood. He is invited to the Pennytown annual reunion at the Freewill Baptist Church. He addresses the congregation. He makes copies of archival photos of the lost ancestors of some Pennytown residents and gives them to descendants. A decade later, he and Virginia Huston (a cousin of Elmer Jackson) meet in Montgomery, Alabama and walk together through the National Memorial for Peace and Justice.

Serene Jones felt the weight during a candidate's job talk for a position in African American religious thought at Yale. A slide of the 1911 double lynching of Mary Nelson and her son L. D., in Okemah, Oklahoma, appeared as part of the candidate's talk. She felt her breath leave her body when she heard the word "Okemah." Her grandfather grew up in Okemah. She did the math. She connected the dots. At once the past came up to claim her and the unforgetting began. There was more than a good chance that members of the Jones family witnessed this double execution. Her grandfather would have been six years old at the time. How did the horrors of that afternoon sediment themselves into her family line? How did they shape the collective body of Okemah? How did the community tolerance for vigilante justice become high enough to permit a few men to lynch a mother and her son in broad daylight in the first place? Jones remarks:

> Cutting, whipping, raping, torturing, beating, humiliating, shaming, ignoring, killing, chaining, imprisoning, and violating people . . . are skills that take practice and constant training. White people need to own the fact that for hundreds of years this is what they have been trained to do. . . .White families who owned enslaved Africans or who participated in their enslavement had to master the skill of not seeing them as human beings but animals. They had to convince not just their minds, but their bodies and their souls that this was the case. . . .They had to fight off any guilt that might linger in them about the moral outrage of slavery. . . .They had to master the embodiment of cruelty.[35]

What remnants of her ancestors' high tolerance for violence remain in her body? Human beings are not naturally cruel. We are wired for connection. So, what has to happen to a person, a family, or a community to make them fear black, indigenous, or Mexican Oklahomans to the point where their public execution becomes a spectator sport?

Katrina Browne felt the weight when she read her grandmother's DeWolf family history and came across the line: "I haven't stomach enough to describe the ensuing slave trade."[36] Before the words settled, she realized that on some level she already knew this but had somehow buried it along the way. The DeWolf family were known as "The Great Ones," a prominent family who, for generations, lived and made their fortunes in Bristol, Rhode Island. Bristol was a major shipping port and the DeWolfs were the largest slave-trading family in U.S. history. How was such legacy forgotten? At what point did the DeWolf descendants become desensitized to the weight? We release the weight when it is too traumatic to bear, but it always leaves the imprint of its origins. For Browne, the traces of the trade were tucked quietly into the African names of the family nursery rhymes she learned as a child. They peered attentively through the eyes of the embroidered black faces populating the family's heirloom needlework. They waited patiently to be rediscovered between the letters of the Africans names on headstones in the family cemetery. The bread-crumb trail leading back to the wound was there all along, but Browne lacked the sensitivity to feel it. She later confesses that it never occurred to her to ask how the DeWolf family became so established in the first place.

In December 2000, Browne sent a weighty invitation to her extended family, asking them to join her in re-tracing the route of triangle trade for her documentary film project *Traces of the Trade: A Story from the Deep North*. This was not an invitation to a family reunion. It was an invitation to take up the weight of the immense suffering caused by their DeWolf ancestors and to embark on a collective healing project, a journey that took them to the lived sites of historical trauma in Bristol, Cuba, and along the coast of Africa. Remarking on the stubborn persistence of racial inequality Brown tells her family that she wants to "begin with our family and try to better understand the whole can of worms: privilege, shelteredness, protective feelings of guilt, unproductive feelings of guilt, fear, etc."[37] This is not a general white guilt; it's a unique texture of family guilt born from being related to Mark Anthony DeWolf, who began the trade. She asks a series of heavy questions. "How does this two-hundred-year-old story connect to who I am today? How does it shape my conscious and unconscious sense of myself? I've started to research the past so that I might find traces of it in the present."[38] The family discusses what they must do to repair the enormous harms perpetrated by their ancestors. Keilia DePoorter shares this: "Talking about history, I feel the heaviness pulling generations between slave trade business and now. And, it just feels like a heavy load or repression. What kind of crazy partnership do we have to silence?[39] Thomas DeWolf describes the anesthesia that kept him from feeling this partnership. The "story of an enslaved South and a free North is willful and constructed amnesia: whites, who a few generations removed, had no recollectionor knowledge of northern slavery, reasoned that blacks were disproportionately poor and illiterate due to innate inferiority."[40] At the end of the film, the group returns to Bristol, Rhode Island, where Browne gives a guest sermon at the Episcopal church. She begins,

> It seems, that as white people, we have only two choices. We can listen to African Americans' calls to deal with the history, which can make us feel guilty and bad about ourselves, or shut it all out so we don't have to feel bad. As we bring attention to the question of what will bring wholeness to people of African descent, we can also ask what will create wholeness for us a people of European descent. What are the scars and legacies that we hold? They are different, but they are there.[41]

Katrina Browne's experience resonates deeply with my own. On some level, I was already aware of my family's deep colonial roots in North America, but I'd somehow suppressed them. As a young adult, I remember visiting the open archives in the Metropolitan Museum of Art in New York City and responding indifferently to the magnificent display of eighteenth-century household objects. They did not spark the historical wonder they did in most visitors. They were unremarkable. I grew up seeing eighteenth-century pewter tankards and plates, portraits, and furniture in my grandparent's house. Some of the furniture in my childhood home was over two-hundred years old. Traces of ancestral wealth. How were my ancestors able to afford these luxuries? There must be a story behind the wealth, but I didn't suspect that trafficking black bodies would be part of my family's story. My roots are solidly northern, I assured myself; they extend deeply into the New Jersey clay.

HOLDING SPACE WITH OUR ANCESTORS

We cannot hold space with our ancestors if we allow fear and shame to prune our family trees into pleasing topiaries designed to comfort and flatter us. Warren Read, Serene Jones, Katrina Browne, and many of the DeWolf family descendants held space with their ancestors in ways that caused the anesthesia to lift. There is an implicit request in the act of "holding space" for someone. The phrase frequently appears in the literature on addiction, trauma, and recovery. Holding space with someone requires a focused presence of mind and being. We slow down. We sit. We keep company. We listen without judgment. We hear. We hold. We process. We connect the dots and yes, sometimes we crumble.

The request to hold space with our ancestors is a plea to take up the weighty invitation by settling in with what unsettles us. The invitation extends to genealogical projects George Yancy's request that white people "tarry with the space of an existential burden, the burden of having to claim one's humanity."[42] Tarrying exposes white people to the idea that we *don't know who [we] are*.[43] Holding space with our ancestors exposes white people to the idea that *we don't know from whom we came*, and so, are insensitive to the wounds we inherit from our ancestors.[44] The act of holding space is a weight-bearing gesture. It foregrounds the role that trauma plays in shaping the anesthetized pedigree. Familiar narratives rupture; and, we find ourselves straddling the stories we inherit and the stories that reach up to claim us. When our family stories are in tension with one another, the wound is poked. The shock pulls us from our heads into our hearts and bodies. Gloria Anzaldúa describes the shock as *el arrebato* (an outburst or a soul-stirring experience) that pulls you from the safety of familiar terrain and into the cyclone of liminal spaces. In her words:

> [Each] *arrebatada* (snatching) turns your world upside down and cracks the walls of your reality, resulting in a great sense of loss, grief, and emptiness.... You are no longer who you used to be.... With each *arrebatamiento* you suffer "un susto," a shock that knocks one of your souls out of your body, causing estrangement. With the loss of the familiar and the unknown ahead, you struggle to regain your balance, reintegrate yourself, and repair the damage.[45]

Serene Jones, Warren Read, and Katrina Browne's genealogical discoveries pull them from the safety and familiarity of their official family histories. The crisis here is unquestionably existential, but I don't want to ignore the fact that there are traces of historical trauma present. The process of surrendering your humanity in the name of belonging, or accumulating wealth, is nothing short of traumatizing. Medicinal white genealogies touch that trauma. When our ancestral pasts come up to claim us we are thrown suddenly into spaces where our stories lose their narrative grip. A stormy breeze blows through the limbs of our family trees and shakes loose hidden rotten fruit.

Medicinal genealogies invite us into liminal spaces. They foment a crackling and crumbling that initially produces anxiety, fear, and panic, but this should not give us a reason to avoid these terrains. As James Baldwin notes, "accepting the past—one's history—is not the same as drowning in it; it is learning how to use it. An invented past can never be used; it cracks and crumbles under the pressure of life like clay in a season of drought."[46] It begins with an urgent tug. We may feel pulled to repair our legacies by restoring them *exactly* to the way they were before we felt the rupture. I'm working with a specific understanding of crisis and repair here, one that is transformative rather than restorative. I'm not interested in restoring the comfort of the anesthetized pedigree I've inherited. I yearn for a shift in being, not another dose of anesthesia. Feeling what I'd rather not feel has a transformative effect. I want to know what it takes to break the anesthesia? What does it take for me to finally fall apart? What pulls me to seek out and gather with others who share the weight, and to mourn what we have collectively lost?

Holding space with our ancestors requires resilience. It invites us to suspend our judgment about the kinds of people our ancestors were and worlds they inhabited. Suspending judgment is an important feature of holding space. Judgment pulls us back into the safety of our heads. When we rush to pass judgment about what our ancestors did, we can't fully feel the complexity of their worlds. When we hold space with our ancestors we slow down long enough to become sensitive to the times and spaces they inhabited, and the people with whom they shared those spaces. Warren Read's description of his experience at the Duluth memorial comes to mind. He stands on sacred ground and his ancestral past comes up to engage him. He remains still long enough to absorb and wonder about the complicated worlds his ancestors animated on that fateful day, and what brought them to that place.

Suspending judgment is not the same as forgiveness. There is a difference between deciding that our ancestors were moral monsters whose evil doings are artifacts of a different time, and pardoning them for those deeds. Suspending judgment is not absolution. It does not mean that our ancestors are beyond judgment; it just means that judgment is not the first order of business. The rush to judgment is a weight shifting move. It returns the burden to its origins in hopes of releasing descendants from the weight of our inheritance. Judgments function as end points, as a verdict aimed at laying matters to rest. And, I assure you these matters are alive and afoot. In her conversation with Ta-Nehisi Coates, Krista Tippett asks: "[You say that] in America it is traditional to destroy the black body. It is heritage. And, you are right. And, I carry that in my body, right? In my white body, I carry that cruelty and that violence . . . what do I do with the legacy of my whiteness?"[47]

When we hold space with our ancestors we attend to the ways our ancestor's cruel deeds remain in us.

It's not possible to hold space with our ancestors in solitude. Holding space is a collective endeavor. When we hold space with our ancestors, we hold space with their communities, which means that we are holding space with all the descendants of those communities. Some white medicinal genealogies have done this. Edward Ball pushed the weight of his pedigree into the service of collective healing when he made public the story of how his Ball ancestors operated a dynasty of twenty-five rice plantations for six generations. His book, *Slaves in the Family*, tells that story openly and, at first, without apology, as a means of coming to terms with a family past that his father (willfully?) did not know much about. He interviews Ball family elders and asks them for the names of any black people their extended families knew growing up. He combs through ten thousand pages of archived family documents. He locates and contacts descendants of the people his family enslaved. Some respond and others don't. He attends black genealogy conferences and meets people who have traced their ancestry to the Ball family plantations. He meets up with the descendants of those people his Ball ancestors enslaved. He is invited to their homes. They share meals. They walk together into the pain of their shared family histories as they sift through boxes of Ball family documents. They come to understand that their ability to recover their shared past lies collectively in their hands. They are the keepers of one another's deep ancestral selves. Eventually, they visit the remaining Ball family plantation sites together. As Ball remarks: "The plantation heritage was not 'ours,' like a piece of family property, and not 'theirs,' belonging to black families, but a shared history. The progeny of slaves and slave owners are forever linked. We have been in each other's lives. We have been in each other's dreams. We have been in each other's beds. . . . I thought we should meet, share our recollections, feelings, and dreams and make the story whole."[48] Broadening the genealogical gaze is what moves Ball to work collectively with the Gadsden, Harleston, Heyward, Martin, Lucas, and Poyas families, so the healing can begin.

My own pedigree is heavy. Holding its weight has been painful, humbling, and yet strangely settling. It has forced me to sit uncomfortably with the knowledge that my family tree—my trophy pedigree as someone once called it—was planted in indigenous soil and nourished with indigenous and African blood. I'm descended from a tight cluster of Dutch, English, Scottish, and Welsh settlers, who left the Dutch colony of New Netherland for the fertile soil and timbered lands of East Jersey in the mid-seventeenth century. The Hendrickson, Johnstone, Morgan, Peacock, Schenck, Van Dorn, Van Kouwenhoven, Van Mater, and Van Wickle families were among the first nonindigenous people to set foot on the land the Leni Lenape people called home for thousands of years. My ancestors came to make money and genocide, slave labor, theft of indigenous lands, deforestation, and aggressive agricultural and mining practices were an essential part of that equation. Viewing my family's ancestral worlds through the lens of medicinal genealogy has broken me, but that's the point. Telling the truth about my ancestry breaks what Sara Ahmed calls "the happiness seal": "the past can be what is sealed. When the seal has been broken, the pain floods in."[49] The trick is to "make that pain sacred, so that the rest of your life can be transformed by it."[50] The stories I've inherited crack and crumble and I sift through the dust. I want to excavate what has been lost and to use it in the service of collective growth and transformation.[51] So, I return to New Jersey, the land where the wound was made.

SLAVERY IN THE PROVINCE OF NEW JERSEY

Slavery in New Jersey was especially harsh and slow to end. For most people it is a forgotten history. New Jersey was a "slave state" from its inception. The Dutch West Indian Company began shipping enslaved African people to their North American colonies in about 1625. The English assumed control of the colony in 1664, changing the name from New Amsterdam to New York. They followed the Dutch economic model, which encouraged African slavery as a route to opening up the territory that would become New Jersey to further settlement and trade. The original proprietors offered sixty acres of land for every enslaved person brought into the western settlements. The Monmouth Patent (1665), which includes the land my Morgan ancestors settled, required colonizers to maintain "an able bodied Man servant or two such weaker Servants," and granted additional land to masters with more servants.[52] By 1680, enslaved Africans counted for twelve percent of the East Jersey population.[53] In 1702, when New Jersey became a crown colony, Queen Anne instructed Lord Cornbury, the first royal governor, to report on "the present number of . . . Masters and Servants, free and unfree, and of the slaves in our said Province." The governor was told, moreover, to be prompt in paying the Royal African Company for their human merchandise in order that the province "may have a constant and sufficient supply of Merchantable Negroes, at moderate rates."[54] The instructions became policy, and the trafficking of enslaved Africans became such an essential part of the area's economy that the Provincial Council struck down a 1744 proposed tariff on their importation. High manumission taxes were imposed to discourage emancipation. The Monmouth Patent lands are directly south of Perth Amboy, the region's main shipping port. From the early 1700s through 1818, thousands of African and African-descended people worked and were trafficked through, Perth Amboy. My father's maternal line took root in this avaricious and cruel colony.

HOLDING SPACE WITH MY MORGAN AND VAN WICKLE ANCESTORS

The Morgan family burial ground is all that remains of the original 600+ acres of land and marsh that was Charles Morgan's (1648--1720) original allotment along the Raritan Bay. My partner, my father, and I visit the cemetery on a muggy June afternoon with a local historian. The grounds are shady, cool, and a bit overgrown. If you stand in the right place by the cemetery fence line you can see Perth Amboy, Staten Island, the lower tip of Manhattan, and Long Island. The British occupied Perth Amboy during the American Revolution. My fifth great-grandfather, Captain James Morgan, Sr. (1734–1784) almost certainly sat near this spot on the days leading up to the Battle of Monmouth (1778). From here he penned six reconnaissance letters, sending them by courier, to General George Washington, alerting him to British naval traffic in the Lower Bay.

We stood quietly listening to the wind blow through the trees until our guide spoke. "The Morgan family had their hands on everything that moved, and what didn't move, they already owned." They were entrepreneurs who got in on the ground floor of the emerging colonial economy. Sherriff Charles Morgan I (?–1668) left Newport, England, to settle at Gravesend, New Amsterdam, a Dutch colony established at the Canarsie peoples' village of Massabraken. In 1644, he served as a cadet in the West India Company in Jamaica. In December 1663, a group of English Puritans received permission from Governor Stuyvesant to settle the land across the Raritan Bay. Twenty men were sent to "purchase" land from the sachem Poppemora and his people. The Sheriff's son, Charles Morgan II (1648–1720) was among them. On a deed dated May 7, 1710, a man named Richard Townley transferred a big part of what is now Morgan, New Jersey, to my sixth great-grandfather Charles Morgan III (1683–1750). This is the land upon which the Morgans built their homes and their fortunes. That's the story my people tell, and when they do, they are sure to highlight the Morgan's patriotism during the American Revolution and their pottery empire. The family operated a pottery near Old Bridge, which the British destroyed in a 1779 raid. Two years earlier, the British captured Maj. Gen. James Morgan, Jr. and he suffered a year-long imprisonment, under conditions of near-death privation, in the old

MY MORGAN AND VAN WICKLE ANCESTORS
AND THE 1818 NEW JERSEY SLAVE SCANDAL

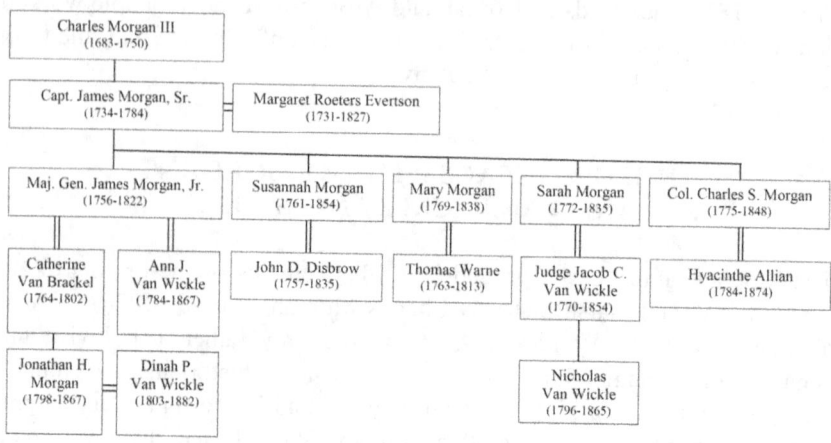

Figure 5.1   Family Tree. The Morgan and Van Wickle families intermarried frequently concentrating their wealth from both family pottery businesses. Judge Jacob C. Van Wickle forged the consent forms permitting his network to illegally move free and enslaved people of African descendent from New Jersey to his brother-in-law Col. Charles S. Morgan's *Morganza* plantation in Pointe Coupée, Louisiana. The judge's son Nicholas acted as their middleman. John D. Disbrow fought with Maj. Gen. James Morgan, Jr. in the Battle of Monmouth and later married Susannah, the general's sister. He used his sloop—the Thorne—to help his brother-in-law Col. Morgan transport enslaved people from New Jersey to Louisiana. A Disbrow family diary notes that Jonathan H. Morgan, was "involved in the trade." After the death of his first wife Catherine, Maj. Gen. James Morgan, Jr. married Ann J. Van Wickle, who was Judge Van Wickle's niece. The judge himself had married the Maj. General's sister Sarah thirteen years earlier. In 1822 Jonathan H. Morgan, married his step-mother's youngest sister Dinah. Van Wickle. Mary Morgan married Thomas Warne whose family also successfully manufactured stoneware in the region. Created by the author.

Sugar House in lower Manhattan. He later served a term in the 12th U.S. Congress (1811–1813) as a Federalist. That's the story my people like to tell (figure 5.1).

We quickly locate the graves of Maj. Gen. James Morgan, Jr. (1756–1822) and his second wife Ann J. Van Wickle (1784-1869). His parents, Captain James Morgan, Sr. (1734–1784) and Margaret Roeters Evertson (1731–1827), are interned nearby. The tiny plastic American flag that was pushed into the Amboy clay near his grave by the Sons of the American Revolution has already faded. The guide redirects our attention to a new cyclone fence surrounding the private burial ground and mumbles something about a bad decision. He points to three small white granite stones, now overgrown with poison ivy and moss, and mentions that an old oak tree was blown over during the last big storm. The cemetery keepers discussed whether to include the three monuments within the cemetery fence line when they rebuilt the barrier. He says something about these being the graves of three Morgan slaves. I crawl through the laurel to read the inscriptions on the stones. They are illegible. I run my fingers across them, hoping to feel their names into being, but I'm unable give them voice.

Major General James Morgan, Jr. was extremely wealthy and his will was extensive. It contains a room-by-room description of the family's worldly goods, most of which were luxuries at the time. It also mentions "an old Negro slave named Kate, no value." And a "Negro slave for life, named Hannah, $75." Under the heading, "In front of the Barn" is an additional listing for "one black man, a slave for life named Ben, $175." Three names and three stones, but there is no way of knowing whether they mark Kate, Hannah and Ben's final resting places. For the purposes of our guide's story, however, all that matters is that some of the descendants *believed* these were slave graves and *decided* to fence them out. They don't belong. They are not family. The anesthesia is with them. If the three white stones truly mark the graves of Kate, Hannah, and Ben, then this would be unusual. In Monmouth (and Middlesex) County, slaves who died prior to receiving their freedom were "often buried in backyards in unmarked graves."[55] I stare down at the Amboy clay sticking to my shoes and wonder—Slaves were valuable, clay was valuable. It turns out that there is a connection. The history of American colonial stoneware is tightly intertwined with the history of the New York and New Jersey slave trade.

The story of the Morgan Pottery empire begins with the rich clay beds along the Cheesequake Creek that were part of Charles Morgan's original 1710 deed. Twenty years after Charles Morgan III died, his son, Captain James Morgan, Sr. established the Morgan Pottery, which he managed from 1775 to 1784. Like his father, James was more businessman than potter. He increased the family fortune by selling clay, finding skilled potters to make stoneware, and transporting the finished pieces to regional markets. Cheesequake clay was valuable. For years the phrase "clay as good as Morgan's" described all high-quality stoneware clay. The Morgans shipped their raw clay to potteries from Maine to Georgia, and as far away as western New York and Canada.[56] My fourth great-grandfather, Maj. Gen. James Morgan, Jr., managed the pottery from the time of his father's death until about 1801, but he never really left the stoneware business. Later, with Jacob C. Van Wickle and Branch Green, he established the James Morgan and Company stoneware manufacturing plant in Old Bridge, New Jersey. He also purchased the Warne & Letts pottery, which he managed from about 1815 until his death in 1822; and, here's where things get interesting.

The Morgan family operated many successful stoneware businesses for decades, but I doubt any of them knew how to throw, glaze, and fire a pot (figures 5.2 and 5.3). The vessels produced at the Morgan Pottery were made by potters trained in the German tradition of wheel-thrown gray-bodied salt-glazed stoneware accented with deep cobalt-blue designs. Morgan stoneware was frequently decorated with cobalt-blue floral motifs, but the signature design most associated with Morgan stoneware is the so-called "watch spring," a thin linear cobalt-blue double-spiral design. This description always seemed anachronistic to me. Why would Morgan potters choose something that looked like a watchspring for their signature stoneware vessels?

The answer is, they wouldn't . . . unless they were West African.

To European eyes the double-spiral brings to mind a clock mainspring. To African eyes, it is recognizable as the Ghanaian Akan *Dwennimmen* adinkra, a ram's horn motif, symbolizing strength and humbleness. We know that free and enslaved African (and African-descended) potters and German potters worked alongside one another in New York. Pottery shards with African-influenced designs have been discovered in lower Manhattan construction sites, including the World Trade Center, Wall Street, the Financial District, and the African Burial Ground. Some contain traces of the watch-spring motif. The story of enslaved pottery artisans, however, would have been lost had it not been for the descendants of John D. Disbrow, who shared their grandfather's genealogical research online. Drawing on these resources, Pearl Duncan offers convincing evidence for the link between the illegal slave trade and the stoneware industry.[57] In a series of articles for *ArtDaily*, she explains how skilled potters were transported across state lines from one stoneware kiln to another. According to Duncan:

> [I]t was not only the skilled workers such as the German owners and employees who moved from one place to place, but the skilled enslaved and free African-American artisans were also transported. Illegal, pirated transportation of enslaved people had always occurred, but by 1818, the states attempted to restrain wealthy merchants from engaging in this trade. Capt. James Morgan, Sr. and his extended family of pottery entrepreneurs participated in the illegal trade of skilled enslaved artisans."[58]

Transporting skilled potters from one kiln to the next was not noteworthy in the late eighteenth and early nineteenth centuries. That changed when New Jersey passed *The Act for the Gradual Abolition of Slavery* in 1804, along with additional laws regulating the movement, leasing, and sale of enslaved people.[59] What was once business as usual had suddenly become a criminal offense. My ancestors would exploit two legal loopholes to continue their business dealings. The first permitted slave owners to extend the period of bondage for

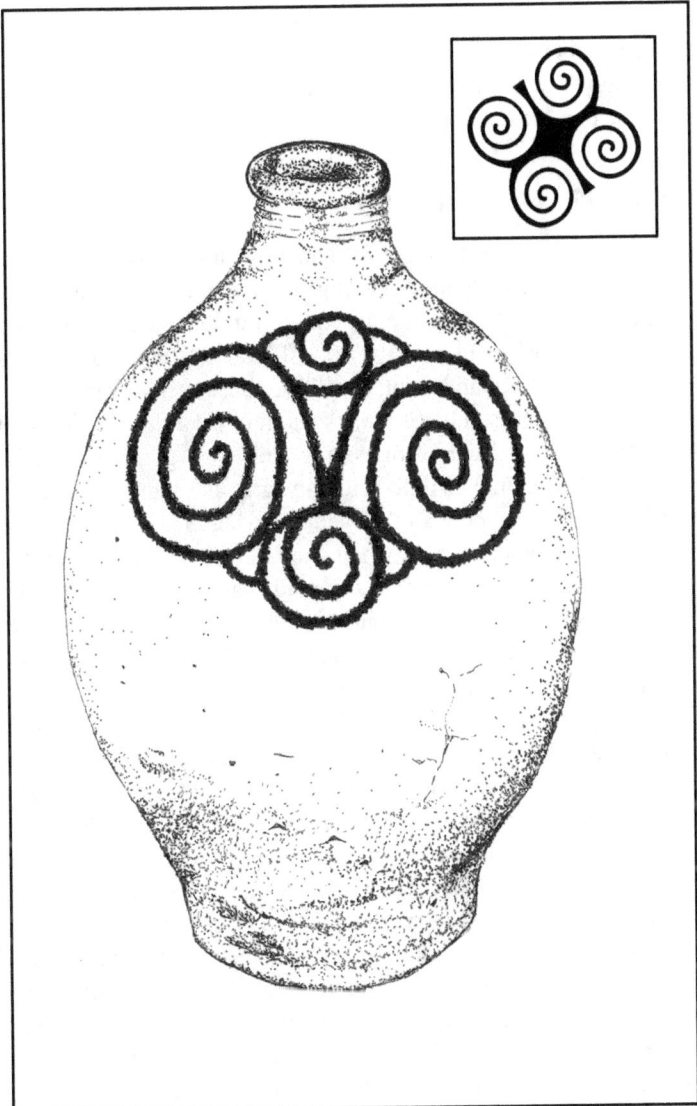

Figure 5.2 Stoneware Pot and Figure 5.3 Adinkra Symbol Comparison. Above: Two-gallon ovoid stoneware jar with vibrant cobalt-colored "watch-spring" design, late eighteenth century, attributed to Capt. James Morgan Pottery, Cheesequake, New Jersey. Insert: An Akan Dwennimmen adinkra, a ram's horn motif, symbolizing strength and humbleness. Pearl Duncan's research offers convincing evidence of the connections between the slave trade and the stoneware industry in New York and New Jersey. Her comparison between the signature Morgan pottery "watch-spring" design, and the adinkra strongly suggests that Morgan used enslaved and free African labor at his pottery, and that potters African-influenced designs had a strong influence on early American decorative ceramic arts. Illustrations by Halie Hugenberg.

enslaved children if the mother was re-sold to a new owner. The second held that enslaved people would remain in bondage if they consented to be moved or sold out of state to serve another owner. The repeated abuse of these loopholes soon gave rise to a local scandal.

The Van Wickle and Morgan Slave Scandal (1818)

The pastel portraits of Jonathan H. Morgan and Dinah Van Wickle hung over the bookcases in my grandparent's living room when I was a child. I remember asking about them. "Those are my great grandparents," my grandmother told me, "Jonathan Morgan was the son of Major General James Morgan, who fought in the American Revolution." Maybe she knew more. My grandmother was born and raised fifteen miles south of the original Morgan family plantation. Perhaps she heard stories from her own grandmother, Ida Van Wickle Morgan, who moved into with my grandmother's family after her own husband died. The portraits moved with her. I remember feeling the pride in my grandmother's voice when she talked about the portraits. I also recall the look on her face the day she read that the Old Morgan Inn (est. 1703) in South Amboy caught fire and would be demolished. The last public artifact of the Morgan plantation was gone. I didn't give the Morgans another thought until my father handed me those boxes.

The Morgan and Van Wickle families were intimately connected. They did business together, socialized frequently, and intermarried with astounding regularity. The plot to traffic free and enslaved "black and colored people" from New Jersey into southern markets centered on two men: Judge Jacob C. Van Wickle (1770–1854) and his brother-in-law "Colonel" Charles Morgan (1775–1848).[60] In about 1800, Charles left his native New Jersey to become a land surveyor in Louisiana. He settled in Point Coupée Parish, at the bend of the Mississippi River, where he built *Morganza,* his new sugar and cotton plantation. Louisiana was under Spanish rule and it may have been challenging for the average New Jersey resident to pick up and move into the Mississippi Valley. His Morgan pedigree may have afforded him a level of protection unavailable to other planters.[61] He began planting. After the Louisiana Purchase, he was appointed Sheriff and made a member of the Louisiana Legislature. Five years later he owned twenty-eight enslaved people and his labor needs were rapidly increasing. Sometime in January 1818, with the astounding sum of $45,000 in his pocket, Col. Morgan made plans to travel to Virginia and purchase more enslaved people for his plantation. But first, he decided to visit his family in South Amboy, where he discovered that "New Jersey slaves could be purchased to advantage"[62] (table 5.1).

New Jersey's *Act for the Gradual Abolition of Slavery* failed to bring about the emancipation it was designed to produce. Instead, it fueled an interstate slave

Table 5.1 A Timeline for the 1818 Van Wickle and Morgan Slave Scandal

1704	*An Act for Regulating Negro, Indian and Mulatto Slaves within this Province of NewJersey*, is passed controlling the movement and sale of enslaved people.
1792	Illicit shipping of black people from Elizabethtown, NJ to New Orleans is reported. New Jerseyans seize the opportunity to profit from selling people to southern buyers.
1798	New Jersey legislature passes a statute requiring enslaved peoples' consent before being removed from the state.
1800–1801	'Col.' Charles Morgan leaves South Amboy, NJ. He purchases land for *Morganza*, his sugar and cotton plantation in Point Coupée, LA.
1804	Charles Morgan is appointed sheriff of Point Coupée Parish. He is also appointed to the Louisiana legislature.
February 15, 1804	The New Jersey *Act for the Gradual Abolition of Slavery* is passed.
1808	U.S. Congress abolishes the slave trade, but not the thriving interstate trade.
1809	Col. Charles Morgan's *Morganza* lists 28 enslaved people on his property schedules.
February 1, 1812	*New Jersey Supplement to 1804 Gradual Abolition Act* specifies that "no negro, other slave or servant of color for life or years, shall be removed out of this state without his or her consent." It specifies that bonded and enslaved people must both consent to emigration and be examined by two impartial local officials to affirm their consent.
January 1818	Charles Morgan leaves Louisiana to purchase additional enslaved people. He partners with Judge Jacob C. Van Wickle to illegally remove enslaved and bonded people to Louisiana.
March 10–11, 1818	*First Group:* Thirty-nine "consenting slaves" board the brig *Mary Ann* at Sandy Hook and sail to the port at New Orleans
May 25, 1818	*Second Group* leaves Judge Van Wickle's Estate. Col. Charles Morgan leaves Perth Amboy for New Orleans aboard the sloop *Thorn* with thirty-nine enslaved people.
May 25, 1818	The brig *Mary Ann* arrives in New Orleans and is seized by customs officials for "falsification of manifests."
June 13, 1818	Grand Jury of Middlesex County, NJ hands down 17 indictments charging Col. Charles Morgan with removing 16 black children and one adult man from New Jersey without their consent. An arrest warrant is issued.
July 1818	*New Orleans Chronicle* lists the arrival of 36 enslaved people aboard the brig *Mary Ann*, and 39 on the sloop *Thorne* from the second voyage.
Late July 1818	*Third Group:* The *Bliss* departs New Jersey for New Orleans with 39 enslaved people.
August 1818	Judge Van Wickle sends letters and affidavits to New Jersey and Philadelphia newspapers to clear his name.

(Continued)

Table 5.1 A Timeline for the 1818 Van Wickle and Morgan Slave Scandal (*Continued*)

October 25–26, 1818	*Fourth Group:* The Schoharie departs Perth Amboy with 48 enslaved people on board. It is the last documented slave ship to leave the port.
November 5, 1818	Middlesex County freeholders successfully petition the NJ state legislature to defend "servants for years" from illegal trafficking, and to enforce penalties against people who traffic or transfer enslaved people and servants.
November 7, 1818	*Fifth Group:* An unknown number of enslaved people are transported by land through Philadelphia to an unknown southern location.
November 13–17, 1818	In a Philadelphia courtroom Lewis Compton, James Brown, Col. Charles Morgan, Nicholas C. Van Wickle, and others answer charges of removing people of color from New Jersey and New York without their proper consent,
December 1818	The State of New Jersey fails to convict Judge Van Wickle.

trade, driven by a combination of high poverty among emancipated black people and the rapidly declining market for enslaved labor in what is now the tri-state area. Enslaved Africans were still property. And, slave holders retained both the right to sell them in states where slavery was legal and to contract them into long-term indentures. There were also a sizeable number of free people of color in New Jersey and New York, but most were liberated into poverty, homelessness, and privation, making them easy pickings for traffickers. Other emancipated people of color became wards of the state, which usually rented them back to their former owners in order to defray the costs of their upkeep. Given these complexities, most New Jersey slave owners cut their losses by either selling the people they owned into southern markets, or moving them into states where they might continue to profit from their labor.[63] To minimize trafficking, the New Jersey legislature passed an 1812 law declaring that bonded and enslaved people could not be moved out of state without their consent. Their removal would require "a private examination of the slave by two impartial local officials, usually justices of the peace or interior court judges."[64] This complicated Col. Morgan's plan to purchase "Jersey Negroes," inexpensively and ship them to *Morganza*. The obstacles these new laws created, however, could be easily removed if your brother-in-law was a judge with a long-standing interest in the family business.

Judge Jacob C. Van Wickle owned a large estate on the South River near Old Bridge, where he served as a judge on the Middlesex County Court of Common Pleas. He was married to Sarah Morgan, the Colonel's sister. All Col. Morgan needed to transport his newly purchased slaves to New Orleans was evidence that they consented to move to Louisiana with him. Judge Van Wickle used his judicial power to falsify the consent forms, and the judge's son, Nicolas Van Wickle (1796–1865), brokered the transactions. The Judge and the Colonel were part of an extended cartel. They used family, friends, and business connections to locate families who would be willing to sell the people they enslaved.⁶⁵ It was alleged that bribes, false promises of freedom, paid work, and fear pressured many black people to agree to leave New Jersey.⁶⁶ The judge used his South River estate as the central location to gather, process, and hold free, bonded, and enslaved people until they could be transported south. Many captives were women with young children, who may have decided that moving to Louisiana with their children was less risky than being separated from them in New Jersey. Their consent was falsely manufactured during their captivity at Van Wickle's estate. "The children 'interviewed' were between six-weeks and nine-years old," and according to Judge Van Wickle, "as far as they could answer . . . declared their willingness to move to Louisiana."⁶⁷ One six-week-old child's cries were interpreted as consent to a life of bondage in the deep south.-

Jay W. Sterner's research on his Disbrow family ancestors offers the only known account of what happened next. On March 15, the first group of captives was transported by wagon from the Van Wickle estate to a dock in South Amboy, just north of the Morgan plantation. According to the Disbrow papers,

> From Wilmurt's Dock, between eight and nine that same night of the fifteenth, the sloop *Thorn* slipped away into the darkness and headed down the bay with her contraband cargo. [Col.] Charles Morgan was abroad and directed [John D.] Disbrow in stowing the blacks. Thomas Day and William Gordan Abrahams came aboard after the sloop had left the wharf, bringing four or five—some female slaves—with them in a small boat. Jonathan Morgan was with this consignment.⁶⁸

The last line breaks me. My third great-grandfather was part of this first consignment. The portraits that hung in my grandparent's living room were commissioned six short years after the events of 1818. Two years after, Jonathan Morgan married Dinah Van Wickle, the judge's niece. It makes sense that he was called to help move enslaved people from the judge's estate to the dock that night. He was almost twenty years old and well positioned to inherit his share of the Morgan businesses and fortune. Wilmurt's dock lies less than two miles north of the home where he lives with his father, step-mother Ann Van Wickle, and seven siblings. His father James and his unmarried 33-year-old sister Alice "Elsey" Morgan were also working with Van Wickle.⁶⁹

The gravitational pull of whiteness is strong even in the face of this clear fact pattern. *Well, maybe he was just there helping out that one night. He was young; he probably was just trying to please his family. He wanted to be a part of the excitement. He wanted to prove that he belonged . . . it's not as if he was one of the key players.* Whiteness drags me away from the obvious. It's highly unlikely that Jonathan made a cameo appearance on that March evening. It's more likely that he assisted his father, sister, uncle, and their associates with this abominable business on a regular basis. The pull slackens and I fall back on Serene Jones's remark about how her ancestors had to "master the embodiment of cruelty." Wonder brings my third great-grandfather's deeds to life. What kind of person did Jonathan H. Morgan have to become to be emotionally capable of moving people from his step-uncle's garrison to the wagons, and from the wagons onto the *Thorn*, and into a life of permanent bondage? What did he say and do to them to get them to board the sloop? Did he call them names that were not their own? Was he forceful and cruel? All I know is that the following morning the sloop sailed out to Sandy Hook and transferred her human cargo to the brig *Mary Ann*. When the winds rose the brig set sail for New Orleans with

> Peter 15 years old, Simon a freeman, Margaret Coven a free woman,[70]
> Sarah 21 and her daughter Dianna 7 months, Rachel 22 and her daughter Regina 6 weeks, Hagar 29 with daughter Roda 14, daughter Mary 2, and son Augustus 4 . . .
> Florah age 23 and her daughter Susan 7 months . . .
> Harry 14 years of age, James 21, Elmirah 14, George 16 and Susan Watt 35, Moses 16, Lydia 18, Betty 22, Patty 22, Bass 19 years of age . . .
> Christeen 27 and her daughters Diannah 9 and Dorcas one-year old.
> Clareese 22, her son Hercules 2, Lidia 22 and her daughter Harriett,
> Jane 3, Bob, Rosanna, Closs (Claus), Jenette,
> Ann and her son Rosino,
> Charles a child, Elias a child, Robert a child . . . .[71]

Customs officials seized the *Mary Ann* upon its arrival in New Orleans on May 25, 1818. They charged Col. Morgan with transporting enslaved people without a valid manifest. His actions were at once punishable and praiseworthy. Two months later the *New Orleans Chronicle* reported that "the slave market appears to be very brisk." And, that the community is "much indebted to the enterprising and successful exertions of Charles Morgan, for the copiousness of the present supply" of "Jersey negroes," who, "appear to be peculiarly adapted to this market—especially those who bear the mark of Judge Vanwickle."[72] In early June, the Middlesex County grand jury handed down seventeen indictments against Col. Charles Morgan and nine indictments against Nicholas Van Wickle. They arraigned seven more prominent South Amboy citizens, including my fourth great-grandfather Maj. Gen. James Morgan, Jr. and his daughter "Elsie." Judge Van Wickle escaped indictment, because he placed the people he trafficked in the name of his son and other members of his New Jersey cartel. They would organize four more voyages before the year ended (figure 5.4).

The loss of the *Mary Ann* taught Col. Morgan a valuable lesson. He decided to hire a ship for the second voyage south.[73] On the afternoon of May 25, 1818, a second group of captives were loaded onto horse-drawn wagons. The wagon train left Van Wickle's South River estate and headed toward

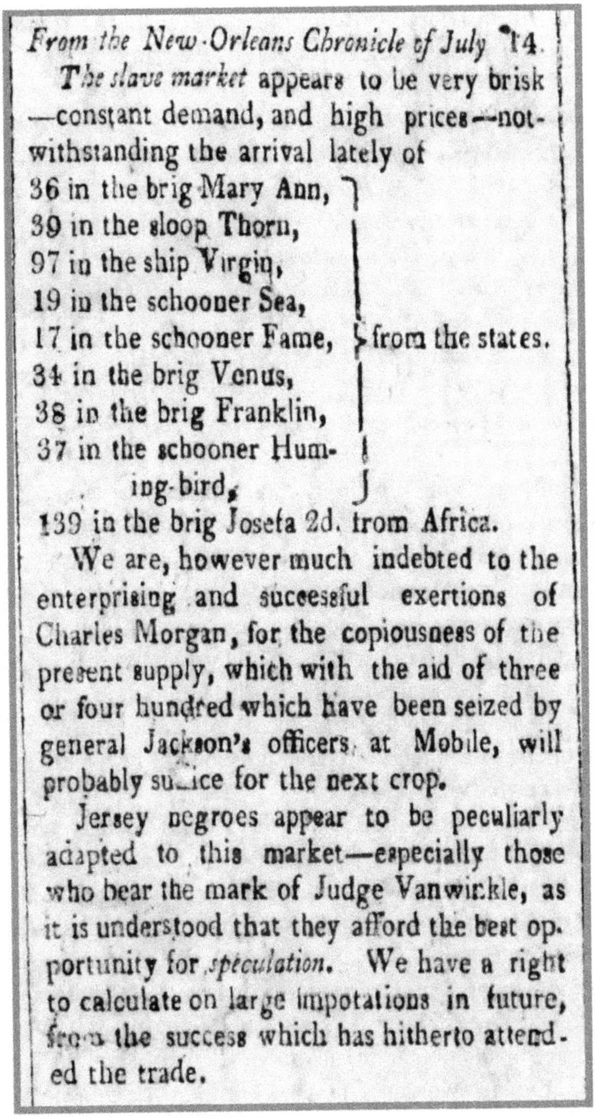

> From the *New-Orleans Chronicle of July* 14.
>
> The *slave market* appears to be very brisk—constant demand, and high prices—notwithstanding the arrival lately of
>
> 36 in the brig Mary Ann,
> 39 in the sloop Thorn,
> 97 in the ship Virgin,
> 19 in the schooner Sea,
> 17 in the schooner Fame, } from the states.
> 34 in the brig Venus,
> 38 in the brig Franklin,
> 37 in the schooner Huming-bird,
>
> 139 in the brig Josefa 2d. from Africa.
>
> We are, however much indebted to the enterprising and successful exertions of Charles Morgan, for the copiousness of the present supply, which with the aid of three or four hundred which have been seized by general Jackson's officers, at Mobile, will probably suffice for the next crop.
>
> Jersey negroes appear to be peculiarly adapted to this market—especially those who bear the mark of Judge Vanwinkle, as it is understood that they afford the best opportunity for *speculation*. We have a right to calculate on large importations in future, from the success which has hitherto attended the trade.

Figure 5.4 *New Orleans Chronicle* **Slave Market News Article.** Reprint of an original story from the *New Orleans Chronicle* announcing the arrival of *the Mary Ann, Thorne,* and other ships carrying enslaved people to New Orleans. Source: Vermont Watchman and State Journal (Montpelier, Vermont, August 25, 1818). Public Domain.

Perth Amboy. The 39 captives were unloaded at the port and herded onto John D. Disbrow's sloop. They set sail on that warm afternoon with:

> Leta 21, Dorcas 16, Sam Johnson 32, and Margaret age 21, and Mary Davis age 23,
> Jane 25 and her son John aged 4 years, Phyllis 25 and her son Charles age one,
> Jack age 16, and Harvey 22, and Elizer (female) 19, Frank 21, Hester 18,
> Peter 21, Susan Silvey 30 and her son Jacob only 18 months . . . .
> Betsey 22, Jonas 16 a free person, and Sam 16-years old.
> William 22, Henry 21, and Amey 22, Juda (female) 26, and her son Samuel age 2 years old . . .
> James aged 22, Sam 32, George Byron 18, Hannah 16,
> Nancy 22 and a child, Joseph only two days old.
> Peter 17 a free person, Hannah 14, Jack Danielly 21 years old, Jude (no certificate),
> Caroline and Ann both 18 years old, Jeanette 12, and Mose.

If you ran your eyes quickly cross their names, then the anesthesia has returned. A brisk read affords the reader distance and comfort. I'm asking you to slow down and to hold space with these names. These are the names local historians and members of the Lost Souls Memorial Project have taken time and care to resurrect. Read them out loud, so that you feel each syllable glide from your heart to your mouth. Let the names rest on your tongue. Take a breath and speak them into the world. Giving voice to their names is an antidote to the anesthesia. Hearing their names spoken two centuries after their erasure opens us to their collective presence. It keeps alive the spirits of those sold into permanent bondage.

The events of 1818 did not end with the second voyage. The Van Wickle and Morgan names had already become associated with quality human merchandise in Louisiana. There was more money to be made. Three more groups of African-descended people would be sold into permanent slavery before the year was out.[74] In late July, a third group was herded aboard the *Bliss*. A fourth group of 48 people was smuggled onto the *Schoharie* at the Perth Amboy port on October 26. Two weeks later, on November 7, a fifth group was transported by land through Philadelphia to an unknown southern location.

I want to return to Morgan's pottery kilns. Pearl Duncan's research on enslaved skilled artisans convinces me that the events of 1818 cannot be explained independently of the infrastructure put in place by the regional stoneware and clay industry. Our cemetery guide's words return to me: "The Morgan family had their hands on *everything* that moved, and what didn't move, they already owned." It's too easy to conclude that the events of 1818 were just the dreams and schemes of an avaricious planter, a corrupt Judge, and their friends. However, I really think that the scandal has to be understood systemically. The Morgan and Van Wickle families already had a well-oiled regional network for transporting labor, material, and goods from state to state. The economic machinery of colonialism made the plan possible long before Col. Morgan returned for his family visit. The story of the pottery-making trade intersects tightly with the abominable business of slavery and piracy, because it's a story about how the descendants of early settlers collectively used their family connections and pooled their resources over generations to preserve and grow their wealth. The Cheesequake region of Middlesex County was "the epicenter of the colonial stoneware industry."[75] Capt. James Morgan, Sr., Maj. Gen. James Morgan, Jr., Judge Van Wickle and his son Nicholas were all in the stoneware business. The Morgan and Van Wickle families also intermarried with the Warne and Letts families, who also owned profitable potteries.[76] And, their family connections extended beyond the kiln sites. The Morgan and Disbrow plantations shared a common property line. As a child, John D. Disbrow most certainly played with the Morgan children. As an adult he was a farmer, a sailor, and for a time, a soldier who fought loyally alongside Captain James Morgan during the American Revolution. He married Susannah Morgan, the Captain's daughter. He owned the *Thorn*.[77] When he was not plowing, planting, and harvesting, he may have made extra money transporting potter's clay and stoneware to New York potteries, and skilled potters and goods to New Jersey on his return trip.[78] As Duncan explains:

> Judge Van Wickle and the wealthy merchants who owned the mansions and estates adjoining New Jersey's stoneware factories and clay pits were instrumental in the illegal activities, because they hid the kidnapped skilled artisans, their families and others in the basements of the mansions on their plantations. . . . Prior to the 1811 law being enacted, [Maj Gen.] Morgan's extended family owned, transported, and kidnapped other owners' skilled and unskilled enslaved artisans and their families, whom they sold locally and in other colonies, and later in other states.[79]

The events of 1818 then, were not a stand-alone business opportunity. They were an artifact of a long-standing business network, a regional triangle trade that moved clay, stoneware, and potters from one market or pottery kiln to another. They were, in the words of one Disbrow descendent, a "closed corporation."[80] And, as such, their business practices and connections were easily recalibrated to accommodate Col. Morgan's request.

Holding Space as Mourning

I've been holding space with my Morgan and VanWickle ancestors for over eight years now. It's taken me that long get a feeling for how to navigate the gravitational pull of my trophy pedigree. I'll never be completely free of the weight I inherit, and to be clear, this is not my goal. Weightlessness is not liberation. My ancestry will always contain a mixture of anesthesia and tears. Yet the tears somehow feel differently than they did before my ancestors came up to claim me. They are now the tears of mourning. Mourning and crisis share many features. They are both breaking points. They pull us apart in ways that resist re-assemblage. The stoneware vessel that is shattered and mended is similar to, but not identical with, its original condition. It can never be restored flawlessly. It can never return to the wholeness it once knew. It can only be transformed. Like Silas Marner's pot in George Eliot novel, the pieces of the vessel have been gathered, reassembled and glued back together, and returned to the space where the pot sat before it was broken.[81] Its traumatic fissures humbly on display. When we mourn, we hold space with the pain that breaks us until we feel it shift, subside, and settle into a new way of being. As Serene Jones observes: "To move from grief, from mourning, is to move from a place of sheer loss to a place of acknowledging the loss, and in mourning the permanence of the loss, it can't be fixed, but also, it creates a space, in mourning, for you to make sacred the pain so that the rest of your life is transformed by it."[82]

Crises have a curious way of conjuring up healing resources when we most need them. Medicinal genealogies have taught me that collective healing can only happen in one another's company. Our ancestral histories survive in fragments. The terrain under our feet holds scattered shreds of our ancestral pasts that wait patiently to be reassembled anew, and to have their stories told side by side. How might we summon a healing community from these fragments?

I have been typing "Van Wickle and Morgan Slave Scandal (1818)" into search engines and databases for a very long time. Like the impatient fisher who repeatedly casts her line into murky waters only to come up empty handed, I find scholarship but not community. I make a last-ditch effort to determine whether anyone has gathered as a community process the residue of my ancestor's unfinished business. I type the terms again. I'm astonished when my search engine conjures up the Facebook page for the Lost Souls Memorial Project, which describes the group as a grass-roots community-based effort to remember the 137+ African American people whose freedom was stolen by corrupt Middlesex, New Jersey judge and his extended network. Seriously, the page wasn't there a week ago. The project is dedicated to preserving the memory of those souls lost to the Van Wickle Slave Ring. They are raising funds to design and build a public memorial to remember them back home. They are designing an educational curriculum, to ensure that this part of New Jersey history will be taught in local schools. For two years, they have gathered to recite the 137+ names of those people whose freedom was stolen by my ancestors. I sheepishly message the group. I identify myself as a descendent and say something about how excited I am to have found them. Reverend Karen G. Johnston replies with a warm welcome and a generous offer to continue our conversation. I read the names of the people my ancestor's trafficked aloud to myself from their website. I watch two video recordings of the first two Recitations of Names events. There is an affective difference between reading those sacred names to myself as I sit at my computer in Illinois, and hearing them spoken into the world. Listening to African American members of the project speak them into the world hits me particularly hard. I hold as much space as I can with the names. The numbness subsides and I can feel the full weight of my Morgan and Van Wickle ancestors' imprint on the lost souls' worlds. The weight increases six months later when I open up the *New York Times Magazine* and read Anne C. Bailey's a photo essay for the 1619 Project, chronicling unmarked slave auction sites. Judge Van Wickle's South River estate is featured prominently.[83]

The Third Recitation of Names is planned for May 30, 2020.[84] The COVID-19 pandemic makes public gatherings potentially fatal, so the recitation, like everything else this season, will be held online. George Floyd is murdered by four Minneapolis policemen five days before the event and the world is filled with the righteous anger of the mournful. Days later, Trump deploys militarized police to beat and tear gas Black Lives Matter activist protesting peacefully in Lafayette Square across from the White House. In southern cities, the statues of confederate leaders are being tagged, defaced, and pulled down by protestors. I feel the Newark lessons stir again, but this time I feel hopeful. Once again, the past has come up to claim us. The Lost Souls Project asks for volunteers willing to record themselves reciting a short list of names. The recordings will be edited into a compilation video, a virtual assembly of voices "speaking the Lost Souls into visibility, an act of liberatory memory."[85] As fate would have it, I'm assigned to recite the names of nine people from the group that Jonathan H. Morgan transported from Van Wickle's garrison to Wilmurt's Dock. I set up my laptop on a card table in the hallway. I pull up a slat-backed chair with hand-painted yellow roses on it and sit. This is the chair Dinah Van Wickle Morgan sat in for the pastel portrait that used to hang in my grandmother's living room. I take a slow deep breath, click the record button, and say their names.

Betty, 22 . . . Patty, 22 . . . Bass, 19,
    Christine, age 27 with her two children: Diannah, 9 years and Dorcas, 1 year . . .
        Chareesse, 22, with her son Hercules, age 2 years . . .
           Bob.

NOTES

1. Alison Bailey, *Monmouth Girl: Leola Crawford Bailey's Monmouth County Ancestors* (San Francisco, CA: Blurb Books, 2014); And, *Edgar Henry Summerfield Bailey, Aravesta Trumbauer, and Their Ancestors: An Illustrated Genealogy* (San Francisco, CA: Blurb Books, 2018).

2. Charles Mills, *The Racial Contract* (Ithaca, NY: Cornell University Press), 13.

3. Alexis Shotwell, "Unforgetting as a Collective Tactic," in *White Self-Criticality beyond Anti-Racism: How Does It Feel to Be a White Problem?*, ed. George Yancy (Lanham, MD: Lexington Books, 2015), 58.

4. Warren Read, *The Lyncher in Me: A Search for Redemption in the Face of History* (St. Paul, MN: Borealis Books, 2008), 24.

5. My comments are addressed primarily to descendants of settler colonists. Readers can decide for themselves whether they offer a helpful entry point into their own ancestral pasts.

6. Aurora Levins Morales, "The Historian as Curandera," in *Medicine Stories: Essays for Radicals* (Durham, NC: Duke University Press, 2019), 72.

7. François Weil, *Family Trees: A History of Genealogy in America* (Cambridge, MA: Harvard University Press, 2013), 11–15.

8. The Daughters of the American Revolution (DAR) limited membership to people who could offer proof colonial or Revolutionary War era descent. In the interest of keeping out the riffraff they also considered whether the nominees were "personally acceptable." Morgan observes, that "a right-thinking, truly elite membership ultimately mattered more to such an organization than did the ability to document colonial or Revolutionary descent." Many DAR chapters contacted women they wanted as members first, then began documenting their pedigrees. Francesca Morgan, "A Noble Pursuit: Bourgeois America's Uses of Lineage," in *The American Bourgeoise: Distinction and Identity in the Nineteenth Century*, ed. Sven Beckert and Julia B. Rosenbaum (New York, NY: Palgrave MacMillan, 2010), 142–43.

9. Weil, *Family Trees*, 140.

10. Morgan, "A Noble Pursuit," 140.

11. Morgan, 141.

12. Christine E. Sleeter, "Critical Family History: Situating Family within Contexts of Power Relationships," *Journal of Multidisciplinary Research* 8, no. 1 (Spring 2016), 20.

13. Jenn Selby, "Ben Affleck: The Deleted Segment about His Slave-Owning Ancestry He Didn't Want You to See," *The Independent*, April 23, 2015, https://www.independent.co.uk/news/people/ben-affleck-the-deleted-segment-about-his-slave-owning-ancestry-he-didn-t-want-you-to-see-10198131.html

14. Selby, "Ben Affleck."

15. Sara Ahmed, *Living a Feminist Life* (Durham, NC: Duke University Press, 2017), 123.

16. Daniel Krepps, "PBS Suspends 'Finding Your Roots' After Ben Affleck Slave Controversy," *Rolling Stone*, June 25, 2015, https://www.rollingstone.com/tv/tv-news/pbs-suspends-finding-your-roots-after-ben-affleck-slave-controversy-43610/

17. It's telling that PBS removed the entire Affleck episode from its distribution. I can't find footage of the interview anywhere.

18. Shannon Sullivan, *Good White People: The Problem with White Middle-Class Anti-Racism* (Albany, NY: SUNY Press, 2014), 67. My italics.

19. Sullivan, *Good White People*, 68.

20. Alice Walker, *The Way Forward is with A Broken Heart* (New York: Random House, 2000), 200.

21. Catherine Nash, "Genealogical Relatedness: Geographies of Shared Descent and Difference," *Genealogy* 1, no. 7 (2017), 2–3.

22. Eduardo Duran, *Healing the Soul Wound: Counseling with American Indian and Other Native Peoples* (New York: Teachers College Press, 2006), 27.

23. Morales, "The Historian as Curandera," 72.

24. Morales, 72.

25. Joy DeGruy, *Post-Traumatic Slave Syndrome: America's Legacy of Enduring Injury and Healing* (Portland, OR: Joy DeGruy Publications, Inc., 2017), 120, 153. Erykah Badu cautioned Black women about the costs associated with carrying too much cultural and historical baggage. Summarizing Badu's observations, Brittney Cooper remarks, "Our lives are strewn with structurally deposited baggage. If we assume the radical position that it isn't ours to carry, we are called lazy. Degenerate. Angry. Irresponsible. The Nation waves its fingers at us in accusation, demanding that we take the weight. And, often, we accede to these demands..." See, *Eloquent Rage: A Black Woman Discovers Her Superpower* (New York: St. Martin's Press, 2018), 110.

26. DeGruy, iv.

27. Albert Memmi addresses the impact of colonization on our collective humanity earlier: It is "the oppressor himself who restores, with his slightest gesture, the humanity he seeks to destroy; and, since he denies humanity in others, he regards it everywhere his enemy. To handle this, the colonizer must assume the opaque rigidity and imperviousness of stone." See, *The Colonizer and the Colonized* (Boston: Beacon Press, 1991), 24.

28. Serena Jones, "On Grace," Interview by Krista Tippett, *On Being*, NPR, December 5, 2019. Transcript, https://onbeing.org/programs/serene-jones-on-grace/

29. Adinkra symbols stand for concepts or aphorisms. They encapsulate traditional wisdom. They also have a decorative function and appear on pottery and fabric, and in architectural elements. W. Bruce Willis, *The Adinkra Dictionary: A Visual Primer on The Language of Adinkra* (n.a.: Pyramid Complex, 1998).

30. I'm treading cautiously here. It's not just the genealogist's racial identity that orients her ancestral journey in a particular way, historical inequalities also shape that path. My project here is not to review genealogy guides that target particular racial demographics, although this would be an interesting project. I approach the connections between genealogy and healing not from the perspective of the literature that helps people of color find their ancestors. Instead I focus on the literature that highlights the role genealogy plays in recovery.

31. Sleeter, "Critical Family History," 12.

32. See, Macky Alston, *Family Name* (New York, NY: First Run/Icarus Films, 1997), DVD; Edward Ball, *Slaves in the Family* (New York: Farrar, Straus, and Giroux, 1998); Katrina Browne, *Traces of the Trade: A Story from the Deep North* (San Francisco, CA: California Newsreel, 2008), DVD; Thomas Norman DeWolf, *Inheriting the Trade: A Northern Family Confronts Its Legacy as the Largest Slave-Trading Dynasty in U.S. History* (Boston: Beacon Press, 2008); Loki Mullholload,

The Uncomfortable Truth (Lehi, UT: The Joan Trumpauer Mulholland Foundation, 2016), retrieved December 3, 2019, from Kanopy; and, Christine Sleeter, "Becoming White: Reinterpreting a Family Story by Putting Race Back into the Picture," *Race, Ethnicity and Education* 14, no. 4 (September 2001), 423.

33. Read, *The Lyncher in Me*, 11.

34. Read, 129.

35. Serene Jones, *Trauma and Grace: Theology in a Ruptured World* (Louisville, KY: John Knox Press, 2009), 174–75.

36. From 1789 to 1820 DeWolf family ships traced the well-worn routes of the triangle trade. They moved rum from the port at Bristol, Rhode Island to West Africa where they traded it for Africans. The captives were then transported to Cuba where they were forced to work on family sugar cane plantations and sold at auction in Havana. The ships were filled with sugar and molasses and returned to Bristol where the cargo was unloaded and distilled into rum. James DeWolf and three generations of DeWolfs transported over 10,000 slaves during this time. He later became a U.S senator and was reportedly the second-richest person in the United States. My summary of the DeWolf family history follows Katrina Browne, *Traces of the Trade: A Story from the Deep North* (San Francisco, CA: California Newsreel, 2008), DVD; and, Thomas Norman DeWolf's *Inheriting the Trade: A Northern Family Confronts Its Legacy as the Largest Slave-Trading Dynasty in U.S. History* (Boston: Beacon Press, 2008).

37. DeWolf, *Inheriting the Trade*, 7.

38. DeWolf, 52.

39. Browne, *Traces of the Trade* (00:10:06).

40. DeWolf, *Inheriting the Trade*, 68.

41. Browne, *Traces of the Trade* (01:17:01).

42. George Yancy, *Backlash: What Happens When We Talk Honestly about Racism in America* (Lanham, MD: Rowman and Littlefield, 2018), 4.

43. George Yancy, "Introduction: Unsuttered," in *White Self-Criticality: How Does It Feel to Be a White Problem?*, ed. George Yancy (Lanham: MD: Lexington Books, 2015), xv.

44. Yancy's call to tarry within the space of existential burden does not address trauma directly, but it is does not exclude it either. I speak in terms of "holding space" because it focuses more directly on what's at stake for me in these liminal spaces.

45. I'm drawing on Gloria Anzaldúa's account of the ruptures that pull us into liminal spaces (*nepantla*). See, "Now Let Us Shift...The Path of Conocimento... Inner work, Public Acts," in *The Bridge We Call Home: Radical Visions of Transformation*, eds. Gloria E. Anzaldúa and Analouise Keating (New York: Routledge, 2002), 540–79.

46. James Baldwin, "The Fire Next Time: My Dungeon Shook," in *The Price of the Ticket: Collected Nonfiction 1948–1985* (New York, St. Martin's Press, 1985), 368.

47. Ta-Nehesi Coates, "Imagining a New America," Interview with Krista Tippett, *On Being*, NPR, September 12, 2019.

48. Ball, *Slaves in the Family*, 14.

49. Ahmed, *Living a Feminist Life*, 61.

50. I'm drawing on Serene Jones's insights on how pain and trauma spark healing.

51. My comments come from conversations with George Yancy. See, "Race and the Naming of Whiteness: "Alison Bailey" *On Race: Thirty-Four Conversations in a Time of Crisis*, ed. George Yancy (Oxford: Oxford University Press, 2017), 61–71.

52. Graham Russell Hodges, *Slavery and Freedom in the Rural North: African Americans in Monmouth County, New Jersey, 1665–1865* (Lanham, MD: Madison House, 1997), 2.

53. Hodges, *Slavery and Freedom*, 12.

54. Edgar J. McManus, *Black Bondage in the North* (Syracuse, NY: Syracuse University Press, 1973), 13.

55. This is Sue Kozel's observation. See Jennifer Kohlhepp, "A Journey into the Shadow History of a Community," *Central New Jersey Digital Archives 2000–2015*, posted March 8, 2015, http://www1.gmnews.com/2007/03/08/a-journey-into-the-shadow-history-of-a-community/

56. See, n.a. "The Morgan Pottery: Road Widening Spares 18th-Century Kiln Site," *Cultural Resources Digest, New Jersey Department of Transportation* (January 2008), 2.

57. My account combines Pearl Duncan's research with online conversations I've had with Deirdre McIntosh, a Disbrow descendant.

58. Pearl Duncan, "Magnificent, Mysterious Designs in American Folk Art Revealed in African Iconography," *ArtDaily*, January 25, 2020, https://artdaily.cc/news/56187/Magnificent—mysterious-designs-in-American-Folk-Art-revealed-in-African-iconography#.XizMCBNKiu4

59. The law declared that "every child born of a slave within this state, after the fourth day of July next, shall be free; but shall remain the servant of the owner of his or her mother, and the executors, administrators or assigns of such owner, in the same manner as if such child had been bound to service by the trustees or overseers of the poor, and shall continue in such service, if a male, until the age of twenty five years; and if a female until the age of twenty one years." Ultimately, slavery in New Jersey, was not abolished fully until the Thirteenth Amendment was passed 1865. Geneva Smith, "Legislating Slavery in New Jersey," *Princeton and Slavery*, https://slavery.princeton.edu/stories/legislating-slavery-in-new-jersey

60. My summary of the scandal follows Frances D. Pingeon, "An Abominable Business: The New Jersey Slave Trade, 1818," *New Jersey History* 109 (1991), 15–36; James J. Gigantino, "Trading in Jersey Souls: New Jersey and The Interstate Slave Trade," *Pennsylvania History: A Journal of Mid-Atlantic Studies* 17, no. 3 (2010), 281–302; Calvin Schermerhorn, *The Business of Slavery and the Rise of American Capitalism, 1815–1860* (New Haven: Yale University Press, 2015); Edgar J. MacManus, *Black Bondage in the North* (Syracuse, NY: Syracuse University Press, 1973); and, Francis Amorosi, *Index to Slaves and Servants in The New Jersey Calendar of Wills 1670–1817*.

61. See Jarrett M. Drake, "Off the Record: The Production of Evidence in 19th Century New Jersey," *NJS: An Interdisciplinary Journal* (Summer 2015), 109.

62. Col. Morgan "could buy at minimum 150 slaves as the highest advertised prices for a slave for life in New Jersey between 1804 and 1818. In May 1816, *The New Jersey Journal* advertised "a nineteen-year-old smart and active male," for $300. The same able-bodied male would sell for $800 or more in New Orleans. Gigantino, "Trading in Jersey Souls," 285.

63. My summary follows Hodges's *Slavery and Freedom in the Rural North*.

64. See, Smith, "Legislating Slavery in New Jersey," https://slavery.princeton.edu/stories/legislating-slavery-in-new-jersey

65. Emerging evidence suggests that Judge Van Wickle and Col. Charles Morgan also acquired people to traffic from the "city jails as far away as Newark, NJ. Black people unable to prove their free status were routinely classified as runaways and imprisoned. To recoup the cost of imprisonment, government officials like New Jersey Governor Isaac H. William sold the people they imprisoned if their masters didn't claim them within ten days. Jacob Van Wickle advanced funds to government officials to acquire those individuals." Kristal C. Langford, "Exposing the Scene of Villainy," Lost Souls Memorial Project website: https://lostsoulsmemorialnj.org/wp-content/uploads/Inside-Van-Wickles-Slave-Ring.pdf

66. Pingeon, "An Abominable Business," 18.

67. Gigantino, "Trading in Jersey Souls," 285.

68. Jay W. Sterner, "John D. Disbrow," *Todd Sherman's Genealogy page*, http://www.afn.org/~afn09444/genealog/index.html

69. Pingeon, "An Abominable Business," 19. Pingeon's archival work reveals that a Middlesex County Grand Jury arraigned "James Morgan and his daughter Elsie." Until recently, Elsie's identity was a mystery to me. I now believe that Elsey/Elsie was the nickname of Alice Morgan (1785–1853), Maj. Gen. Morgan's oldest daughter. In 1818 she was thirty-three years old and unmarried. No Morgan women had Elsie as their given name, and, all of the Morgan women and girls (except Alice) were under ten years old. Also, "Eley Morgan" (Elsie/Elsey) is listed as living with her siblings and half-siblings in South Amboy on the July 20, 1838 Tax Assessment roles. See, Alvia Disbrow Martin, *At the Headwaters of the Cheesequake* (South Amboy, NJ: Raritan Printing Co., 1971), 159.

70. Simon was once the property of my fourth great grandfather, Major Gen. James Morgan, Jr.. He allegedly consented to serve Col. Charles Morgan for a term of "two years, two months, and eighteen days." Pingeon, "An Abominable Business," 20.

71. The earliest list of names from the first group comes from George J. Miller's collection of three short papers, "The Printing of the Elizabethtown Bill in Chancery. The Quadrant and Circumferentor. Flesh for Sale," (Perth Amboy, NJ: Board of Proprietors of the Eastern Division of New Jersey, 1942), 35–44. With gratitude to the Lost Souls Memorial Project, New Brunswick, NJ for the extensive archival work they've done to bring home the remaining names and memory of the people my ancestors sold into slavery. The names appearing in this chapter are the fruit of their loving labors. Many thanks to Kristal Langford for our conversation and for her work on the Project website; https://lostsoulsmemorialnj.org/. See also, Teresa Vega, "The Insidiousness of Slavery: No Justice and the Van Wickle Slave Ring," *Radiant Roots: Boricua Branches*, 2013, http://radiantrootsboricuabranches.com/the-insidio

usness-of-slavery-no-justice-and-the-van-wickle-slave-ring/. Many "consent forms" for Louisiana slaves involving the Van Wickle and Morgan families can be found in the *Slave Manumissions Volume*, Middlesex County, Record Group 2127, Special Collections Archives (Jersey Room), Rutgers University.

72. *New Orleans Chronicle*, July 14, 1818.
73. George J. Miller, cited in Pingeon, "An Abominable Business," 26.
74. Considerations of space and conflicting historical narratives in the literature prevent me from recounting the exact details of the three remaining incidents. This history is literally being excavated as I write. For an up-to-date account of the names of people trafficked see, the "Victims," and "Timeline of Events" tabs on the Lost Souls Memorial Project website; https://lostsoulsmemorialnj.org/
75. n.a. "The Morgan Pottery," 2.
76. Maj. Gen. James Morgan's sister, Mary Morgan (1769–1838) married Thomas Warne (1763–1813), who founded and operated a pottery near Morgan's pottery in South Amboy.
77. Thanks to Deirdre McIntosh (Sterner's granddaughter) for sharing information on John D. Disbrow and the *Thorn*.
78. Sherman's Genealogy Page, "John D. Disbrow," 62.
79. Pearl Duncan, "Colonial African-American Stoneware Artists, Stolen, Hidden, Now Rediscovered," *ArtDaily*, December 8, 2019, https://artdaily.cc/news/56820/Colonial-African-American-stoneware-artists—stolen—hidden—now-rediscovered #.Xe1SN5JKiu5
80. Sherman's Genealogy Page, "John D. Disbrow," 58.
81. I'm drawing on Sara Ahmed's discussion George Eliot's *Silas Marner* here. See, *Living a Feminist Life*, 165.
82. Serena Jones, "On Grace," https://onbeing.org/programs/serene-jones-on-grace/
83. Anne C. Bailey, "Invisible Wounds," *The New York Times Magazine*, February 16, 2020, 38–53.
84. The complete video of the Third Annual Recitation of Names can be found at: https://www.youtube.com/watch?v=iuRztV9Upfg&t=1095s
85. Rev. Karen G. Johnston, personal correspondence, April 10, 2020.

Bibliography

Ahmed, Sara. "A Phenomenology of Whiteness," *Feminist Theory* 8, no. 2 (2007), 149–68.
Ahmed, Sara. "Declarations of Whiteness: The Non-Performativity of Anti-Racism," *Borderlands* 3, no. 2 (2004), http://www.borderlands.net.au/vol3no2_2004/ahmed_declarations.html.
Ahmed, Sara. *Living a Feminist Life*. Durham, NC: Duke University Press, 2017.
Ahmed, Sara. "Snap," *Feminist Killjoys*, May 21, 2017, https://feministkilljoys.com/2017/05/21/snap/.
Angelou, Maya. "Iconoclast: Maya Angelou," Interview with Dave Chapell, Filmed November 30, 2006, RadicalMedia video, 22:35. Posted May 29, 2014, https://www.youtube.com/watch?v=okc6COsgzoE.
Anzaldúa, Gloria E. *Making Face, Making Soul: Haciendo Caras*. San Francisco: Aunt Lute Books, 1990.
Anzaldúa, Gloría E. "Now Let Us Shift ... The Path of Conocimento ... Inner work, Public Acts," In *This Bridge We Call Home: Radical Visions of Transformation*, eds. Gloria E. Anzaldúa, and Analouise Keating. New York: Routledge, 2002, 540–79.
Applebaum, Barbara. *Being White, Being Good: White Complicity, Moral Responsibility and Social Justice Pedagogy*. Lanham, MD: Lexington Books, 2010.
Bailey, Alison. "Newark Lessons: A Reply to George Yancy's *Backlash*," *Philosophy Today* 62, no. 4 (2019), 1213–18.
Bailey, Alison. "Privilege: Expanding on Marilyn Frye's 'Oppression.'" *Journal of Social Philosophy* 29, no. 3 (Winter 1998), 104–19.
Bailey, Alison. "Strategic Ignorance," In *Race and Epistemologies of Ignorance*, eds. Nancy Tuana, and Shannon Sullivan. Albany, NY: SUNY Press, 2007, 77–94.
Bailey, Alison. "The Unlevel Knowing Field: An Engagement with Dotson's Third-Order Epistemic Oppression," *Social Epistemology Review and Reply Collective* 3, no. 10 (2014), 62–68.

Bailey, Alison. "Tracking Privilege-Preserving Epistemic Pushback in Feminist and Critical Race Philosophy Classes," *Hypatia* 32, no. 4 (2017), 876–92.

Bailey, Alison. "White Talk as a Barrier to Understanding the Problem of Whiteness," In *White Self-Criticality Beyond Anti-Racism: What Is It Like to Be a White Problem?*, ed. George Yancy. Lanham, MD: Lexington Books, 2015, 37–57.

Bailey, Ann C. "The 1619 Project: Slave Auction Sites," *The New York Times Magazine*, February 12, 2020, https://www.nytimes.com/interactive/2020/02/12/magazine/1619-project-slave-auction-sites.html.

Baldwin, James. "On Being White and Other Lies," *Essence* (April 1984), 90–92.

Baldwin, James. *The Price of the Ticket: Collected Nonfiction 1948–1985*. New York: St. Martin's Press, 1985.

Ball, Edward. *Slaves in the Family*. New York: Farrar, Straus, and Giroux, 1998.

Bambara, Toni Cade. *The Salt Eaters*. New York: Vintage Books, 1980.

Bayoumi, Moustafa. *How Does It Feel to Be a Problem: Being Young and Arab in America*. New York: Penguin Press, 2009.

Bennett, Lerone. "The White Problem in America," *Ebony* (August 1965), 29–36.

Berenstain, Nora. "Epistemic Exploitation," *Ergo* 3, no. 22 (2016), 569–90.

Berila, Beth. *Integrating Mindfulness into Anti-Oppression Pedagogy: Social Justice Pedagogy in Higher Education*. New York: Routledge, 2016.

Biss, Eula. "Let's Talk about Whiteness," Interview by Krista Tippett, *On Being*, NPR, September 13, 2018. Transcript, https://onbeing.org/programs/eula-biss-lets-talk-about-whiteness-sep2018/#transcript.

Biss, Eula. "White Debt: Reckoning with What is Owed—And What Can Never Be Repaid—for Race Privilege," *New York Times*, December 5, 2015, https://www.nytimes.com/2015/12/06/magazine/white-debt.html.

Boler, Megan. *Feeling Power: Emotions and Education*. New York: Routledge, 1999.

Bonita-Silva, Eduardo. "The Invisible Weight of Whiteness: The Racial Grammar of Everyday Life in Contemporary America," *Ethnic and Racial Studies* 35, no. 2 (September 2011), 173–94.

Brandt, Joseph R. *Dismantling Racism: The Continuing Challenge to White America*. Minneapolis, MN: Ausburger Books, 1991.

Brown, Brené. "The Price of Invulnerability," TEDx Talk, Kansas City, October 12, 2010, http://www.TEDxKC.org/.

Browne, Katrina. *Traces of the Trade: A Story from the Deep North*. San Francisco, CA: California Newsreel, 2008. DVD.

Burbules, Nicholas, and Rupert Bert. "Critical Thinking and Critical Pedagogy: Relations, Differences and Limits," In *Critical Theories in Education: Changing Terrains of Knowledge and Politics*, eds. Thomas S. Popkewitz and Lynn Fendler. New York: Routledge, 1999, 45–67.

Butler, Judith. *Precarious Life: The Power of Mourning and Violence*. New York: Verso, 2014.

Card, Claudia. "Rape as a Terrorist Institution," In *Violence, Terrorism and Justice*, eds. R. G. Frey, and Christopher W. Morris. Cambridge, UK: Cambridge University Press, 1991, 296–319.

Cargle, Rachel Elizabeth. "When Feminism Is White Supremacy in Heels," *Bazaar*, August 16, 2018, https://www.harpersbazaar.com/culture/politics/a22717725/what-is-toxic-white-feminism/.

Chödrön, Pema. *The Places That Scare You: A Guide to Fearlessness in Difficult Times*. Boston: Shambala Press, 2001.

Coates, Ta-Nehisi. *Between The World and Me*. New York: Spiegel and Grau, 2015.

Coates, Ta-Nehisi. "Imagining a New America," Interview with Krista Tippett, *On Being*, NPR, September 12, 2019.

Code, Lorraine. *Rhetorical Spaces: Essays on Gendered Locations*. New York: Routledge, 1995.

Crosley-Corcoran, Gina. "Explaining White Privilege to a Broke White Person," *Huffington Post*, May 8, 2014, https://www.huffingtonpost.com/gina-crosleycorcoran/explaining-white-privilege-to-a-broke-white-person_b_5269255.html.

Crenshaw, Kimberlé. "Mapping the Margins: Intersectionality, Identity Politics and Violence against Women of Color," *Stanford Law Review* 43, no. 6 (July 1991), 1241–99.

Dana, Deb. *The Polyvagal Theory in Therapy: Engaging the Rhythm of Regulation*. New York: W.W. Norton and Company, 2018.

Dean, David. "Healing the Dominant Group: Breaking the Cycle of Violence," *White Awake* (blog), August 31, 2016, https://whiteawake.org/2016/08/31/healing-the-dominant-group-breaking-the-cycle-of-violence/.

DeGruy, Joy. *Post-Traumatic Slave Syndrome: America's Legacy of Enduring Injury and Healing*. Portland, OR: Joy DeGruy Publications, Inc., 2017.

DeWolf, Thomas Norman. *Inheriting the Trade: A Northern Family Confronts its Legacy as the Largest Slave-Trading Dynasty in U.S. History*. Boston: Beacon, 2008.

DeWolf, Thomas, and Sharon Leslie Morgan. *Gather at the Table: The Healing Journey of a Daughter of Slavery and a Son of the Slave Trade*. Boston: Beacon, 2012.

DiAngelo, Robin. *White Fragility: Why It Is So Hard for White People to Talk about Racism*. Boston: Beacon, 2018.

Dotson, Kristie. "Tracking Epistemic Violence, Tracking Practices of Silencing," *Hypatia* 26, no. 2 (2011), 236–57.

Douglass, Frederick. *Narrative of the Life of Frederick Douglass*. New York: Dover Publications, 1995.

DuBois, William Edward Burghardt. *Black Reconstruction in America: Toward a History of the Part Which Black Folk Play in the Attempt to Reconstruct Democracy in American, 1860–1880*. New York: Routledge, 2017.

DuBois, William Edward Burghardt. *The Souls of Black Folk*. New York: Dover Publications, Inc., 1994.

Duncan, Pearl. "Colonial African-American Stoneware Artists, Stolen, Hidden, Now Rediscovered," *ArtDaily*, December 8, 2019, https://artdaily.cc/news/56820/Colonial-African-American-stoneware-artists--stolen--hidden--now-rediscovered#.Xe1SN5JKiu5.

Duncan, Pearl. "Is One of America's Leading Potters Related to the Family of Potters WhoOwned Him as a Slave?" *ArtDaily*, December 2, 2019, https://artdaily.cc/

news/55726/Is-one-of-America-s-leading-potters-related-to-the-family-of-potters-who-owned-him-as-a-slave-#.Xe1TR5JKhN0.

Duncan, Pearl. "Magnificent, Mysterious Designs in American Folk Art Revealed in African Iconography," *ArtDaily*, January 25, 2020, https://artdaily.cc/news/56187/Magnificent--mysterious-designs-in-American-Folk-Art-revealed-in-African-iconography#.XizMCBNKiu4.

Duncan, Pearl. "On Wall Street: Slavery Lost, Found, and Remembered," *History News Network*, July 7, 2015, https://historynewsnetwork.org/article/159898.

Duran, Eduardo. *Healing the Soul Wound: Counseling with American Indian and Other Native Peoples*. New York: Teachers College Press, 2006.

Eddo-Lodge, Reni. *Why I'm No Longer Talking to White People about Race*. London: Bloomsbury Publishing, 2018.

Elliott, Shanti. "Recovering from 'the Anesthesia of Power': Conflict Healing and Dialogue," *Teaching While White*, December 13, 2017, https://teachingwhilewhite.org/blog/2017/12/12/recovering-from-the-anesthesia-of-power-conflict-and-healing-in-dialogue.

Fanon, Franz. *Black Skin, White Masks*. London: Pluto Press, 1986.

Feinberg, Joel. *Social Philosophy*. Englewood Cliffs, NJ: Prentice Hall, 1963.

Frye, Marilyn. "Oppression," In *The Politics of Reality: Essays in Feminist Theory*. Freedom, CA: The Crossing Press, 1983, 1–16.

Frye, Marilyn. "White Woman Feminist." In *Willful Virgin: Essays in Feminism*. Freedom, CA: The Crossing Press, 1992, 147–169.

Gigantino, James J. "Trading in Jersey Souls: New Jersey and the Interstate Slave Trade," *Pennsylvania History: A Journal of Mid-Atlantic Studies* 77, no. 3 (2010), 281–302.

Gilman, Charlotte Perkins. *The Living of Charlotte Perkins Gilman: An Autobiography*. New York: Appleton-Century Company, 1935.

Gilson, Erinn. "Vulnerability, Ignorance, and Oppression," *Hypatia* 26, no. 2 (2011), 308–32.

Gordon, Lewis. "Critical Reflections on Three Popular Tropes in The Study of Whiteness," In *What White Looks Like: African American Philosophers on the Whiteness Question*, ed. George Yancy. New York: Routledge, 2004, 173–94.

Gwaltney, John Langston. *Drylongso: A Self-Portrait of Black America*. New York: Random House, 1980.

Hacker, Andrew. *Two Nations: Black and White, Separate, Hostile, and Unequal*. New York: Scribners, 1992.

Hage, Ghassan. *Against Paranoid Nationalism: Searching for Hope in a Shrinking Society*. North Melbourne, Australia: Pluto Press, 2003.

Hannah-Jones, Nikole. "The 1619 Project: Introduction," *The New York Times Magazine*, August 18, 2019, 14–21, https://pulitzercenter.org/sites/default/files/full_issue_of_the_1619_project.pdf.

Hirsh, Jacob B. "The Weight of Being: Psychological Perspectives on the Existential Moment," *New Ideas in Psychology* 28 (2010), 28–36.

Hoagland, Sarah L. *Lesbian Ethics: Toward New Value*. Palo Alto, CA: Institute of Lesbian Studies, 1988.

Hodges, Graham Russell. *Slavery and Freedom in the Rural North: African Americans in Monmouth County, New Jersey, 1665–1865*. New York: Rowman and Littlefield, 1997.

hooks, bell. *Black Looks: Race and Representation*. New York: Routledge, 2014.

hooks, bell. *Killing Rage: Ending Racism*. New York: Henry Holt, 1995.

Hunter, Marcus Anthony. "Racial Physics or a Theory for Everything that Happened," *Ethnic and Racial Studies* 40, no. 8 (2017), 1173–83.

Jacobs, Harriet A. *Incidents in the Life of a Slave Girl: Written by Herself*. Cambridge, MA: Harvard University Press, 2000.

James, Joy. "Contort Yourself: Music, Whiteness, and the Politics of Disorientation," In *White Self-Criticality: How Does it Feel to Be a White Problem?*, ed. George Yancy. Lanham, MD: Lexington Books, 2015, 211–28.

Jensen, Robert. *The Heart of Whiteness: Confronting Race, Racism and White Privilege*. San Francisco: City Lights, 2005.

Jones, Kenneth, and Tema Okun, "White Supremacy Culture," In *Dismantling Racism: 2016 Workbook*. dRworks Books, 2016, 28–35, https://resourcegeneration.org/wp-content/uploads/2018/01/2016-dRworks-workbook.pdf.

Jones, Serena. *Call It Grace: Finding Meaning in a Fractured World*. New York: Viking Press, 2019.

Jones, Serena. "On Grace," Interview by Krista Tippett, *On Being*, NPR, December 5, 2019. Transcript, https://onbeing.org/programs/serene-jones-on-grace/.

Jones, Serena. *Trauma and Grace: Theology in a Ruptured World*, Second edition. Louisville, KY: Westminster John Knox Press, 2019.

Kendell, Frances E. *Understanding White Privilege: Creating Pathways to Authentic Relationships across Race*. New York: Routledge, 2006.

Kipling, Rudyard. *Poems*. New York: Alfred Knopf, 2007.

Kupenda, Angela Mae. "Facing Down Spooks," In *Presumed Incompetent: Intersections of Race and Class for Women in Academia*, eds. Gabriella Gutiérrez y Muhs, Yolanda Flores Niemann, Carmen G. González, and Angela P. Harris. Boulder, CO: University Press of Colorado, 2012, 20–29.

Lee, Mun Wah, dir. *The Color of Fear*. Berkeley, CA: Stir Fry Productions, 1994. DVD.

Lee, Mun Wah. *If These Halls Could Talk*. Berkeley, CA: Stir Fry Productions, 2014. DVD.

Lee, Mun Wah. *The Art of Mindful Facilitation*. Berkeley, CA: StirFry Seminars and Counseling, 2011.

Lee, Mun Wah. "The Numbness," In *If These Halls Could Talk*. Filmed 2014. YouTube video, 1:03. Posted July 28, 2018, https://www.youtube.com/watch?v=BHvtryad_J0&t=2s.

Levine, Peter. *In an Unspoken Voice: How the Body Releases Trauma and Restores Goodness*. Berkeley, CA: North Atlantic Books, 2010.

Lockard, Joe. *Watching Slavery: Witness Texts and Travel Reports*, Second edition. New York: Peter Lang, 2008.

Lorde, Audre. *Sister Outsider: Essays and Speeches*. Berkeley, CA: The Crossing Press, 1984.

Lugones, Maria C. "On The Logic of Pluralist Feminism," In *Feminist Ethics*, ed. Claudia Card. Lawrence: University of Kansas Press, 1991, 35–45.

Lugones, María C. *Pilgrimages/Pereginajes: Theorizing Coalition against Multiple Oppressions*. Lanham, MD: Rowman and Littlefield, 2003.

MacMullan, Terrance. *The Habits of Whiteness: A Pragmatist Reconstruction*. Bloomington, IN: Indiana University Press, 2009.

Manne, Kate. *Down Girl!: The Logic of Misogyny*. New York: Oxford University Press, 2017.

Marilyn Frye, "White Woman Feminist." In Willful Virgin: Essays in Feminism (Freedom, CA: The Crossing Press, 1992), 147–169.

McIntosh, Peggy. "White Privilege and Male Privilege: A Personal Account of Coming to See Correspondences through Work in Women's Studies," In *The Feminist Philosophy Reader*, eds. Alison Bailey and Chris J. Cuomo. New York: McGraw-Hill, 2008, 61–69.

McIntyre, Alice. *Making Meaning of Whiteness: Exploring Racial Identities with White Teachers*. Albany, NY: SUNY Press, 1997.

Medina, José. "Color Blindness, Meta-Ignorance, and the Racial Imagination," *Critical Philosophy of Race* 1, no. 1 (2013), 38–67.

Medina, José. *The Epistemology of Resistance: Gender and Racial Oppression, Epistemic Injustice, and Resistant Imaginations*. New York: Oxford University Press, 2015.

Menakem, Resmaa. *My Grandmother's Hands: Racialized Trauma and the Pathway to Mending Our Hearts and Bodies*. Las Vegas, NV: Central Recovery Press, 2017.

Mills, Charles W. "Alternative Epistemologies," In *Blackness Visible: Essays on The Philosophy of Race*. Ithaca, NY: Cornell University Press, 1989, 21–41.

Mills, Charles W. *The Racial Contract*. Ithaca, NY: Cornell University Press, 1997.

Mohanty, Chandra Talpade. *Feminism without Borders: Decolonizing Theory, Practicing Solidarity*. Durham, NC: Duke University Press, 2006.

Monahan, Michael J. "The Concept of Privilege: A Critical Appraisal," *The South African Journal of Philosophy* 33, no. 1 (2014), 73–83.

Moraga, Cherríe. *Loving in the War Years: Lo Que Nunca Paso por Sus Labios*. Boston: South End Press, 1983.

Moraga, Cherríe L., and Gloria E. Anzaldúa, eds. *This Bridge Called My Back: Writings by Radical Women of Color*. Berkeley, CA: Third Woman Press, 2002.

Morales, Aurora Levins. *Medicine Stories: Essays for Radicals*. Durham, NC: Duke University Press, 2019.

Morgan, Francesca. "A Noble Pursuit: Bourgeois America's Use of Lineage," In *The American Bourgeoise: Distinction and Identity in the Nineteenth Century*, eds. Sven Beckert and Julia B. Rosenbaum. New York, NY: Palgrave MacMillan, 2010, 135–51.

National Coalition against Domestic Violence. "Domestic Violence Fact Sheet," 2014, https://www.speakcdn.com/assets/2497/domestic_violence2.pdf.

No More. "Domestic Violence in the Transgender Community," *No More Blog*. April 29, 2016, https://nomore.org/domestic-violence-transgender-community/.

Olsson, Jona. "White Privilege Workshop, 19th Annual Womyn's Music Festival," Hart, Michigan, August 10, 1994.

Perkins Gilman, Charlotte. *The Living of Charlotte Perkins Gilman: An Autobiography*. New York: Appleton-Century Company, 1935.

Pingeon, Frances D. "An Abominable Business: The New Jersey Slave Trade, 1818," *New Jersey History* 109, no. 3–4 (Fall/Winter 1991), 15–35.

Pohlhaus, Gaile. "Discerning the Primary Epistemic Harm in Cases of Testimonial Injustice," *Social Epistemology* 28, no. 2 (2014), 99–114.

Rankine, Claudia. *Citizen: An American Lyric*. Minneapolis, MN: Greywolf Press, 2014.

Rankine, Claudia. "The Condition of Black Life is One of Mourning," *New York Times*, June 22, 2015, https://www.nytimes.com/2015/06/22/magazine/the-condition-of-black-life-is-one-of-mourning.html.

Read, Warren. *The Lyncher in Me: A Search for Redemption in the Face of History*. St. Paul, MN: Borealis Books, 2008.

Roediger, David R., ed. *Black on White: Black Writers on What It Means to Be White*. New York: Schocken Books, 1998.

Roy, Arundhati. "The Pandemic is a Portal," *Yes! Magazine*, April 17, 2020, https://www.yesmagazine.org/video/coronavirus-pandemic-arundhati-roy/.

Russo, Ann. *Feminist Accountability: Disrupting Violence and Transforming Power*. New York: New York University Press, 2019.

Schermerhorn, Calvin. *The Business of Slavery and the Rise of American Capitalism, 1815–1860*. New Haven: Yale University Press, 2015.

Segrest, Mab. "Of Soul and White Folks," In *Born to Belonging: Writings on Spirit and Justice*. New Brunswick: Rutgers University Press, 2002, 157–76.

Shotwell, Alexis. "Unforgetting as a Collective Tactic," In *White Self-Criticality beyond Anti-Racism: How Does it Feel to Be a White Problem?*, ed. George Yancy. Lanham, MD: Lexington Books, 2015, 57–68.

Sleeter, Christine E. "Becoming White: Reinterpreting a Family Story by Putting Race Back into the Picture," *Race, Ethnicity and Education* 14, no. 4 (September 2011), 421–33.

Sleeter, Christine E. "Critical Family History: Situating Family within Context of Power Relationships," *Journal of Multidisciplinary Research* 8, no. 1 (Spring 2016), 11–23.

Smith, Barbara. "Racism and Women's Studies," *Frontiers: A Journal of Women's Studies* 5, no. 1 (Spring 1980), 48–49.

Smith, Lillian. *Killers of the Dream*. New York: W.W. Norton and Company, 1961.

Solnit, Rebecca. "Milestones in Misogyny," In *Call Them by Their True Names*. Chicago: Haymarket Books, 2018, 21–32.

Spelman, Elizabeth V. *Inessential Woman: Problems of Exclusion in Feminist Thought*. Boston: Beacon Press, 1988.

Spelman, Elizabeth V. "Managing Ignorance," In *Race and Epistemologies of Ignorance*, eds. Shannon Sullivan, and Nancy Tuana. Albany: State University of New York Press, 2007, 119–35.

Sullivan, Shannon. *Good White People: The Problem with White Middle-Class Anti-Racism*. Albany, NY: SUNY Press, 2014.

Sullivan, Shannon. *The Physiology of Sexist and Racist Oppression*. New York: Oxford University Press, 2015.

Sullivan, Shannon and Nancy Tuana, eds. *Race and the Epistemologies of Ignorance*. Albany, NY: SUNY Press, 2007.

Tannen, Deborah. "Our Impossible Expectations of Hillary Clinton and All Women in Authority," *The Washington Post*, February 20, 2016, https://www.washingtonpost.com/opinions/our-impossible-expectations-of-hillary-clinton-and-all-women-in-authority/2016/02/19/35e416d0-d5ba-11e5-be55-2cc3c1e4b76b_story.html?noredirect=on&utm_term=.645dfb9546f2.

Teters, Charlene, interview. In *In Whose Honor?: American Indian Mascots in Sports*, dir. Jay Rosenstein, New Day Films, 1997 [5:00–5:56].

Thandeka. *Learning to Be White: Money, Race, and God in America*. New York: Continuum, 1999.

Thandeka. "Whites: Made in America: Advancing American Philosophers' Discourse on Race," *The Pluralist* 13, no. 1 (Spring 2018), 26–50.

Thompson, Becky, and Veronica T. Watson. "Theorizing White Racial Trauma and Its Remedies," In *The Construction of Whiteness: An Interdisciplinary Analysis of Race Formation and the Meaning of White Identity*, eds. Stephen Middleton, David R. Roediger, and Donald M. Shaffer. Jackson, MS: University of Mississippi Press, 2016, 234–56.

Tuana, Nancy. "The Speculum of Ignorance: The Women's Health Movement and Epistemologies of Ignorance," *Hypatia* 21, no 3 (Summer 2006), 1–19.

Van der Kolk, Bessel. *The Body Keeps the Score: Brain, Mind, and Body in the Healing of Trauma*. New York: Penguin Books, 2015.

Van Dernoot Lipsky, Laura with Connie Burk. *Trauma Stewardship: An Everyday Guide to Caring for Self While Caring for Others*. San Francisco: Berrett-Koeler, 2009.

Watson, Veronica T. *The Souls of White Folk: African American Writers Theorize Whiteness*. Jackson, MS: University Press of Mississippi, 2013.

Watson, Veronica T., and Becky Thompson. "Theorizing White Racial Trauma and its Remedies," In *The Construction of Whiteness: An Interdisciplinary Analysis of Race Formation and the Meaning of White Identity*, eds. Stephen Middleton, David R. Roediger, and Donald M. Shaffer. Jackson, MS: University Press of Mississippi, 2016, 234–55.

Weil, François. *Family Trees: A History of Genealogy in America*. Cambridge, MA: Harvard University Press, 2013.

Welch, Sharon. *Sweet Dreams in America: Making Ethics and Spirituality Work*. New York: Routledge, 1999.

Wise, Tim. "The Pathology of Privilege: Racism, White Denial and the Costs of Inequality," DVD, produced by Sut Jhally, Media Education Foundation, 2008.

Wise, Tim. *White Like Me*. New York: Soft Skull Press, 2006.

Wright, Richard. "The Ethics of Living Jim Crow," In *Uncle Tom's Children*. New York: Harper Perrenial, 2008, 1–16.

Wright, Richard. "The Man Who Went to Chicago," In *Eight Men*, introduction by Paul Gilroy New York: Harper Perennial, 1996, 202–237.

Yancy, George. *Backlash: What Happens When We Talk Honestly about Racism in America*. Lanham, MD: Rowman and Littlefield, 2018.

Yancy, George. *Black Bodies, White Gazes: The Continuing Significance of Race*. Lanham, MD: Rowman & Littlefield Publishers, 2008.

Yancy, George. *Look, a White!: Philosophical Essays on Whiteness*. Philadelphia: Temple University Press, 2012.

Yancy, George. "Loving Wisdom and the Effort to Make Philosophy 'Unsafe,'" *Epistemologies Humanities Journal* (2011), http://c961210.r10.cf2.rackcnd.com/wp-content/uploads/2010/12/Essay-Yancy-Loving-Wisdom.pdf.

Zack, Naomi, and George Yancy. "What White Privilege Really Means," The Stone, *The New York Times*, November 5, 2014, https://opinionator.blogs.nytimes.com/2014/11/05/what-white-privilege-really-means/.

Index

Page references for figures are italicized.

Act for the Gradual Abolition of Slavery, The (1804), 146, 148
advantage. *See* privilege
affirmative action, 23–24
Affleck, Ben, 125, 128–30, 134
Ahmed, Sara, 4, 11–12, 18, 25n13, 88, 89, 129, 142; whiteness as orientation, 41
Allain, Hyacinthe (1784–1874), *141*
ancestors, holding space with, xix, 125, 135, 138–56
ancestral amnesia, xviii, 107, 124, 128–29, 134
anesthesia, xiii, xvii–xviii, 42, 50, 80, 82, 87, 91, 96–100; 'anesthesia of power,' 125, 131, 134. *See* Segrest, Mab; habits of whiteness, 109–15, 129; as trauma response, 93, 99–100, 119–15. *See also* trauma
anesthetized pedigree, 127–30, 139
Angelou, Maya, 67–68
Anzaldúa, Gloria, 59, 85, 139
Applebaum, Barbara, 39, 43, 47, 56n31, 62

Baldwin, James, 35, 38, 49, 56n41, 93, 132, 140; disagreeable mirrors, xii, 45, 94, 95, 118n62

Ball, Edward, 141
Bambara, Toni, 79, 80, 109, 114
the Battle of Monmouth (1778), 143
Bayoumi, Moustafa, 44
belonging, 80, 83–84, 93, 98, 124–25, 139, 145
Berenstain, Nora, 65–66
Biss, Eula, 13–14, 17, 85
Black Lives Matter, xii, 63, 157
Bennett, Lerone, 35
Berila, Beth, 7, 63
Berk, Rupert, 64
Bland, Sandra, 14
Blasey Ford, Christine, 12
Brandt, Joseph, 95–96
Brown, Brené, 100
Browne, Katrina, 137–39
Burbules, Nicholas C., 64

Card, Claudia, 60
Chesnut, Mary Bokin, 96–97
Chödrön, Pema, 48
Clinton, Hilary, 5, 7
Coates, Ta-Nehisi, 4, 7, 140
Code, Lorraine, 61–62
cognitive dissonance, 80

colonization, xix, 74, 107, 124–25, 128, 132–33; ontological alchemy of, 43–44; privilege and, 29n27, 159n27
colorblind racism, 20, 84, 86, 99
critical pedagogy, 64–65
Crosely-Corcoran, Gina, 11, 22

Dana, Deb, 110
Dean, David, 80
DeGruy, Joy, xix, 132–33
DeWolf, Thomas, 91–92, 137–38, 160n36
DiAngelo, Robin, 37, 101; white fragility, xv, 37–38, 42, 63, 88, 98, 129
Disbrow, John D., 146, 151, 154, 155
Dotson, Kristie, 73–74
Douglass, Frederick, 84
DuBois, W. E. B, xv, 7–8, 34–36, 84, 112
Duncan, Pearl, 146, 147, 154, 155

Eddo-Lodge, Reni, 41
epistemic exploitation. *See* Berenstain, Nora
epistemic home turf, 59, 61–62, 67. *See also* Code, Lorraine
epistemic violence, 73–74
Evertson, Margaret Roeters (1731–1827), *144*

Fanon, Frantz, 89
Feinberg, Joel, 8
Finding Your Roots (PBS), xix, 123
Floyd, George, xii, xiii, xv, 35, 89, 157
fluttering, xv, 34–36, 40, 51, 53
Franklin, John Hope, 107
Frye, Marilyn, 2–7, 9, 14, 47, 51

Gates, Henry Louis, Jr., xviii–xix, 123, 125, 128–30
genealogy: *curandera genealogist*, 132; history of, xix–xx, 126–27; medicinal genealogies, xix, 131–34, 135, 140, 156; medicinal white

genealogies, xix, 134–39. *See also* pedigree
Gilman, Charlotte Perkins, 21
Gilson, Erinn, 50
goodness and innocence, white xv, 20, 38–39, 41–43, 47, 62–63, 68; good/bad white person binary, 46, 94–95
Gwaltney, John Langston, 45–46

Hacker, Andrew, 19–20
Hage, Ghassan, 102
heteropatriarchy, 6, 9, 21, 23–26
historical amnesia, xviii, 84, 91, 107–8, 124, 126
historical trauma. *See* trauma
Hoagland, Sarah, 22
hooks, bell, 16, 38

ignorance, 16, 88; as epistemic closure, 46, 48–49; white ignorance, 18, 94; willful ignorance, xv, 41, 49–50, 60, 64, 69, 73–74, 128. *See also* privilege-preserving epistemic pushback
intersectionality, 6–7, 11, 29n21

Jacobs, Harriet, 84
James, Joy, 87
Jim Crow laws and etiquette, 4, 22
Jones, Kenneth, 85–86
Jones, Serena, 93, 136–37, 139, 152, 156
Jones, Van, xii

Kavanaugh, Brent, 12
Kim, Sandra, x, 55n21, 113
Kipling, Rudyard, 91
Kupenda, Angela Mae, 4, 7

Lee, Muh Wah, 50–54, 55n21, 99–100
Levine, Peter, 90
liminal spaces, xi, 139–40
Lipsky, Laura van Dernoot, 111
Lorde, Audre, xiii, 1, 22, 65, 113

Lost Souls Memorial Project, 154, 156–57
Loving v. Commonwealth of Virginia (1967), 13
Lugones, María, 19; faithful mirrors, 45–46; logic of purity, 43; plural selves, 46, 95

MacIntyre, Alice, xv, 34, 36, 38, 39
MacMullan, Terrance, 9
McIntosh, Peggy, xiv, 1–2, 7, 9–10, 14–17, 19, 115n2; invisible and weightless knapsack, xvi, 1, 79, 88. *See also* privilege, white privilege
Medina, José, 70, 75, 87, 99, 106, 117; beneficial epistemic friction, 66, 70; cognitive self-protection, 62–63; insensitivity to our insensitivity, 87
Menakem, Resmaa, xviii, 86–87; pain, dirty and clean, 113–14, 131; soul nerve, 111, 112; white-body supremacy, 112, 113, 127
Metacom (King Phillip), 107
Mills, Charles, 34, 43, 55n9, 105
Moraga, Cherríe, 17, 40
Morales, Aurora Levins, xix, 90, 104, 134; curandera historian, 131–32
Morgan, Alice 'Elsey', 151, 152
Morgan, Capt. James, Sr. (1734–1784), 143, *144*, 145, 147, 155
Morgan, Charles II (1648–1720), 143
Morgan, Charles III (1683–1750), 143, *144*, 145
Morgan, 'Colonel' Charles S., (1775–1848), 148, *149*, 150–52
Morgan, Francesca, 127, 158n8
Morgan, Jonathan H., *144*, 148, 151, 152
Morgan, Maj. Gen. James, Jr. (1756–1822), 143, *144*, 145, 152, 155
Morgan, Mary (1769–1838), *144*
Morgan, Sarah (1772–1835), 150
Morgan, Susannah (1761–1854), 155
mourning, 92, 155–57

Nash, Catherine, 131
Newark lessons, xvii, 81–84, 86, 96, 101–3, 106, 108–10, 112, 124
Newark Race Riots (Rebellion/Uprising), xviii, 81
numbness. *See* anesthesia
"n"-word, 57n41, 61, 74, 76n22; use-mention distinction, 67–68, 70

Okun, Tema, 85–86
Olsson, Jona, 14–15
oppression: double-bind feature of, 3–6, 20, 25n12, 29n20; intersectionality and, 22–27; non-oppressive harm, 6–7

pain, dirty and clean. *See* Menakem, Resmaa
pedigree: anesthetized pedigree, xviii–xix, 127–30; gravitational pull of whiteness on, 125, 151, 155
Plessy vs. Ferguson (1896), 2
plural white selves, 45–46, 94–95
Pohlhaus, Gaile, Jr., 65
polyvagal theory, xviii. *See also* Menakem, Resmaa; Dana, Deb
post-traumatic stress disorder (PTSD). *See* trauma
potteries, 145–46, 154–55
privilege: capriciously granted and unjustifiable, 10, 13–14; check proof, xiv, 1–3, 14, 22–23; earned advantages and perks, xiv, 7–12, 23; intersectional (thick) account of, 2, 22–27; invisible assets, 14–19; legal usage, rights, and entitlements, 8–9, 12–13, 24; light skin privilege, 17; male privilege, 3, 21–22; positive and negative dimensions of, xiv, 20–22; private law, 13–14; stretch-resistant account of, xiv, 3, 27; unearned power conferred systemically, 2, 9–10; wild card

value analogy, xiv, 17, 19–20, 23, 24, 27. *See also* white privilege; privilege-preserving epistemic pushback

privilege-preserving epistemic pushback, xiv–xvi, 60, 84; critical thinking and skepticism, 60, 64–68, 72; definition and examples, 60–62; normative dimensions, 62–63; tracking ignorance, 71–72. *See also* 'shadow texts'

Rankine, Claudia, 17–18, 83
Read, Warren, 125, 135–36, 139, 140
Rice, Tamir, 106
Richards, Ann, 12
Roediger, David, 108
Roy, Arundhati, xii
Russo, Ann, 93

Saar, Betye, ix
Sankofa adinkra, 133–34, *147*
scales, faithful but disagreeable, 94–96
Segrest, Mab, 96–97
sexual violence, 21, 25–26, 60, 67, 73, 104–5, 120n86
shadow texts, xvi, 60, 77n30; pedagogy, 68–72, 74
Shotwell, Alexis, 124
silence and silencing, xiv, 46–48, 72, 87, 124–25; epistemic silencing, 73–74. *See also* Dotson, Kristie
Siyonbola, Lolade, 89
slavery: moral damage to white owners, 84, 96–97; New Jersey, in, 142–43, 161n59. *See also* Van Wickle and Morgan Slave Scandal (1818)
Smith, Barbara, 85
Smith, Lillian, 82, 83
soul nerve. *See* Menakem, Resmaa
Spelman, Elizabeth, 38, 49–51
Spivak, Gayatri, 73
Sullivan, Shannon, 110, 129–30

Take Back the Night, 21

Tannen, Deborah, 5
Taylor, Breonna, xii, xv, 89
testimonial injustice, 50, 59, 72–74
testimonial smothering and quieting. *See* Dotson, Kristie
Teters, Charlene, 89
Thandeka, 45, 83
the 1619 Project, 43
Thompson, Becky, 102, 110–11
Tippett, Krista, 140
trauma, xvii; exposure signs of, 111; historical, 82, 86, 90, 132–33, 139; post-traumatic stress disorder (PTSD), 90; trauma and pedigree, xviii, 127–28. *See also* anesthesia; whiteness, wound at the heart of
Tuana, Nancy, 49, 69

unlevel knowing field, xv, 59, 62, 72

Van Brackel, Catherine (1764–1802), *144*
Van Wickle, Ann J. (1784–1867), *144*, 151
Van Wickle, Dinah (1803–1882), 148, 151, 157
Van Wickle, Judge Jacob C., (1770–1854), 145, 148, 150, 152, *153*, 155
Van Wickle, Nicholas (1796–1865), 152, 155
Van Wickle and Morgan Slave Scandal (1818), 134, *144*, *149–50*, 148–55, 156
vulnerability, xi, xv, 36, 48–54, 80

Walker, Alice, 130
Watson, Veronica T., 102, 110–11
weight of whiteness, the: defined, 91–92; gravitational pull of, xiii, xviii, 94–95, 151. *See also* pedigree; holding space with, xiii, xvi, 79–80, 125. *See also* ancestors; imprint on bodies of color, 16–18, 84–86, 88–90; language of racial gravity, xvii, 80, 85, 87, 92–93, 118n50; material

weight, 103–5; measured as costs and losses, 84–85, 87, 91–92; moral and epistemic weight, 88, 105–7; psychological weight, 101–2; social weight, 102–3; weighty vocabulary, 80, 92–93, 118n62; wholeness, 63, 79–80, 94–95, 114–15, 138

weighty conversation, the: barriers to, xvii, 85–88; invitations to, xiii, xvi–xvii, 84–85, 125, 130, 132–33, 137; token to carry, 88; white comfort, xvii, 48, 51, 63, 69, 85–87, 90, 129–30

weighty epistemology, 80, 87, 92

Weil, François, 126–27, 131

Welch, Sharon, 53

white body: habits of, 91, 98, 110; unsettled, 39–40, 84, 113–14, 127, 140–41; weightlessness, xvi, 84, 87

white-body supremacy. *See* Menakem, Resmaa

white debt. *See* Biss, Eula

white fragility. *See* DiAngelo, Robin

white minds, 86–88

whiteness, wound at the heart of, xx, 79–80, 82–84, 86–87, 89–90, 92, 109–15, 125–27, 130

white privilege: class oppression, 11–12; critique of McIntosh's list, 14–17; energy-saving feature of, 18, 20; overexposed and under exposed sides of, xiii, xvi, 28n4, 79, 88; value and functions of, 15–17. *See also* anesthesia; DuBois, W. E. B; McIntosh, Peggy

white problem in America, 35

white supremacy, 96; collateral damage, 91–92, 109; costs and losses, 100–109; culture, 85–88, 93, 110–11; damage to humanity, xviii, 38, 79–80, 83, 92–93, 97–98; values, 16, 30n3

white talk, xiv, 86, 98; alternatives to, 51–54; boomerang discourse, 38–39, 41, 47; definition and properties of, 33–34, 37–38; epistemic dimensions, xv, 41, 46–50; fluttering grammar of, xv, 38, 40–42, 45, 50, 52, 98; history of, 34–35; impact on people of color, 37, 40, 89; moral rewards of, xv, 42–43, 47, 50; non-verbal dimensions of, 39–41; objections, xiv, 46–48; ontological dimensions, xv, 36, 43–45. *See also* goodness and innocence, white

Wise, Tim, 91

Wright, Richard, 4, 7, 103

Yancy, George, 34, 57n42, 82, 85, 93, 115n10, 139

Zack, Naomi, 9

About the Author

Alison Bailey is a professor of philosophy at Illinois State University where she directs the Women's, Gender, and Sexuality Studies Program. Her scholarship engages issues at the intersections of feminist theories, philosophy of race, critical whiteness studies, and social epistemology (especially questions epistemic injustice and ignorance). She co-edited *The Feminist Philosophy Reader* (2007) with Chris J. Cuomo. Her scholarship on whiteness and ignorance has appeared in *Hypatia: A Journal of Feminist Philosophy*, *Social Epistemology Review and Reply Collective*, *Philosophy Today*, and a variety of edited collections. Her scholarship anger and epistemic injustice appears in the Royal Institute of Philosophy's supplemental volume on "The Harms and Wrongs of Epistemic Practice," and in *The Logic of Racial Practice: Embodiment, Habitus, and Implicit Bias*. Her current scholarship engages whiteness through an autobiographical genealogically focused lens that invites white people to wade slowly and mindfully into the inherited weight of whiteness and to hold space with the ways that white supremacy works to anesthetize white people from the damage it does to our collective humanity.

www.ingramcontent.com/pod-product-compliance
Lightning Source LLC
Chambersburg PA
CBHW061715300426
44115CB00014B/2695